Joseph C. Sweeney

KINSALE

*The Spanish Intervention
in Ireland at the End of the
Elizabethan Wars*

JOHN J. SILKE

KINSALE

*The Spanish Intervention
in Ireland at the End of the
Elizabethan Wars*

LIVERPOOL UNIVERSITY PRESS

1970

Published by
LIVERPOOL UNIVERSITY PRESS
123 Grove Street, Liverpool L7 7AF

ISBN 0 85323 090 0

First published 1970

Printed and bound in Great Britain by
William Clowes and Sons Ltd
London and Beccles

IN MEMORIAM MATRIS ET PATRIS

FOREWORD

by

D. B. QUINN

*Professor of Modern History
in the University of Liverpool*

THE OCCUPATION of the Irish port of Kinsale by a Spanish force in
1601 and its surrender to an English army early in 1602 is an event of
both European and Irish significance. It marked the last attempt by
Spain to force a decision in the long sea war with England which had
lasted since 1585. It was intended to demonstrate that the Spanish
fleet, wounded in 1588 and subsequently suffering rather more rebuffs
than successes, was still a formidable threat to English security. It was
a reminder, too, though rather a tardy one, that while England could
aid the United Provinces to the detriment of Spain, Spain could re-
taliate by assisting Irish opponents of English authority. Perhaps, also,
the taking of San Juan de Puerto Rico by Cumberland in 1598, the
first of a series of damaging sackings of Caribbean towns, had something to do with this counter-attack against an English dependency.

The failure at Kinsale was not, in itself, a serious blow to anything
except Spanish prestige, but it was the last aggressive thrust at England before the death of Elizabeth I enabled effective peace negotiations to take place. On the Irish side the nature and result of Spanish
intervention had more far-reaching consequences. Promises of Spanish
aid from 1596 onwards had helped to sustain Hugh O'Neill's lengthy
struggle for autonomy in Ulster and had been a factor in spreading
over two-thirds of Ireland what had begun as a provincial revolt, so
that it became the nearest approach in the sixteenth century to an all-
Ireland attempt to eliminate English rule. The English military build-
up after 1598 had converted Ireland into a major theatre of war, but
the fiasco of Essex's campaign in 1599 aroused serious apprehension in
England so that immense responsibilities were laid on Mountjoy
when he succeeded Essex in Ireland in 1600. Up to the time of the
Spanish arrival at Kinsale, Mountjoy had had very substantial though

not decisive successes and could reasonably hope to finish off the insurgents in another campaign.

The Spanish force, once installed in Kinsale, changed all this. It presented the English commander with a challenge to which he must rise. It gave O'Neill a chance—though a difficult one—to break the siege and open up a way of using the Spanish infantry in mobile warfare, and so of having the opportunity to defeat Mountjoy in the field. The failure of the Irish attack, and no less the absence of effective coordination with the Spaniards, forced the latter to capitulate and O'Neill to retire to Ulster. For Ireland the battle of Kinsale and the year 1602 marked the end of serious resistance to English rule, though O'Neill was able to hold out until he obtained not inglorious terms in 1603. But Ireland, at the accession of James I, was fully at the disposal of the king of Great Britain and Ireland.

Kinsale has been extensively written on from the Irish side and it is treated in most histories of Spain and some of Europe, but it has never been examined systematically from the Spanish side. Father Silke, already known for his more specialized studies of the period, has been able to consult the Spanish records which provide a full account of the inception of the Irish-invasion project, its political setting, and the logistics of the dispatch of the expedition as well as the story of its fortunes in Ireland. He answers a great many questions which have hitherto remained obscure and places the episode squarely in its European and its Irish setting. His book will take its place as a standard treatment of the subject for students of Irish and of European history alike.

CONTENTS

ILLUSTRATIONS

PLATES

MAPS

PREFACE

THE PRESENT WORK has been written in the hope that a treatment, based on Spanish sources, of the Kinsale episode may fill a gap in Irish (and to some slight extent, perhaps, in European) historiography. Among those to whom I am indebted for assistance in preparing the work mention must in the first place be made of the Directors and staffs of the Archivo General, Simancas; of the Biblioteca Nacional, Madrid; of the National Library of Ireland; and of the British Museum. I gratefully acknowledge the permission of the Director to quote from the documents in the Archivo General, Simancas.

I must also thank Mr. Michael Mulcahy, Cork, who very generously made his unpublished researches into the battle of Kinsale available to me; Mr. S. P. Ó Mórdha, Dublin, for the stimulation of his conversation on Irish history; Mr. A. N. Ryan, of the School of History, University of Liverpool, for his advice on Chapter I; and above all Professor David Quinn, who gave me the encouragement without which the book might never have been written. In drawing up the index, I benefited from the expert advice given me by Mrs. Alison Quinn. Any faults that remain in the book are my sole responsibility.

Kinsale had origin in a thesis prepared, under the direction of Professor R. Dudley Edwards, for the National University of Ireland, and I welcome the opportunity to acknowledge a generous grant-in-aid towards publication made by the Senate of the University.

J. J. S.

New York
January 1970

ABBREVIATIONS

<small>PRINCIPAL SOURCES</small> are described and listed in the bibliography under the headings: I. Spanish sources, pp. 182–6, and II. Other sources, pp. 186–91. The following abbreviations are used in the footnotes, and in the bibliography.

A.F.M.	*Annals of the Four Masters* (*Annála Ríoghachta Éireann*)
AGS	Archivo General de Simancas
AGS, Estado	AGS, *fondo* Estado, *sección* Secretaría de Estado
AGS, Guerra Antigua	AGS, *fondo* Guerra y Marina, *sección* Guerra Antigua
Anal. Hib.	*Analecta Hibernica* (IMC, 1930–)
Archiv. Hib.	*Archivium Hibernicum* (Catholic Record Society of Ireland, 1912–)
Archiv. Hist. Soc. Iesu	*Archivium Historicum Societatis Iesu*
BM	British Museum
Cal. Carew MSS.	*Calendar of Carew papers in the Lambeth library*
Cal. S.P. Ire.	*Calendar of state papers relating to Ireland*
Cal. S.P. Spain	*The letters and state papers relating to English affairs . . . in . . . Simancas*
Cal. S.P. Venice	*Calendar of state papers and manuscripts relating to English affairs . . . in . . . Venice*
CRS	Catholic Record Society, Publications
CSIC	Consejo Superior de Investigaciones Científicas
Codoin	*Colección de documentos inéditos para la historia de España*
D.H.E.	*Diccionario de historia de España*
D.N.B.	*Dictionary of National Biography*
E.H.R.	*English Historical Review*
Galway Arch. Soc. J.	*Galway Archaeological Society, Journal*
HMC	Historical Manuscripts Commission
I.C.H.S. Bull.	*Irish Committee for Historical Sciences, Bulletin* (1939–)
I.E.R.	*Irish Ecclesiastical Record*
I.H.S.	*Irish Historical Studies*
IMC	Irish Manuscripts Commission
Inst. Hist. Res. Bull.	*Institute of Historical Research, Bulletin*
Ir. Sword	*Irish Sword*
Ir. Theol. Quart.	*Irish Theological Quarterly*
NLI	National Library of Ireland
NUI	National University of Ireland

Pac. Hib.	[Stafford, Thomas], *Pacata Hibernia*
PROL	Public Record Office, London
RAH	Real Academia de Historia
R.E.	*Revista de España* (149 vols., Madrid, 1869–1904)
Rep. Nov.	*Reportorium Novum*
Rév. d'Hist. Dipl.	*Révue d'Histoire Diplomatique*
RHS	Royal Historical Society
VA, Borghese III	Vatican Archives, Borghese, series III
Vallid.	Valladolid

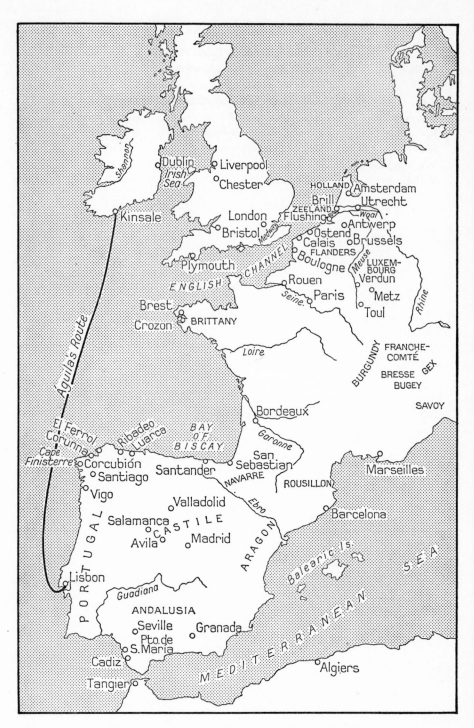

THE ELIZABETHAN WARS: I. THE EUROPEAN THEATRE

THE ELIZABETHAN WARS: II. THE IRISH THEATRE

RÓISÍN DUBH

Hugh O'Donnell addresses Ireland

A Róisín, na bíodh brón ort fár éirigh dhuit:
tá na bráithre ag teacht thar sáile 's ag triall ar muir;
tiochfaidh do phárdún on bPapa 's on Róimh anoir
's ní spárálfar fíon Spáinneach ar mo Róisín Dubh.
Mhairbh tú mé, a bhrídeach, is nár ba fearrde duit,
is go bhuil m'anam istigh i ngean ort, 's ní hinné ná inniu;
d' fhág tú lag anbhann mé i ngné 's i gcruth —
ná feall orm is mé i ngean ort, a Róisín Dubh.

Anon (sixteenth century)

O, My Dark Rosaleen,
  Do not sigh, do not weep!
The priests are on the ocean green,
  They march along the deep.
There's wine from the royal pope
  Upon the ocean green,
And Spanish ale shall give you hope,
  My Dark Rosaleen!
  My own Rosaleen!
Shall glad your heart, shall give you hope,
Shall give you health, and help, and hope,
  My Dark Rosaleen!

All day long, in unrest.
  To and fro, do I move.
The very soul within my breast
  Is wasted for you, love!
The heart in my bosom faints
  To think of you, my queen,
My life of life, my saint of saints,
  My Dark Rosaleen!
  My own Rosaleen!
To hear your sweet and sad complaints,
My life, my love, my saint of saints,
  My Dark Rosaleen!

James Clarence Mangan (1803–49)

INTRODUCTION

Éigceart na nÉireannach féin
Do threascair iad d'aoinbhéim
Ag spairn fa ceart ghearr chorrach
Ní neart airm na n-eachtrannach.[1]
Fr. Geoffrey Keating (1570–1645)

ON A MORNING in midwinter towards the close of the reign of Queen Elizabeth I one of the decisive battles in Irish history was fought, outside the walled town of Kinsale, in the extreme south of Ireland. There, as the night mists gave way before the dawn of 3 January 1602 (Christmas Day, 1601, with the English, who thought that the revised Gregorian calendar smacked too much of popery), a small English force under Lord Mountjoy, the queen's general and lord deputy in Ireland, routed with the greatest dispatch the entire Irish army, led by Hugh O'Neill. By this singular victory the old queen had virtually achieved an aim cherished by the Tudor monarchy during the century and more of its existence. Ireland, the victim alike of its anarchic, if heroic, Gaelic past and of the fatal mistrust between Gael and Gall, between the 'old Irish' and 'old English', went down before the superior discipline of a modern state. The effect of the great victory gained by O'Neill at the Yellow Ford was now annulled, and although the war, with its benumbing horrors for the native population, was to drag on for over another year the final reduction of the country was now in sight.

While the English victory at Kinsale made certain at last the conquest of Ireland, it was not without effect on the outcome of the Atlantic conflict between Spain and her enemies, now, with France out of the war, reduced to two: England and the Northern Provinces of the Netherlands. Hugh O'Neill had been drawn from the security

1. It was the fault of the Irish themselves—wrangling over petty, worthless claims—which destroyed them at one stroke, and not the armed might of the foreigners.

of his Ulster fastness southwards to give battle at Kinsale by a Spanish occupation of the town. His defeat, followed by the capitulation of the Spanish invaders, prepared the way for the treaty of London (in 1604) between Spain, the Netherlands, and England. Spain had made her peace with France in 1598 (treaty of Vervins); after 1604 there remained for her only the Dutch to deal with. In her eyes the Dutch were rebels; but peacemaking had its own momentum, and in 1609 she concluded a truce of twelve years with them.

The Irish defeat and the Spanish withdrawal from Ireland also provided the Papacy with an opportunity to explore the possibility of gaining from Elizabeth's successor, James I, some amelioration of the disabilities under which his Catholic subjects laboured. The morning's fight, then, at Kinsale had more than local consequences.

Ireland had played a minor but definite role in European politics ever since the Tudors had begun first to assert and then to extend their authority over their colony to the west. The Irish lords in opposing the Tudor attack on their independence had turned for aid to the Catholic powers—first to the empire, then to France, and finally to Spain. The peace of Cateau-Cambrésis (1559) established Spain as the leading power in Europe. At the same time France began to be torn internally by religious strife. It was natural, therefore, that from now on Irish hopes for foreign intervention against the crown rested mainly on Spain. These hopes increased when, by the Spanish annexation of Portugal in 1580, conflict between Elizabeth and Philip II became more open. The Spanish response to Irish appeals is viewed as a rule by Irish writers in the context of their country's struggle against England and by English historians in that of the colonial administration in Ireland. A few writers, however, Professor Manuel Fernández Álvarez in a brief article on Shane O'Neill,[1] and Major Hume and J. B. Kelso at more length,[2] view Spanish intervention in Ireland from the wider perspective of European politics. Both Hume and Kelso, who base their researches on documents in the Spanish state archives at Simancas, concentrate on the period between the 'invincible' armada and the death of Elizabeth. But Hume's contributions and

1. Fernández Álvarez, 'La sublevación de Shane O'Neill contra Isabel de Inglaterra', in *Simancas*, i (1950), 327–33.

2. Hume, 'Españoles e irlandeses', in *Españoles e ingleses en el siglo xvi*, ch. VI; *Treason and plot* (in which Hume relates the Irish opposition to Elizabeth to that of the English and Scottish Catholics); 'Spain under Philip III', *Camb. mod. hist.*, vol. iii, ch. XVI; Kelso, *Die Spanier in Irland 1588–1603*.

Kelso's monograph, however compendious, are not full-scale works; furthermore, they need to be brought up to date in their treatment of both the international and Irish backgrounds to the Spanish intervention. The findings of two generations of research workers since Hume and Kelso have left us in a better position than they were to appreciate the complexity of the factors—political, economic, religious, even geographical and logistical—that determined the nature and extent of Spanish aid to Ireland, just as they have given us a clearer understanding than was possible for scholars of sixty-odd years ago of the changing shifts in royal policy towards Ireland and of the internal Irish political, religious, and military situations.

The present work aims at setting the Spanish invasion of Munster against a backcloth of the contemporary international, colonial, and Irish scenes. It is, surely, owing to the lack of such a study that Irish historiography has not gone beyond a superficial view of Don Juan del Águila's invasion. That invasion is seen as the simple and necessary intervention of Catholic Spain in the Irish struggle for faith and fatherland, almost a fact of nature which could be taken for granted. That the sending of the armada by Spain might not have been such a simple matter, or that, once sent, it might have had difficulty in landing at the port of its choice, or, indeed, in landing at all, are considerations which have not been adverted to.

In fact, the controversies which Águila's expedition has aroused in the past, controversies about his destination and about his conduct of the defence of Kinsale, simply show that the available source-material has not been properly studied. Besides, these disputes overlook the difficulties of raising such an expedition as Águila's and of landing it in Ireland at all, as they overlook the poverty of his resources and the lack of support accorded him. Ignacio Olagüe wrote to the point when he observed that it would have been a miracle if the 'invincible' armada and the two later expeditions (one against England and the other against Ireland) sent by Philip II had succeeded. Olagüe (who wrote thus in 1938) compared the launching of these expeditions to the sending of a squadron of planes from Europe to cross the Atlantic in one flight and bombard New York.[1]

Águila's expedition, it may then be agreed, is mainly of interest, not for the issues around which the controversies alluded to above have raged, but for more fundamental reasons, namely why was it sent at

1. Olagüe, *La decadencia española*, i. 355.

all? need it necessarily have been sent? and what light does a study of it throw on the nature of the struggle in Ireland and on the place of Ireland in contemporary power politics?

Fault is found by historians with the Spanish expedition to Munster on four standard counts: it was too little, it was too late, it came to the wrong place, and it was incompetently led by Águila. The first three charges, or the first and third at any rate, may be readily admitted. But if we are to guard against the danger of making facile judgements, it would be well for us here to recall the warning sounded by Fernand Braudel, in connection with the duke of Alba's movement of troops to the Netherlands in 1567. The recruiting of infantry, the mobiliza-tion and victualling of round ships, the movement of troops from far-away Andalusia, and the navigation, 'continental' in extent, that was demanded by the operation, presented, Braudel points out, a tremendous problem in logistics in the sixteenth century.[1] And granted that Águila's little force was far less calculated to strain the resources of the Spanish empire (even in decline) than was Alba's army of 25,000 men, yet the movement (directed at times from Madrid, at times from Valladolid) of 4,000 infantry (camp-followers do not appear on the official list of those going to Ireland) from Guipúzcoa, Andalusia, and the remote Azores by way of Lisbon to Ireland was not achieved without considerable difficulty.

But the sending of the expedition was determined by considerations not merely of logistics but also of the political objectives to be gained. Contemporary Irish leaders were realistic enough to see that they could not secure Spanish aid on the plea of Irish need alone; the Spaniards, however altruistic they were, however Catholic, naturally considered their own interests, and these interests were primary in their calculations. Accustomed as Irish historians are to seeing the nine years' war as the game on the board and the Spanish intervention as the moving of one piece (however important) by Hugh O'Neill, it might be salutary for them to realize that the Spanish outlook was not necessarily so restricted; Spanish friendship for Ireland and Spanish concern at the threat to Catholicism in Ireland did not blind Spaniards to Ireland's importance as the English 'Netherlands' and to Hugh O'Neill's value as a pawn to be used in the game against Elizabeth. As his advisers, in a key-statement, put it to Philip III:

1. Braudel, *Méditeranée et monde méditerranéen*, p. 883.

Spanish aid to Ireland will save our holy faith in that country. Besides, by aiding Ireland His Majesty will at very little cost achieve the same effect as Queen Elizabeth does by aiding the Dutch rebels. This is a matter whose importance we ought to rate very highly and to which we ought to attend with great care and diligence . . .[1]

What Braudel has said of Philip II after 1559 is true also of Philip III: it is from Spain that the king views and judges events; it is within a climate morally Spanish that his policy is elaborated, because Spanish interests and Spanish statesmen are closest to him.[2]

This is not to say that Philip III was hypocritical in his attitude towards Ireland; the justice and the utility of intervention in Ireland could very easily be reconciled. Ideally, of course, Spain was committed to the defence of Catholicism, and her obligations as Catholic champion were a too-continually recurring theme on the lips of her statesmen to be dismissed as mere platitudes. But however much they sought in theory the restoration of the old Christian unity of Europe, and however much the crusade remained an aspiration for them, the policy of the Spanish Habsburgs was in practice determined rather by reasons of state than by the crusading ideal. It is perhaps necessary to stress this in an age which has seen a secular and professedly more liberal society wage total war on an 'evil' enemy, offering him no choice but unconditional surrender.

The succouring of the persecuted Irish Catholics appealed to the piety of the young Philip III, as the honouring of his father's promise made in 1596 to the Irish appealed to his pride. But the invasion of Munster resulted not so much from Philip's wish as from the decision of the duke of Lerma, the king's first minister, to favour it. Lerma's decision, in turn, was consequent on the fact that the accident of peace between France and Savoy had made available two thousand men in Lisbon to become the nucleus of the invading force. A study of the expedition illustrates, as to certain vital elements, the working of the Spanish administration, for the councils of state, of war, and of finance were all engaged in its direction. The difficulties which the preparation of the invasion encountered reveal in turn the administrative chaos of Spain, the weakness of the naval arm, and Philip III's

---

1. . . . demas de que dello resulterá conservasse allá nuestra sancta fe por aquella mano podrá su magestad hazer el mesmo effecto que la reyna haze por la de los rebeldes a muy poca costa, que es cosa de tanta consideración que se deve stimar en mucho, y acudir a ella con extraordinario cuydado y diligencia . . . AGS, Estado 840, f. 288: Council of state to Philip III, 8 June 1600.

2. Braudel, *Méditerranée et monde méditerranéen*, pp. 773–4.

inability to meet the demands of such a comparatively modest expedition at a time when money was being squandered on frivolities; just as the efforts made by a dedicated few to surmount these difficulties reveal the concern of individuals for Spain and for her mission. The story of the expedition makes clear also the essential subordination by Spain of Irish interests to her own, at a time when her chief concern was to make England yield good peace terms.

Spain, when in 1601 she sent an army to Ireland, was paradoxically really interested in disengagement. But while she had concluded peace with France, had sent out overtures to England, was seeking to extricate herself from the costly Dutch war, and was conducting negotiations even with Constantinople, she yet maintained a jealous care for her greatness. Thus she prepared herself for war with France, if that country should attack Savoy; she continued to aid Archduke Albert, sovereign of the Netherlands, in his struggle against the United Provinces; she sought to support the emperor's eastern war against the Turk by attacking the Berbers in the western Mediterranean; and she tried by creating a diversion in Ireland to extract better peace terms from England.

For the English and Spaniards had already in 1600 come to the conference table. But the peace-talks at Boulogne, at which the archduke, who in fact had taken the initiative on the discussions, was also represented, had proved to be premature. There were at least two good reasons why Elizabeth saw more to be gained from a continuation of the war than from peace. In the first place France was threatening to attack Savoy; such an attack would endanger Spanish possession of Milan and probably lead to a renewal of hostilities between France and Spain. Secondly, the Dutch inflicted a crushing defeat on Albert at Nieuport on 2 July, providing Sir Francis Vere, the English general, with an opportunity to strengthen Ostend. With the Spaniards and the archduke so hard pressed the English envoys at Boulogne proved unyielding, and the negotiations broke off, *re infecta*, in August.

Then in January 1601 France and Savoy made peace, and the French threat to the Milanese lifted. Spain had intended to transport troops from Lisbon to the relief of Albert; she now could send men overland from Milan instead, and the 2,000 infantry assembled at Lisbon were made ready for call. The Spaniards decided to raise this force, by the addition of further levies, to 6,000 men to go to the aid of Hugh

O'Neill. Philip III also decided to send the Genoese brothers Fedérico and Ambrosio Spínola with another army of 6,000 men to invade England. Elizabeth was to be brought to her knees.

The army which sailed from Belém for Ireland on 3 September 1601 numbered only 4,432 men, far short of the expected 6,000. It was too small therefore to take the field and attack the Munster towns, and its immediate aim should have been to join forces with the Irish. Its destination for that reason should have been Killybegs or Teelin or, at the very furthest south, Limerick. But owing to a combination of inexpert advice and ill-chance it landed at Kinsale instead. The Spaniards were thus at the furthest remove in Ireland from O'Neill and his ally, Hugh O'Donnell, who were now taken in the rear at Loch Foyle and Lifford and had lost again the allegiance of Leinster and Munster. The chances that the Spanish and Irish forces might effect a junction were thus very remote. Moreover, by sending their ships home the Spaniards gave up control of Kinsale harbour and thereby considerably reduced their ability to stand siege against a well-armed, well-provisioned, and determined enemy. Pope Clement VIII finally refused to make it a matter of conscience for Catholics to support the invasion, so that the Munster lords (apart from a number in the south-west) and townsmen did not come out in support of the Spaniards.

The reasons why many (but not all) of the lords of the south-west did declare for the Spaniards were these: a further small force of Spanish infantry occupied the ports of Castlehaven, Baltimore, and Berehaven in December, and O'Neill and O'Donnell against all probability broke through the encircling enemy and reached the neighbourhood of Kinsale and cut off the besiegers' land-approaches.

O'Neill sensibly wished to avoid an engagement with the English on open ground, and to let starvation and exposure defeat them instead. However, he was forced to attack by Águila, the Spanish general, and by O'Donnell. In the ensuing fight, which does not merit the name of battle, the Irish were utterly routed. Nine days later the Spaniards in Kinsale capitulated. Spain withdrew from the Irish theatre of war, and Philip's plan of invading England was defeated by the exigencies of the war in Flanders. Spain in any case was now dedicating her energies to peacemaking. Philip had ratified the treaty of Vervins in 1601. When Elizabeth died and O'Neill had submitted, it was easy to come to terms with the peacefully inclined James I. The peace of London of 1604 together with the truce of 1609 between Spain and the Dutch brought about a general disengagement in Europe. Irish hopes of further Spanish aid faded to become a dream of the poets, 'the tellers of the tale and myth'.

I · THE EMPEROR CHARLES V AND PHILIP II OF SPAIN

Now for reasons of state there was armed intervention in France and in Brittany. In spite of the considerable loss suffered, this was very proper. It follows that some intervention in Ireland would be of no less value.

Don Martín de la Cerdá, 1600[1]

CHARLES I OF SPAIN (1516–56) outbid his competitors and secured election as Holy Roman Emperor in 1519. Charles V (his imperial title) now united under his personal rule a vast number of heterogeneous dominions sprawling over Europe and the New World. His maternal grandfather Ferdinand had bequeathed to him the kingship of Aragon, with Naples, Sicily, Sardinia, and Corsica, and a claim to the duchy of Milan, which was in 1519 held by the French but was technically a fief of the empire. Ferdinand had also left to his grandson certain stations in North Africa, together with Cerdagne and Rousillon; these latter were two Catalan counties which lay on the French side of the Pyrenees and were claimed by France. With his imbecile mother Joanna, Charles was joint ruler of Castile, to which was annexed Navarre and the rapidly growing American empire. As heir to his father, Philip the handsome, he was duke of Burgundy; this title made him lord of Artois and Flanders (both of them French fiefs), the Netherlands, Luxembourg, and Franche-Comté, and claimant to the duchy of Burgundy, which had reverted to the crown of France. Finally, as head of the house of Habsburg, Charles ruled over the five duchies of Austria, Tyrol, Styria, Carinthia, and Carniola, together with Alsace and expected the reversions of the other Habsburg hereditary lands, the kingdoms of Bohemia and Hungary.

1. *Pues, por razón destado se metió la guerra en Francia, siendo muy acertado, y en Bretaña, donde se ha perdido tanto. De donde se sigue no ser de menos conveniencia meter alguna en esta isla* ... AGS, Estado 185.

Each of these varied and extensive dominions had its own problems, and their interests were often in conflict and were indeed irreconcilable. Castile, for instance, now needed to establish her power in North Africa and to make secure possession of her Atlantic discoveries. But her partner Aragon had designs on Italy, so that Castile was distracted by the demands of her alliance from serving her real interests. Italy was a battle-ground between Aragon and France. The Italian peninsula, with its rich cities, developed economy, and political weakness, invited conquest, and the struggle between France and Spain for its possession was the central issue on which Europe divided between the years 1494 and 1559. In order to maintain the Spanish hold on Italy and to keep the French out of the country, Charles V like Ferdinand before him sought to contain France within a system of alliances embracing chiefly Spain, England, and Austria.[1]

If Spanish policy was at odds with itself, Germany was now presented with a great opportunity to achieve her goal of unification, for her king could draw on the resources of Germany's borderlands, the Burgundian Netherlands and Austria, to impose centralization on the Reich. But unfortunately Charles had too many other preoccupations to be able to devote himself single-mindedly to this task, and the favourable moment was lost.

Unappalled, however, by the magnitude of the problems of his far-spreading empire, and undeterred by the tensions from within and without which constantly threatened to rend it asunder, Charles worked steadily and patiently for almost forty years to keep his dominions together and to transmit them intact to his heir. His strategy was essentially conservative, his outlook that of the medieval emperors, of whom in fact he was the last. As Caesar, as Charlemagne, he saw it as his sacred charge to maintain the unity of Catholic and feudal Europe and to defend it against its external foes, the Ottoman Turks, and later against its internal enemies, the Lutheran princes.[2]

If the strategy of Charles V was to maintain the politico-religious unity of Europe under pope and emperor, his tactics were, in the first place and in true medieval fashion, to form dynastic alliances, and only when danger threatened the security of the Habsburg possessions to resort to war with other Christian powers. In the second place

1. Lynch, *Spain under the Habsburgs*, i. 34.
2. Cf. Koenigsberger, in *New Camb. mod. hist.*, ii. 302–3.

Charles sought to isolate his problems and to deal with them one at a time, to find a compromise solution for one problem which would leave him free to deal with another; thus he hoped eventually to settle them all.

But the enemies of the emperor's design were too numerous for these tactics to succeed. Islam, France, the Lutherans, England, and even the Papacy: his opponents were a Hydra who grew heads faster than he could cut them off. To put the matter in another way: Europe was now in a ferment, seething with new nationalism and old dynasticism, novel heresies and old Guelph notions, and it would not be contained within the mould which Charles sought to impose upon it.

Already, indeed, western Europe had taken on a new mould, in which four major territorial units were engaged in a struggle for power, a struggle which was now complicated by the religious divisions which followed upon the Lutheran revolt. These four units were France, England, and, united under the Habsburg rule of Charles V, the two power-aggregates of Burgundy–Austria and Castile–Aragon. Between these two power-aggregates lay, as has been said, the German empire.

France, even if she could not compare in extent with the Habsburg empire, was undoubtedly first and greatest of the new powers. With a coastline bordering the Mediterranean, the Atlantic, the English Channel, and the North Sea, she outshone even Spain as a maritime power. Her developed urban life, her wealth of corn and vines, her great waterways, all ensured her commercial strength. The crown of France was hereditary in the male line, a factor which gave stability. The crown had secured control over all the great fiefs and had at command a standing army, which it could support by imposing taxation without reference to the States-General. France occupied a central position in Europe, with internal communications, and with England, Italy, and Spain arranged symmetrically around her. Her population of perhaps fifteen million was twice that of Spain, four times that of England.

England was a small nation indeed, but her people were well-endowed with the requisite qualities of daring for making the most of the great opportunities that were now offered them for advancement in political and commercial strength. England, too, was well-placed for developing her ocean trade and she could exploit the fact that her friendship was eagerly sought by both the emperor and the king of France.

The imperial objective was to maintain the *status quo*, that of the other powers to disrupt it; and the advantage lay with them. Lutheranism found strong support from the princes and cities of Germany, who wished to guard their autonomy against the emperor and to emulate the autocracy of the 'new' monarchies, in England, France, and Spain. Civil and religious disobedience thus combined against Charles in Germany. The French, in order to escape from Habsburg encirclement and to win back control of Italy, turned this situation to their own advantage, as they did also the fears of the Papacy. Rome, seeing in the growth of Charles's influence in Italy the greatest threat to her independence of action, resisted that growth by whatever means she could; but in so doing she gave aid to the forces of disintegration within the universal church. The Holy See thus found itself in the unpleasant dilemma of either losing its independence or assisting in the disruption of Christianity.

England saw in a balance between Habsburg imperialism and France the best guarantee of her own liberty, and in order to maintain this equilibrium sometimes supported the emperor in his war with France, sometimes opposed him. Europe was dividing politically into the two great masses of the Habsburg empire and France, which attracted within their orbits all the lesser powers, and England wavered between the two. Then in the mid 1530s Henry VIII, fearful of losing his independence to the emperor, sought to build up alliances with Charles's enemies in Germany. This policy proved a failure, and Henry in the end threw in his lot with Charles against Francis I, the Valois king of France. It was difficult for England to avoid committing her support to one or other of the giant powers. In the reign of Edward VI she patched up a truce with France, but under Mary she was again drawn into the imperial orbit.

It was essential for Henry VIII, seeking as he did from the 1520s to arbitrate between Habsburg and Valois, that he should not be open to attack from the European enemy of the moment through Ireland. To reduce the independence of the Irish lords, both Norman and Gaelic, therefore became his policy across the Irish Sea. It was a policy which naturally provoked resistance. But Ireland's success in obstructing Henry's policy of political and religious centralization depended on two factors, namely, a positive response of the European powers to Ireland's appeals for help and a measure of political unity among the princes. Unfortunately, both of these factors were missing.

The Geraldines, greatest of the Anglo-Norman houses and dominant power in Ireland, were the first victims of Henry's new policy of centralization; and under attack James Fitzmaurice Fitzgerald, tenth earl of Desmond, 'Silken' Thomas, and the lords of the Geraldine League[1] all in turn appealed to the continental powers for help. James of Desmond sought aid first, in 1523, from Francis I and then, in 1527, from Charles V. Unfortunately for the success of Desmond's intrigues, Habsburg and Valois were engaged in the Italian wars, and Desmond died in the year in which peace between the two was signed (1529). When in 1534 the rebel 'Silken' Thomas, Lord Offaly, appealed to the emperor for support, the latter was too busy fighting with the corsairs in the Mediterranean to think of going to his assistance; then the Habsburg–Valois conflict drew on once more and two years afterwards, in 1536, the emperor was at war again with his great enemy Francis, in Italy. Henry VIII was thus left free to destroy the power of the once-great house of the Leinster Geraldines.

The stern lesson taught by the king, who executed together Thomas of Offaly and his five uncles, was not lost on the Irish lords. To both Gael and Norman it was now apparent that Henry no longer intended to tolerate any independent power in Ireland. A number of the lords, therefore, drew together in the Geraldine League, organized by Manus O'Donnell, lord of Tyrconnell. But the League's attempts to secure foreign intervention also failed. The year 1538 saw Francis signing a truce with Charles, but it was recognized as only a temporary cessation of hostilities; there was no possibility that the two monarchs would co-operate in any action against Henry. The latter placated Charles by dropping Cromwell's policies of protestantizing England and of forming alliances with the emperor's German opponents. He then felt secure enough to deal with Ireland in a more conciliatory fashion. His moderate policy of 'surrender and regrant' which he followed between 1540 and his death in 1547 secured acceptance. The Irish lords received their lands by feudal tenure from the Crown and in return acknowledged Henry as king of Ireland. The monarch could feel well content with the success of his new colonial policy, which had secured

1. On the Geraldine revolts cf. Read (ed.), *Bibliog. Br. hist., Tudor Period*, for sources. *Ir. hist. documents 1172–1922*, eds. Curtis and McDowell, pp. 77–125, gives a representative selection of documents.

on paper at least, and for the moment, the submission of Ireland.

It was easy for the king to out-manoeuvre the Irish nobility, as Ireland was a jungle of inter-sept and inter-racial rivalries. The lords of this jungle were unable to set aside their feuds in favour of combined action against the king. Their inability to present a common front also made it impossible for them to exploit either Habsburg or Valois against England. Their lack of political sophistication allowed the crown to isolate them one after the other, and the outcome of their revolts was only to secure more firmly royal control of Ireland.

With the west divided against itself the emperor was prevented from meeting, with the united forces of Europe, the Turkish attack in the east and south. The Turks had made Constantinople their new capital, renaming it Istanbul, and from there as base they advanced into Europe in a crescent-shaped attack. One horn of the crescent moved up the Danube valley into Hungary and in the direction of Vienna, while the other penetrated into the central and western Mediterranean, the preserve of the Aragonese.

Thus harassed on all sides the emperor failed to realize his grand design for Europe: the formation of a front by France, the Empire, and the Papacy aimed at the crushing of Protestantism and the conquest of England, the liberation of Hungary from the Turk, and the transmission to his son Philip of the imperial dignity in addition to the kingship of Spain, which Philip had enjoyed since 1542.[1]

Charles V abdicated in 1556, dividing his territories. Philip II, already king of Spain and since 1554 joint ruler with Mary of England, received the Netherlands; his uncle, Ferdinand, added Germany and the imperial title to his dominions of Austria, Bohemia, and Hungary. The death of Mary Tudor in 1558 dissolved the union of England and Spain and shattered another Habsburg dream, that of an Anglo-Flemish state based on the North Sea. France might have lost Milan for good,[2] but with the incorporation of Calais, Metz, Toul, and Verdun into the state she was more unified and powerful than ever.

But Spain had gained from her release from the union with Germany, which in any case was still in the possession of the junior branch of the Habsburg family. Philip was ruler of a more compact empire than his father: made up of the Mediterranean lands and the Americas,

1. Lynch, *Spain under the Habsburgs*, i. 68–100.
2. Francesco, the last Sforza duke of Milan, died in 1535, and the duchy reverted to the emperor as an imperial fief. Charles invested his son, Prince Philip, with the duchy in 1540, and thereafter it remained a Spanish possession.

with the Netherlands, its composition was now more logical, and its opportunities for development could be realized. Spaniards, at first antipathetic towards Charles V, and frustrated by seeing the Reconquest checked, had eventually under his rule come to accept their 'destiny' as leaders of the Christian world-empire. Now with Philip II began their great century of military, intellectual, and artistic predominance. The movement towards unification in Iberia received a new impetus, which had effect in the annexation of Portugal and the Portuguese maritime empire. Ruler of the whole peninsula and of a vast empire, both in the old world and the new, the Catholic king could believe that it was his mission to shape the destinies of the globe. And this belief was shared by Spaniards in general.

But Spanish hegemony did not go undisputed. If the two power blocs which for forty years had sundered Europe between them had now broken up, the continent was dividing even more sharply into two new hostile camps, at issue with each other on the question of religion. Reluctantly Spain was driven to become champion of Catholicism, and, just as reluctantly, England, facing Spain across the Atlantic, was forced to become the upholder of the Protestant challenge to Catholicism. The fires of religious conflict were fed by other fuel: the growing Spanish preponderance, commercial rivalry, the struggle for control in France, and the efforts by the Dutch and Irish to gain independence. For a hundred years the fires blazed throughout Europe, until the peace of Westphalia in 1648 at last officially acknowledged the passing of the old medieval unity. Even then the confessional passion was not spent, but continued to smoulder for many years to come, making the air of Europe and the world foul with the intolerance shown by most temporal and spiritual authorities at a national level towards dissident minorities.

At war on the Atlantic front, Spain had to maintain a vigilant guard against the Turk in the south as well. Philip II had to bear the brunt of the infidel assault on the western Mediterranean. Inheriting bankruptcy and heresy from the previous reign, her attention diverted from the more pressing and rewarding task of putting her own house in order, the Spain of Philip II found herself unhappily engaged with both north and south in fateful hostility. In the south she checked the advance of Islam, but France, England, and the United Provinces successfully contested her supremacy in the north and established themselves as her rivals.

Philip won the victory of Saint Quentin and forced the French to sign the definitive peace of Cateau-Cambrésis in 1559. With peace established in the north, the king of Spain used the opportunity afforded him to launch a counter-attack against the Turks, whose Berber allies had taken possession of Algiers and Tripoli. But the expedition which Philip sent against Tripoli in 1560 was defeated with heavy loss. Philip, however, built up his fleet and at Lepanto (1571) endangered Turkish supremacy in the Mediterranean.

Forced to meet the challenge from the Turks and bankrupted, Philip had other preoccupations as well. He feared that Spain was to be the victim of the next attack from Protestantism, now again on the march in its Calvinist form. He was concerned too, since Mary Stuart was queen of France, that the French might gain control of England and Scotland, a control that would endanger Spanish possession of the Netherlands. Apart from his many concerns Philip's outlook was conservative. He made no response therefore in 1559 to an offer of the throne of Ireland to a king of his choice, in return for a Spanish force sent to liberate the country. This offer did not in any case come from any national confederacy, and Philip was shrewd enough to realize this. In fact, it is doubtful if the alleged national league of bishops and nobles which made it had any existence other than in the perfervid imagination of James Fitzmaurice Fitzgerald, cousin of the earl of Desmond.[1]

To the appeals which continued to come from Ireland during the early sixties Philip turned a deaf ear.[2] These appeals now came from Shane O'Neill, who had made himself master of Ulster and then had sought Spain's assistance against the crown. Philip did not find Shane's suggestions 'desirable' and instructed his ambassador in England to 'cut them short gently'. Disappointed in Spain, O'Neill in his later years turned to the Guises and their cousin, Mary Stuart, for help in driving out the English. But the Guise party was no longer in the ascendancy in France, and in the period of calm (1559–65) that succeeded the great series of wars in Europe, the waters were too untroubled for Irish malcontents to fish in. Death found Shane in 1567 with nothing to show for his overtures to France.

Shane O'Neill, essentially provincial rather than national in outlook, was typical of the Irish nobility, who gave no serious indication that

1. Cf. Silke, *Ireland and Europe 1559–1607*, pp. 5–8.
2. *Cal. S.P. Spain, 1558–67*, p. 370: Philip to Silva, 6 Aug. 1564.

they would rally to support any Spanish or French force sent to liberate the country from English rule. This was demonstrated once more
when, as a result of the expropriations which followed upon the earl
of Desmond's forced surrender of his palatinate into the queen's hands
(February 1568), James Fitzmaurice Fitzgerald dispatched the archbishop of Cashel, Maurice Fitzgibbon, to Spain as his envoy in 1569[1].
The archbishop presented a memorial to Philip II, which declared that
Elizabeth, against the wishes of all the Irish leaders and people, was
seeking to impose heresy on the country. The memorial went on to
ask that Philip nominate a Spanish or Burgundian prince as king of
Ireland, whose appointment would be confirmed by the pope,
suzerain of Ireland. There followed a list of bishops and nobles who,
it was claimed, favoured this request. The list contained the names of
the four archbishops and of eight bishops, as well as of every leading
lord, old English and old Irish.

There are striking similarities between Fitzgibbon's appeal to
Philip and that made in 1559. Both refer to a vast Irish confederacy, in
which Desmond's name takes first place; in both Philip is asked to
appoint a prince of his blood as king of Ireland; and in both the motive
for the Irish appeal is stated to be religious alone. But in each case the
list of supporters is less that of an actual confederacy than of one that,
it was felt, the arrival of Spanish aid would bring into being. Fitzmaurice, whose aims were transparent enough, sought to rally all
Ireland in the cause of religion, but with little success.

Philip in any case returned no favourable answer to the appeal of
Archbishop Fitzgibbon. A Spanish victory at Malta (1565), the death
of Sultan Sulaiman, and Turkish losses in Hungary (1566) had caused
a relaxation of Ottoman pressure in the Mediterranean in 1567. Philip
was therefore free to turn his attention to the northern front. He sent
the duke of Alba with 25,000 men into the Netherlands to reduce them
to obedience. They were in a state of unrest, owing among other
things to Philip's foreign origin and his policies of high taxation and
religious uniformity and to the growth of militant Calvinism. It was
essential for Philip to pacify the Low Countries, as they provided
him with a considerable part of his revenue and were of great
strategic importance to Spain and the emperor in any war with
France.

1. Cf. Binchy, 'An Irish Ambassador at the Spanish court, 1569–74', in *Studies*, x–xiv
(1921–5).

2

The following year, 1568, Mary Queen of Scots fled to England and was kept prisoner by Elizabeth. Now the main threat to England came from the Low Countries, rather than from France through Scotland. The danger was that the main Spanish army under Alba, based just across the Channel from England, in control of the coasts of Holland and Zeeland and their shipping and supported by the industrial resources of Flanders and Brabant, would not only threaten the extinction of English trade but, with the aid of favourable winds achieve the conquest of England itself.[1] The huge concentration of Spanish troops on the new northern front aroused the religious fears of Cecil, the French Huguenot leader Coligny, and the German Protestants.

Being well aware of these fears, Philip had no desire just now to incite the northern powers still further by sending an expedition to Ireland. Besides, the detention of Mary by Elizabeth ended the danger of a united front of England, France, and Scotland against Spain. Philip therefore had hopes of renewing the old alliance with England if Elizabeth could be induced to make restitution for damage from English privateering.[2] The English traded illicitly in the Caribbean, for silver and logwood, and in West Africa for slaves; they appealed to *ius gentium*, the right of nations, against the papal partition of the New World between Spain and Portugal and sought to make contact with negro and Indian rebels; and they attacked, on the ocean and off the Spanish coasts, cargoes returning from the Indies to Spain. The archbishop of Cashel remained in Spain, detained by Philip 'with fair words', while the king waited to see the outcome of his negotiations with Elizabeth.

The negotiations were fruitless, and Philip was led by the ceaseless English attacks on his commerce to think of supporting the Catholic nobles who rebelled against Elizabeth in 1569. But Alba insisted on peace with England while he was engaged in pacifying the Low Countries.

Philip was now, in 1569–70, faced with the great crisis of his reign. Not only were the Netherlands in revolt, but also the Moriscos, or converted Moors, of Granada who broke out at the end of 1568. They were believed, and with some reason, to be in sympathy with their

---

1. Cf. Wernham, *Before the Armada*, pp. 19, 292, 320; and in *Elizabethan government and society*, pp. 340–68; Braudel, *Méditerranée et monde méditerranéen*, pp. 870–6, 882–7.
2. *Cal. S.P. Spain, 1568–79*: Philip II to Alba, 18 Nov. 1569.

co-religionists, the Turks. Philip was convinced that Spain was under attack from two international conspiracies, that of Protestantism and that of Mohammedanism.

But although he still toyed with the idea of intervening in England or, as Archbishop Fitzgibbon suggested, in Ireland, Alba restrained him. Pope Pius V, however, unlike Alba, did not fear provoking Elizabeth. His austere conscience, rather than political expediency, was for Pope Pius the guiding principle of action, and in February 1570 by the Bull *Regnans in excelsis* he excommunicated Elizabeth and deprived her of her rights of sovereignty.

Philip absolutely refused to execute this sentence. Alba seemed to have quelled rebellion in the Netherlands, and Philip, whose reputation for temporizing and for 'prudence' is one of the most curious myths of history, turned back at once to deal with the Turks. Pius and Philip were at one at least on the need to strike at the Ottoman, and a league of the Papacy, Spain, and Venice defeated the Turks in the great sea-battle of Lepanto (7 October 1571).

If Philip had failed him as an instrument for deposing Elizabeth, the pope was comforted to find that there was at least one paladin brave enough to do battle with the English heretics. Or so it seemed to him when Sir Thomas Stukeley, an English soldier of fortune, came to him with a scheme for invading Ireland. Pius, without resources himself, sought to gain Philip's support for Stukeley's plans. But Sir Thomas, although he might deceive the unworldly Pius, was known to the more astute Philip, who had rejected an earlier offer from him to go to conquer Ireland, for the adventurer he was. It was no surprise, therefore, when in January 1572 the king turned down Stukeley's scheme. In any case, with England courting France, Philip was not anxious to antagonize Elizabeth too much. He had shown some favour (although Alba had not) towards the conspirators who, between 1570 and 1572, aimed with Spanish help at dethroning Elizabeth, marrying Mary of Scots to Norfolk and placing her on the throne. But Cecil's vigilance had defeated this plot (the so-called Ridolfi plot), and its only effect was to favour the growth of friendship between England and France, so that the two countries made a defensive pact in 1572 (treaty of Blois).

This was alarming to Philip because of developments in the Netherlands. In 1572 the Dutch exiles, the 'sea-beggars', returned home and captured Brill and Flushing. William of Orange advanced from

Germany into Brabant and there was open revolt in the Low Countries. The French sent forces in to support the Dutch.

Not only Philip but also Elizabeth viewed these developments with
dismay. The queen of England did not desire the total destruction of
Spanish hegemony in the Netherlands, since it would only be replaced
by French control of the Channel coast from Brest to Brill. England's
policy under Elizabeth, as it had been under her father, was to follow
a middle course between the Spanish Scylla and the French Charybdis.
Elizabeth sought without destroying Spanish sovereignty over the
Netherlands to restore to them the securities, political and fiscal, of
which Philip had deprived them, and to gain for the Protestants some
measure of freedom. To get the Spaniards out altogether would only
be to let the French in. For this reason she patched up disputes over
the Netherlands in 1575, and sought to negotiate peace between
William of Orange and Philip.

Meanwhile, Sir John Perrot had arrived in Cork in 1571 to take over
a new office, that of the presidency of Munster. Within two years he
had broken resistance, and in 1575 James Fitzmaurice was driven
abroad. Rebuffed in France he went to Spain, where he had no better
fortune. If either country intervened in Ireland Elizabeth would be
driven into the other's camp.

The war in the Low Countries broke out fiercely again, and Elizabeth's attempt to play the role of honest broker was defeated, as was
the plan of Don John of Austria for dealing with England. Don John
came to the Netherlands as governor in 1576. He hoped to pacify the
rebellious provinces and then go on to lead an invasion of England,
designed to place Mary of Scots on the throne. He failed in his first
objective, and so the second never became a practical possibility. The
Dutch renewed the war with vigour, and called on the duke of Anjou,
brother of Henry III of France, to be their protector (1578). Elizabeth
did not want this, and she re-opened with Anjou marriage negotiations begun in 1572. At the same time she continued to assist the
Dutch; she subsidized Duke John Casimir of the Palatinate, who provided mercenaries for the rebel army, and in 1578 she sent Walsingham over to negotiate with William of Orange. Philip, in order to pay
her back somewhat in her own coin, allowed James Fitzmaurice to
depart for Ireland with a tiny force of not more than fifty or sixty
soldiers.

Fitzmaurice came ashore at Dingle in July 1579 to the chant of litanies, and erected the standard of the Holy Cross. He called on the princes and people of Ireland to rally to this standard for the glory of God. The voice of the military counter-reformation, making up in fervour what it lacked in strength, was now for the first time heard in Ireland. The party went on to fortify themselves in Dún an Óir, the Golden Fort, a promontory overlooking Smerwick harbour. Fitzmaurice went out to raise help but was killed in a skirmish by fellow Irishmen. Fray Mateo de Oviedo, a Spanish Franciscan, had been appointed by the papal nuncio in Spain to come with the expedition. He went back to Spain and reported that the majority of the Irish lords would rebel if only a stronger army came. In spite of his enthusiasm Oviedo failed to arouse the interest of the government. But over a year later Bastiano di San Giuseppi came from Santander to Dún an Óir with another six hundred troops (10 September 1580). San Giuseppi, self-styled colonel, had raised these volunteers on his own initiative without mandate from Philip, although he had a papal commission. About two hundred were Spaniards, the rest mainly Italians. Dún an Óir, however, was easily taken by the deputy, Lord Grey of Wilton, who massacred the entire garrison (10 November).[1]

The coming of the foreign aid, small though it was, sparked off risings, not only in Munster, but also in Ulster, Connacht, and even the Pale. These risings were easily suppressed, but they gave evidence of the unifying effect which religion was beginning to have. In the Pale Viscount Baltinglass went into revolt in July 1580. He got little support, but this rebellion marked an important stage in the struggle in Ireland and alarmed the government, Baltinglass, like Fitzmaurice, rebelled solely on religious grounds; he had suffered for his loyalty to the mass, and he could not tolerate Elizabeth's claim to spiritual supremacy. But on the whole James Fitzmaurice's appeal did not touch the consciences of the Catholics of the Pale and the south. Elizabeth's policy of restraint in enforcing the religious laws allowed them to remain firm in maintaining their political loyalty to her.

Philip of Spain had not been officially implicated in the Fitzmaurice–San Giuseppi adventure, and he did not intervene when the government took full reprisal on the Desmond palatinate. The territory was first devastated, 'a most populous and plentiful country', testified Spenser, 'suddenly made void of man and beast', and then planted.

---

1. Documentation for the Smerwick episode in VA, Nunciatures, (*Archiv. Hib.*, vii (1922)). Cf. also AGS, Estado 160, for report by Oviedo to Philip II, Mondoñedo, 13 Nov. 1580.

The lesson of Philip's inaction was not lost on Munster, which refused to respond to Don Juan del Águila's call to arms in 1601.[1]

Philip disengaged himself from the Mediterranean war because his main concern was now to suppress the revolt in the Netherlands. He appointed Alexander Farnese, duke of Parma, who was grandson of Charles V, as governor of the Netherlands in 1578 in succession to Don John. Showing rare military and diplomatic genius Parma began to win back the southern provinces for Spain.

Philip now set his face towards the west. The death of King Sebastian of Portugal provided him with a convenient pretext for annexing that kingdom and its maritime empire. Now Spain took on a new direction in policy, a new vitality in purpose. Foiling the French dream of gaining Portugal and Brazil (1582–3), Philip was engaged in a great northern war: face to face with England, at war with the Dutch, in partial occupation of Brittany. Unfortunately for Spain, Philip failed to exploit his possession of Lisbon, where he should have moved his court permanently to direct the war against England and France.

The Spanish conquest of Portugal threatened the balance of power in the Atlantic. Apart from the territorial gains, Spain took over the Portuguese fleets. In 1585 the Spanish merchant marine rivalled, if it did not outrank, the Dutch, doubled the German, and trebled the English and French.[2] In the same year in which Philip annexed Portugal the Catholic Francophile party, under the earl of Lennox, came into control in Scotland again. Lennox worked in conjunction with the French Catholic League, under the leadership of the duke of Guise, and with Mendoza, the Spanish ambassador in London. They planned an invasion of England, by Lennox from Scotland and by Guise from France, in order to place Mary Stuart on the throne. But Lennox was overthrown by the Scottish Protestants in 1582. A revised plan—that Guise alone, at the head of a detachment of Parma's soldiers, should invade England—was revealed under torture by Mary's agent, Francis Throckmorton, to Walsingham in 1583. As a result diplomatic relations between England and Spain were broken off (January 1584).

Anjou died in June and the Protestant Henry of Navarre and Bourbon was now heir presumptive to Henry III. The Catholic League at once made it its object to exclude Navarre, and Philip II joined the

1. O'Rahilly, *The massacre at Smerwick, 1580*; Read, *Walsingham and Elizabeth*, i. 306–422.
2. Hamilton, 'The decline of Spain', in *Econ. Hist. Rev.*, viii (1938), 168.

League in 1585. The Protestant cause in the Low Countries had already received what seemed a mortal blow when on 10 July 1584 William the Silent was assassinated. William, who for a short while had united the Catholics and Protestants in the Low Countries in their struggle for their liberties, had latterly been the inspiration of the northern Union of Utrecht, formed in 1579 with the object of achieving complete independence. William's leadership of the United Provinces devolved on the States-General, a parliament of the representatives of the various provinces; but it was a timid, unwieldy body. With Parma going from success to success south of the Meuse and Philip leagued with the Guises, the counter-reformation gained in momentum.

The Protestant cause looked well-nigh lost. If Brittany and Normandy, as seemed likely, came completely under the control of the Catholic League, and if Flushing and the Scheldt fell to Parma, Spain would have a line of sea bases extending from Lisbon to Flushing, from which, with her superior sea power, she would be able to launch an overwhelming attack on England, the last remaining bastion of Protestantism.

In 1585 Philip seized the English merchant ships in Spanish ports. Elizabeth, now thoroughly alarmed, committed herself by the treaty of Nonsuch (August 1585) to the protection of the United Provinces. Brill, Flushing, and Rammekens, the so-called cautionary towns, were to be security for the money she should spend. In December the earl of Leicester went over to take command of a considerable expeditionary force which had gone to the Netherlands in October.

The acceptance of the title of Governor-General by Leicester was in effect the acceptance for Elizabeth of English sovereignty of the Netherlands.[1] English intervention had one early effect that was ironic, for Sir William Stanley, who had brought over a regiment of Irish to serve under Leicester at the beginning of 1587, went over to Spain with the majority of his troops.[2]

In the growing conflict between England and Spain there were many causes of dispute, both political and economic. The attack by Drake on the Indies in 1585-6 proved the final irritant to Philip. The young James VI of Scotland, already anxious to succeed Elizabeth on the English throne, made a defensive alliance against foreign powers

1. Read, *Walsingham and Elizabeth*, iii. 107–37; Neale, *Essays in Elizabethan history*, p. 171; Handover, *The second Cecil*, p. 47.

2. On Stanley's career cf. *Wild Geese in Spanish Flanders*, ed. Jennings, *passim*; Loomie, *The Spanish Elizabethans*, pp. 130–74.

with the queen in July 1586 (Treaty of Berwick). Feeling confident now of James, Elizabeth consented to the execution of his mother, Mary of Scots, in February 1587 for her complicity in the Babington plot. Mary's death removed the last obstacle to Philip's invasion plans, the 'enterprise of England', for he could not have placed her on the throne without strengthening the French. He therefore launched the 'invincible' armada in 1588, designed not only to conquer England but also to destroy the Dutch.

Medina Sidonia, the armada's commander, adhering rigidly to the strategy worked out for him, failed to attempt a landing at Plymouth or the Isle of Wight, and the armada drove on to defeat. Henry III was encouraged to attack the Catholic League strongly in France. He was however assassinated in August 1589, and France became a battle-ground between the Huguenot Henry of Navarre, claiming the succession as Henry IV, and the League.

If Henry IV were to unite France behind him, both Spanish possession of the Netherlands and Spanish domination in Italy would be endangered. Philip determined to prevent this. He himself as son-in-law of Henry II had a claim to the French throne, which he now sought for his daughter, Isabel Clara Eugenia. He sent 3,000 men to Brittany to serve under the duke of Mercouer, general of the League (October 1590). Elizabeth was frightened lest Philip should renew the attack on England from bases in the Netherlands and France. Spain, foiling English attempts to stop her treasure fleets from coming home, was rebuilding her navy. The queen therefore sent expeditionary forces to Normandy and Brittany. Meanwhile Parma, acting on Philip's orders, had to come twice from the Netherlands to France to relieve the Catholic League strongholds of Paris (1590) and Rouen (1592) from siege by Henry. This prevented his dealing the *coup de grâce* to the two remaining dissident provinces, Holland and Zeeland. The Dutch with English help improved their position and the great Parma died, a disappointed man, on 2 December 1592. Maurice of Nassau, William the Silent's son, was a cool and resolute commander. With the best of Philip's Netherlands troops diverted to France after 1589, Maurice was able to begin the campaign which, six years later, was to see the Spaniards cleared from the provinces north of the Lower Rhine and Waal. Maurice even held Ostend, as a base of operations against Flanders, in the south.[1] The northern Netherlands were in effect lost to Spain.

1. *Elizabethan government and society*, p. 350.

II · THE NINE YEARS' WAR

> If indeed you remain steadfast for the future in your efforts to
> expel altogether from your territories the enemies of God, you
> may expect all the assistance that Alonso Cobos, in whom you
> are to have full trust, will assure you of.
>
> Philip II to Irish Catholic nobles, 14 August 1596[1]

IN FRANCE TOO, where Henry IV became a Catholic in 1593 and thus
began to win the allegiance of the Leaguers, Spain was losing ground.
But Philip still fought for possession of Brest, a valuable revictualling
stage between Spain and Flanders; while Elizabeth, with her own
safety in mind, sought to prevent his getting this port as a base in
which his armadas might refit for the invasion of England. The
Spaniards with 5,000 men on the Blavet faced the combined opposition of Henry's army and an English force under Sir John Norris.

As if it were not enough for Spain to have armies engaged in both
France and the Low Countries, she was now asked to send an expedition to Ireland as well. This request came from the north of Ireland
from a confederacy of bishops and chiefs, of which Edmund Magauran, archbishop of Armagh, and Red Hugh O'Donnell, the vigorous
young prince of Tyrconnell, were the moving spirits. Magauran had
talked with Philip of Spain and had rather rashly formed the convic-
tion that Philip would aid the Irish if they formed a reasonably strong
combination and took up arms. The primate found Red Hugh very
willing to assist him in forming such a combination, and by May 1593
the two had brought it into being.

To the lords of Ulster, spiritual and lay, it seemed, and with good
reason, as if their province, the last stronghold of Gaelic independence
and of the free exercise of the old faith, was about to be conquered. To
gain the support of Philip II for their fight in defence of their liberty,

---

1. . . . *si vero eodem animo in posterum Dei hostes ex ditionibus vestris omnino expellandos
curabitis . . . non est cur minora vobis inde bona promitatis quam ex Alphonso Cobos . . . cognoscetis, cui integram fidem adhibebitis.* AGS, Estado 2604.

political and religious, they sent Archbishop James O'Hely to Spain in 1593.

The confederacy of which Archbishop O'Hely was agent was notable for the absence from its leadership of the most important of the Ulster chiefs, the man whose mid-Ulster lordship was the pivot of the whole province. This was Hugh O'Neill, second earl of Tyrone. O'Neill was in an awkward position. Ties of blood united him to both O'Donnell and young Hugh Maguire, the leading chiefs of the confederacy. But while these young men could hope to wrest concessions from the queen by an exhibition of strength, he, more mature, saw much danger to himself if he provoked her. As things stood he was in the good graces of Elizabeth who recognized his title to the earldom of Tyrone. Should he rebel he incurred the risk of unpleasant consequences. The failure of Philip to support Fitzmaurice's rebellion, the devastation wrought in Munster during and after the Desmond wars, and the introduction of the undertakers into the south were all warnings to him not to indulge in treasonable activities, especially as his 'Irish' rivals, O'Neill (Turloch Luineach) and the sons of Shane, could be counted upon to take advantage of any government action against him.

But Maguire took the field in 1593 and O'Donnell a year later, and the septs of Tyrone began to rally behind them. In order to bring in the other provinces the co-operation (for what it was worth) of the exiles living on Spanish pension in Lisbon was sought and gained. These exiles were Edmund Eustace, claimant to the Baltinglass title, Cahil O'Conor, son of Brian O'Conor Faly, and Maurice and Thomas Fitzgerald of the Munster Geraldines.

But O'Donnell waited in vain for the force of five to ten thousand men that he hoped to see piloted into his waters: Philip had his hands full in the Netherlands and Brittany. In April the Spaniards in Brittany, under Don Juan del Águila, moved north from the Blavet and in an attempt to take Brest built for themselves the fort of Crozon, on the northern part of the Roscanvel peninsula, commanding the harbour of Brest. They were besieged by a large English army under Norris. After a month's siege Norris stormed Crozon (10 November 1594) and Águila had to fall back on the Blavet. England need not now fear invasion from Brest.[1]

Notwithstanding therefore the impression that Primate Magauran

1. Lavisse, *Histoire de France*, vi. 405.

had carried away from Spain two years previously, Philip was now little disposed to embark on a fresh and doubtful venture in Ireland. He evidently did not agree with Archbishop O'Hely's claim that an attack on Elizabeth in Ireland would be the most effective means of countering the aid she gave the rebels in the Low Countries and Philip's enemies in France. As the king pointed out to Juan de Idiáquez, his trusted adviser in the sphere of war:

What the Irish ask . . . is much; and I think they will require much more still. Speak to the archbishop of Tuam and make full enquiry, so as to discover what force in the final analysis they really need. If it be such a small one that we can afford to give it, it will be a very good thing to help them.[1]

But no force, great or small, was sent.[2]

Tyrone, in view of the event, had been wise in playing a waiting game. But because of the energy displayed by Maguire and O'Donnell in maintaining the war of the north against the English, the earl's position on the fence was becoming untenable. In September 1595 he assumed the Irish title O'Neill. Still, however, he played for time, and again submitted to the government in October, saying that he had never 'practised with foreign princes to draw strangers into this kingdom' before. Yet he admitted that he had written to Philip in August.[3]

O'Neill (as we shall henceforth call him) was playing a double game. In fact he had then an agent, Edmund MacDonnell, dean of Armagh, at the Spanish court. And as late as 27 September Hugh O'Donnell and he had written letters (which fell into English hands) to Philip II, Cahil O'Conor, claimant to the lordship of Offaly, and Don Juan del Águila. From King Philip they asked for an army of two or three thousand men. The letters mentioned previous appeals which had gone unanswered and made an offer of the kingdom of Ireland to Philip. The bearer, as he confessed under examination, was instructed to say that the two chiefs would carry on the war if Philip undertook to send help by May.[4]

But Philip was hard pressed. Spain, officially at war with France

---

1. *Lo que piden . . . es mucho, y a mi mucho más lo será. Vos le hablad, y os informad del de todo para ver en lo que a lo ultimo habrán menester, que se les pudiese dar, muy bueno sería ayudarlos.* AGS, Estado, 839, f. 51: Philip II to Idiáquez [autumn of 1593].
2. Silke, 'The Irish appeal of 1593 to Spain', in *I.E.R.*, ser. 5, xcii (1959), 279–90, 362–71.
3. *Cal. Carew MSS. 1589–1600*, p. 126.
4. Ibid., pp. 122–3; *Cal. S.P. Ire., 1592–6*, pp. 406–7, 409–10; Walsh, 'Scots Clann Domhnaill in Ireland', in *I.E.R.*, ser. 5, lviii (1936), 23–42; Ó Lochlainn (ed.), *Tobar fíorghlan Gaedhilge*, pp. 55–6.

since March 1595,[1] was fighting all around France's borders. With this
strain on her resources she became bankrupt again, Philip suspending
payment for the third time in 1596; and the war was going against
Spain Clement VIII absolved Henry IV from excommunication in
1595. Already the majority of the members of the Catholic League
had gone over to Henry, who gained Burgundy and Provence in 1596.
But contrary to what might have been expected Henry was unable to
carry the war into the southern Netherlands. In fact, it was the
Spaniards who crossed the border into Artois and Picardy, where
their successes included the taking of Calais (April 1596). However,
their gains drove England and the Dutch to form a triple alliance with
Henry IV against Spain.

With Brittany saved from the Spaniards, Sir John Norris had
brought over his English veterans to Ireland in 1595. In spite of that
the northern allies had recovered Enniskillen, given Bagenal a reverse
at Clontibret, and gained Sligo and Monaghan. O'Donnell exercised
sway over Connacht outside the garrisons, while O'Neill was giving
Norris plenty to do to maintain communications with the garrisons at
Newry and Armagh by way of the Moyry pass. Philip's interest began
to be aroused. O'Neill was obviously providing Elizabeth with formidable opposition, and now with open war between England and Spain
he should clearly be encouraged. Philip therefore gave the Irish to
understand that in their war for the defence of the faith they might
have any assistance they required from Spain.[2]

This offer, brought to them in May 1596 by Alonso Cobos, raised the
hopes of the confederates. O'Neill and O'Donnell replied at once to
Philip that they would now end the truce (in being since the previous
October and renewed in April) with the English and begin the war
again. They asked for some help at once, to be followed by a full-sized
army as soon as it could be got ready. They offered to make Cardinal
Archduke Albert, son of Maximilian II and governor of the Netherlands since 29 January, king of Ireland, with the proviso that he should
live in the country.

In this summer of 1596 Philip sent, besides Cobos, two other military missions to Ireland, to secure information on the basis of which
he might plan his intended invasion. One of these missions reported

1. Dumont, *Corps universel diplomatique*, vol. v, pt. I, pp. 512, 515: reciprocal declaration
of war by Philip II and Henry IV, Brussels, 7 Mar. 1595.
2. *Cal. Carew MSS. 1589–1600*, p. 141: Philip II to Tyrone, Madrid, 22 Jan. 1596.

that there were many difficulties against landing any expedition in
the north. Donegal was not to be recommended as a port of disembarkation; Carlingford, Killybegs, Teelin, and Sligo all offered possibilities, but Limerick was to be preferred.

This vital question, where should the expedition land, was the subject of discussion between another mission, that of Captains Cisneros
and Medinilla, and the Irish leaders. In this matter various factors had
to be taken into account: the suitability of each harbour itself, whether
it was defended, whether the surrounding terrain offered opportunities for transport, and so on. On the whole, it was agreed in the discussions, Limerick would make the best landing-place; it could berth
a large armada, the 'marquis of Connacht' (probably Tibbot Burke,
son of Walter Ciotach, set up by O'Donnell as MacWilliam in 1595)
would be at hand to aid the Spaniards, and the other chiefs would
keep the enemy occupied until the invaders had established themselves.

The confederate leaders claimed that they commanded 6,000 foot
and 1,200 horse. While admitting that the queen had six or seven
thousand non-Irish troops in the country, they maintained that the
Catholics now subject to her would change allegiance as soon as the
Spaniards struck a blow.[1]

In claiming this the chiefs were making free with the truth, as they
knew it. In 1590 the first specifically Irish college abroad, Alcalá, was
established; and Alcalá was the forerunner of a number of Irish col-
leges set up in Spain and Portugal, the Low Countries, France, and at
Rome. But even by 1590 Irish priests educated on the Continent had
already made sure of the allegiance of the old English to Rome in
spiritual matters. While devotion to the Holy See was confirmed and
grew in strength among the Catholics of the Pale and towns, their
loyalty to the crown in political matters remained unshakeable. Thus
for the most part they ignored James Fitzmaurice's call to arms, and
they were out of sympathy with the aims of the northern rebels. They
considered that O'Neill was bent only on establishing his own supremacy in Ireland, and pointed out that the anti-Catholic laws of 1560
(the oath of supremacy and the fine of one shilling for refusal to attend
Protestant services) were not being pressed against them. In fact, these

---

1. The foregoing is documented in AGS, Estado 839 (*Cal. S.P. Spain, 1587–1603*, pp.
619–27; O'Clery, *Life of Hugh Roe O'Donnell*, ed. Murphy, introd; *Cal. S.P. Ire., 1592–6*, pp.
517, 519, 522, 526, 542–3).

laws were moderately enforced, except on one or two occasions, after the excommunication of Elizabeth, and after the armada. Their priests supported the old English in their stand, if indeed they did not inspire it. The loyalist Irish argued strongly that O'Neill was not a champion of the faith and that the queen was indifferent to the exercise of their religion.

For this reason O'Neill was making efforts to win over the old English and was seeking through the Holy See to exert pressure on them to support him. In the year 1596 he asked Pope Clement VIII to grant him the patronage of Irish sees and benefices. But the old English were able to take advantage of a changing political climate at Rome, and O'Neill did not secure the granting of this or further requests designed to compel the Catholics of Norman descent to join him. In 1580 a Roman declaration concerning the Bull of excommunication of Elizabeth allowed Catholics in effect to accept the queen as their head in the temporal order. Pope Clement VIII (1592–1605) freed the Papacy from domination by the Habsburgs; he sought, however, to conciliate them as well as the French, and in this he was successful. Henry IV was received back into the Church in 1593 and the pope absolved him from heresy two years later. But so prudent had Clement's handling of this affair been that Spain was not estranged. The Papacy under Clement maintained an influence over the two great Catholic powers. Following the same line of policy Clement refrained from judging between the two Catholic parties in Ireland, rebel old Irish and loyal old English.[1]

Philip II has earned a reputation for 'irresolution' which in view of the facts is not justified. He was already at war in the Netherlands and France. Not content with this, he was now seriously thinking of sending an army to Ireland. It was Elizabeth herself who provided him with the final provocation. After the capture of Calais Elizabeth allowed Essex and the war-party in her council to have their way, and on 20 June the earl of Essex appeared before Cadiz. The English fleet with Dutch help captured or burned fifty-seven ships and left on 16 July, taking a spoil estimated at 20,000 or more ducats and leaving the city in flames. The only resistance met with was from Don Pedro de Zubiaur, leader of a squadron which maintained communications between the Iberian peninsula and Brittany. Don Pedro, in his cruise

1. My article, 'Hugh O'Neill, the Catholic question and the papacy', in *I.E.R.*, ser. 5, civ (1965), enlarges on the subject under discussion here.

of the northern sea, engaged six enemy munition ships, sinking two
and taking four captive.

Philip II sought reprisal for the attack on Cadiz. He fell in with the
plan of Don Diego de Brochero, Zubiaur's fellow commander in the
Atlantic, to support O'Neill with an army against Elizabeth. Preparations were made in Cadiz, Lisbon, and El Ferrol, and the veteran
sailor Don Martín de Padilla, Adelantado Mayor of Castile,[1] was in
1596 made general-in-chief of the Ocean or Atlantic fleet and commander of the expedition.

Philip again sent Cobos as his envoy to the two Hughs to advise
them in advance of the proposed expedition. O'Neill and O'Donnell
wanted the Spaniards to land at Galway (near MacWilliam Burke's
lordship) or, if driven into the North Channel by the wind, at Carlingford in O'Neill's territory. Cobos announced that Philip had approved
in principle the suggestion that Archduke Albert be made king of
Ireland, but wanted clarifying discussion on this proposal.

O'Donnell laid in provisions to be ready on 1 November to victual
the Spanish army, but in vain. Padilla left Lisbon with eighty-one
vessels and was joined by nineteen from Seville. He intended to join
with other ships from Ferrol and Vigo. Seeking to round Finisterre, he
ran into an equinoctial tempest off Viana on 28 October. The fleet was
overwhelmed and thirty-two ships, not counting caravels and lesser
vessels, perished between Corcubión and Cape Finisterre. Two
thousand men at least were lost (estimates vary somewhat) and the
surviving ships got with much difficulty into ports of the Gulf of
Cantabria.[2]

Another expedition, which planned to land at Falmouth and intercept Essex's fleet on its return from the Azores, also failed. On 19
October 1597 Padilla, again captain-general, left Corunna with a fleet

1. The office of *adelantado* was established in the middle ages. The *adelantados mayores*,
whose office was hereditary, were those of highest function and exercised civil and judicial
jurisdiction over the provinces, being responsible only to the king. In wartime they had
command of all the military forces of their district. Cf. *Encic. Espasa-Calpe;* Almirante,
Diccionario militar. Don Martín de Padilla Manrique, conde de Buendía (15 . . ?–1602), had
fought against the French, the Moriscos, and at Lepanto. In 1585 he was appointed captain-
general of the galleys of Spain and Adelantado Mayor of Castile; in 1587 he became first
conde de Santa Gadea and a grandee of Spain. Cf. Fernández Duro, *Armada española,* iii. 130;
D.H.E.

2. AGS, Estado 839 (*Cal. S.P. Spain, 1587–1603,* pp. 637–43): 'Despatches brought by Cobos
to the Pardo'; Museo Naval, Madrid, Col. Sans de Barutell, art. 4, nos. 1262, 1263, 1267
(*Codoin,* lxxxviii, f. 242): Padilla's account to Philip II, 14 Dec. Cf. Fernández Duro, *Armada
española,* iii. 118–26, 129–32; *Epistolario de Zubiaur,* pp. 11–26.

of 136 ships. Don Juan del Águila was land commander, with Conde
de Palma in charge of the cavalry. On board were 12,634 men and 300
horses. Again the season was advanced, and in sight of England
Padilla's fleet was driven back by storm and several ships were lost.[1]

It was Philip's last offensive. Feeling his end approaching he sought
only peace for Spain. The prospects for peace had now increased, for if
Philip and, even more so, Archduke Albert were now weary of un-
profitable war, the Dutch, English, and French could feel satisfied with
the successes they had won against Spain. The Dutch were safe behind
the defence barrier formed by the Rhine, with its distributary the
Waal, and the Meuse. Their gain was also a gain for England, now
freed from the fear of a Spanish attack launched from bases on the
Dutch coast. England was also delivered from the danger of an attack
from the French coast, for Albert had been forced to retreat from
Picardy in 1597 and in March 1598 Mercoeur submitted to Henry.
These events also delivered France from the attacks on her unity made
by domestic malcontents and foreign enemies, and it was time for
her king to set about the task of national reconstruction.

But if, as with our advantage of hindsight we are able to say, Europe
was in 1598 moving towards a general disengagement, this was not at
all apparent then. Nor, when over the next eleven years peace had
been painfully established, was it firm enough to resist for more
than a decade afterwards the strains imposed upon it by the jealousies,
antagonisms, and fears with which the peoples of Europe regarded
each other.

But in 1598 the king of Spain and even the king of France were
willing to listen to the archduke's peace overtures. Philip for one
thing had gained nothing from his war with France but his third bankruptcy, and for another he wanted before he died to establish his
daughter Isabel Clara Eugenia in the rule of the Netherlands. And
Henry saw that the aims of his allies were diverging from his. They
wished him to continue immobilizing Spain, which was to their advantage but gained him nothing; for him an attack on Savoy or Bresse or
the Low Countries would be far more practicable. Besides, his country
needed peace for a reconciliation of parties and for economic restoration. And if England and the Dutch need not fear peace, both could
yet gain from a continuation of the war. Both countries were growing

1. González Dávila, *Felipe tercero*, pp. 74–5; Fernández Duro, *Armada española*, iii. 166–7;
Hume, *Españoles e ingleses*, p. 249; *Elizabethan government and society*, pp. 359–61.

rich on the commercial ruin of the southern Netherlands and were gaining for themselves the trade of the Atlantic, Mediterranean, and East Indies. They were even trading in the Caribbean at a time when the American market for Spanish products was beginning to contract. It was in their interest, therefore, to keep Albert and Philip distracted by the French war while they made further economic gains. The Dutch, moreover, were fully aware that neither Albert nor Philip acquiesced in their hard-won independence.

Both England and the United Provinces accordingly sought to prevent Henry IV from making peace with Philip. The Papacy, how-ever, threw its influence against that of the northern powers. Clement VIII saw clearly that the prolongation of war between the Catholic southern powers benefited only the Protestant north. Rome too, which from 1580 had supported the anti-Protestant war, now under Clement felt that this war had reached its conclusion and wished to turn from it to a renewal of the Holy League against the Turk. The war between the emperor and the Turk in the east had recommenced in 1593, and now there was prospect that the imperial forces might gain Buda, the centre of Turkish power on the Danube. The Papacy was the chief architect of the peace between France, Spain, and Savoy which was concluded at Vervins on 2 May 1598.[1]

There was calm in the Mediterranean between 1597 and 1600 and Spain's chief problem was now the Netherlands. Philip in the month of Vervins tried to solve this problem by making over the country as a quasi-autonomous principality under Spanish protection to Isabel and her husband-to-be, Archduke Albert, upon whom Isabel's actual ruling powers were devolved.[2] The archdukes, as Albert and Isabel were known, were married in November. It was the best that Philip could do.

If Philip was concerned about the future of the Low Countries, he was even more worried about the future of Spain under his son and heir, Prince Philip. 'God,' he lamented, 'who has given me so many kingdoms, has denied me a son capable of ruling them.' It was a worry that added to the vexations of his last painful illness, but his faith did not fail him at the end. As he committed his soul to the divine mercy,

1. Braudel, *Méditerranée et monde méditerranéen*, pp. 1070–3; Lynch, *Spain under the Habsburgs*, i. 335–6; Dumont, *Corps universel diplomatique*, vol. v, pt. I, p. 561.
2. Carter, *Secret diplomacy of the Habsburgs*, pp. 79–80; Dumont, *Corps universel diploma-tique*, vol. v, pt. I, p. 573, gives conditons of cession on 6 May 1598 of the Low Countries by Philip II to Isabel Clara Eugenia.

so he committed Spain to the divine guidance, making his testament to his own children that of St. Louis to his son. He breathed his last on 13 September 1598 in the Escorial.

Before he died he had received one last reminder of the war in Ireland, an account brought to him of the victory gained by O'Neill at the Yellow Ford in August. The king dictated a letter congratulating O'Neill and O'Donnell and encouraging them, but in vague terms, for Philip was preoccupied with the unfinished business of peace with England.[1]

1. AGS, Estado 839 (*Cal. S.P. Spain, 1587–1603*, p. 649): Philip to O'Neill and O'Donnell, Madrid, 1598.

III · THE ADMINISTRATION
OF PHILIP III

PHILIP II had reason to feel apprehensive about his son's capacity for ruling. Piously inclined, amiable, and colourless, Philip III had little taste for affairs of state, whose direction he was willing to leave to others. At hand to take advantage of this situation was the first of a series of favourites, who in this reign and the next occupied the chief place in Spain after the king. The first *valido*, or *privado*, was Don Francisco Gómez de Sandoval y Rojas, fifth marquis of Denia, created duke of Lerma by Philip in 1599. Lerma continued in favour until 1618 when he fell from power, dragging down with him in his crash a whole retinue of lesser men. His career was so notorious, marked by scandal, bribery, fortune-building, and the picaresque doings of his followers,[2] and his end was so spectacular that it has been hard for historians to approach with dispassion the question whether his ascendancy was beneficial or harmful for Spain. He is variously seen as a mediocrity (Cánovas del Castillo), a debasing influence (Ferrer del Río), and a peacefully inclined statesman, who, whether his motive was to save Spain from bankruptcy (Gardiner) or merely to line his own pockets (Pérez Bustamante), reversed the warlike tendencies of Philip II and gave Spain a new, pacific direction in policy (Ranke).[3]

1. 'A foolish king, an insolent duke, and an absolving confessor are drawing the whole people down to ruin.' Quoted in *Ciudad de Dios*, cxxx (1922), 15.

2. Antonio Ferrer del Río, 'El duque de Lerma', in *R.E.*, xviii (1871), 161–87, gives a vivid picture of the corruption, bribery, and wasteful expenditure of Lerma's ascendancy, as well as of the disorderly and scandalous lives of the duke's pages and gentlemen. Don García de Pareja, Ferrer thinks, was most probably the writer who left the memoirs, which were published in novel form by Le Sage under the title, *Gil Blas de Santillane*.

3. Gardiner, *History of England . . . 1603–42*, i. (1883), 102; Pérez Bustamante, *Felipe III*, p. 112; Ranke, *L'Espagne sous Charles-Quint, Philippe II et Philippe III ou les Osmanlis et la*

After all this it is not surprising to find a modern writer judiciously deciding, after careful argument, that in fact Lerma did not occupy the seat of power at all.[1]

The 'favourite' or 'first minister'—the special quality of this personage derives as much from his political standing in the kingdom as it does from his personal relationship to the monarch[2]—was now an accepted institution in England and France as in Spain. The development of the *privanza* marked a stage in the evolution of the great powers, which sought by means of this institution to deal with the ever-increasing complexity of government. As absolute royal power developed the need arose for some intermediary, some 'first' minister, between the king, now acquiring as 'the anointed temple of the Lord' a semi-divine status, and the representatives, whether of his own estates or of foreign powers.

In the nature of the case it was not to be expected that the Renaissance sovereigns, forced as they were by the lack of development in the bureaucratic machines to choose as first minister a courtier bound to them by personal ties and depending on them for support, would find ministers of real competence to cope with the problems of state.[3]

For the Spanish empire these problems were grave. No longer dominant in arms, faced with the relentless commercial rivalry of the Dutch, English, and French[4] at a time when her own economy was contracting, encumbered by the increasing weakness of her imperial partner, Spain was perhaps inevitably set on the path of decline.

But the decline might not have been so rapid if Philip III had shown a more positive capacity for ruling. Perhaps it is true, as Pérez Bustamante alleged, that the rigorous restraint by which Philip II had sought to control the weakness and frivolity which marred his son's character had indeed been too severe, so much so as to annul his very character and inhibit his power to govern.[5] At any rate the new king took little personal interest in the routine of government; there was no question any more, as there had been with Philip II, of the king's being his own chief clerk. Very occasionally, in matters which affected

1. Carter, op. cit., pp. 71–2.
2. Ibid., p. 70.
3. Mattingly, *Renaissance diplomacy*, pp. 224–5.
4. *New Camb. mod. hist.*, i. 446, 456–69.
5. Pérez Bustamante, *Felipe III*, pp. 26–31.

---

monarchie espagnole. Translated by J. B. Haiber, pp. 219–23. Quoted, Carter, *Secret diplomacy of the Habsburgs*, pp. 67–8.

his *amour-propre* or devotion, Philip—capriciously and without logic—insisted on his own will. But this was exceptional; the king in the main left the tedious business of ruling to others.

There was no question of a change of direction in the policy of Spain under Philip III; as with Charles V and Philip II the guiding policies continued to be the conservation of the Christian frontiers and their defence against the Turk.[1] The problem is rather whether it was now the favourite or the king's councils (or perhaps the council of state in particular) which exercised the real power in Spain.

For the purposes of the present study the question may be confined to the *privanza* of the duke of Lerma. The duke, in the view of Pérez Bustamante, was the real ruler of Spain until 1618, when the avarice and nepotism which were the characteristic features of his ascendancy brought about his downfall. Lerma himself, as Pérez points out, replaced the royal secretaries on whom Charles V and Philip II had relied; for twenty years he was Philip III's one and universal secretary, enjoying the king's full confidence and alone dispatching business with him orally.

In another view, however, the locus of power is to be sought in the conciliar structure of Spain: in the royal councils in general, as Cánovas del Castillo maintained, or, as C. H. Carter, modifying Cánovas's thesis, suggests, in the council of state in particular.

As in France and England, so also in Spain the king in the exercise of his rule made use of a number of councils. These bodies, whether they were consultative or ministerial in function (a point to be discussed presently), in no way limited the royal prerogative, and their members, chosen (at least under Philip II) from the intellectual aristocracy, were appointed at will by the king.

At the end of the reign of Philip II the councils stood twelve in number. The council of state (*consejo de estado*), analogous to the French *conseil d'en haut*, formed the king's supreme advisory (or ministerial) body, and the king himself nominally presided over it. Its jurisdiction was total and was disseminated through two different types of council, those whose responsibilities were territorial—councils of Castile, Aragon, Italy, Flanders, and Portugal—and those whose functions were departmental—finance, justice, war, military orders, and crusade. Thus, for example, the council of war was simply the

1. Chudoba, *Spain and the empire*, pp. 174–5; Carter, *Secret diplomacy of the Habsburgs*, p. 71, who follows Cánovas del Castillo, *Estudios del reinado de Felipe IV*, i. 258.

council of state, with perhaps the addition of a military or naval expert or two, meeting to discharge the functions of high command.

Another way of stressing the importance of the council of state is to say with Carter[1] that it dealt with all large matters, whether pertaining to the peninsula or to Flanders or to Italy. The other councils were subordinate and referred important issues to the council of state, which might and frequently did bypass them.

All this complexity of government moved Philip II in 1592 to form a junta or private council, analogous to a cabinet. This was the famous 'council of night'. It was formed of three members: the old king's loyal Portuguese servant Don Cristóbal de Moura (affairs of Portugal), the efficient Basque secretary Don Juan de Idiáquez (war, state, and foreign affairs), and the count of Chinchón (affairs of Aragon and Italy). Of these three the first, Moura (1538–1613), had since 1573 been the chief adviser to the king in Portuguese matters and had been chiefly instrumental in attaching Portugal to the Spanish throne.[2] For this he was made marquis of Castel-Rodrigo. Idiáquez had succeeded Antonio Pérez as secretary to the council of state in 1579 and in 1584 had been admitted to that council.[3] The conservative Don Diego Fernández de Cabrera y Bobadilla, third count of Chinchón (d. 1608), favourite and majordomo of Philip II, had represented Spain in Rome and Vienna besides holding many other offices. He had come into the council of state in 1573.

Later, Gómez Dávila, marquis of Velada (a creature of Moura), and Cardinal Albert, the future Philip III's brother-in-law, were added.

In the palace revolution engineered by Lerma at the change of reign the more intimate councillors of Philip II were sent away from court. Archbishop Loiasa of Toledo went off, as did also the count of Fuensalida, Don Pedro Portocarrero, who was bishop of Cuenca, and Don Pedro de Guzmán, while Moura was removed a safe distance to the governorship of Portugal. Velada and Idiáquez both remained; they offered no danger to him, and Idiáquez in particular was too efficient a servant to lose.

Philip III, who thus foolishly rid himself of the corps of loyal and experienced servants bequeathed to him by his father, placated the nobility passed over in the previous reign by choosing from their ranks

1. Carter, *Secret diplomacy of the Habsburgs*, pp. 72–3.
2. Biography by Dánvila y Burguero, *Don Cristóbal de Moura* (Madrid, 1900); also a seventeenth-century account in *Codoin*, vi. 23–7.
3. Idiáquez died in 1614. Cf. Pérez-Mínguez, *Don Juan de Idiáquez* (San Sebastian, 1935).

new councillors. Lerma himself came on the council, and most of those newly appointed were his friends and partisans: the count of Miranda, relative of Lerma by marriage, who in May 1598 became president of the council of Castile;[1] the duke of Medina Sidonia; the duke of Nájera; the Adelantado Mayor of Castile; and Don Juan de Borja.[2] The archbishopric of Toledo went to Lerma's uncle, Bernardo de Rojas y Sandoval, who was also now made cardinal. Rojas was already bishop of Ciudad Rodrigo (since 1585), Pamplona (since 1588), and Jaén (since 1595). Soranzo, the Venetian ambassador, had a low opinion of his experience and administrative capability. An important influence on the king was Fray Gaspar de Córdoba, O.P., his confessor since some years before Philip's accession and now a councillor. Fray Gaspar, as Ottaviano Bon, another Venetian ambassador, observed,[3] had a great reputation for having the ear of the king at all times, for being devoted to Lerma, and for being one of those who advised the duke in the most intimate matters of state. However this may be, Lerma in the matter of aiding Ireland at least was not so enthusiastic as Gaspar wished.

In approaching the question whether the reality of power lay with the favourite Lerma or with the councils, one may begin by noting that within the councils themselves power lay with the council of state. To it the other councils were subordinated, and its jurisdiction over them and over the Spanish empire was total. But before the main question can be tackled there is a further issue to be disposed of, namely what was the status of the councils? Opinions among historians range from the view that the councils were merely advisory bodies[4] to the view that they were ministries.[5] An intermediate position is held by a recent historian, J. Lynch, who maintains that the council of state was purely consultative, but that the regional councils, while they were not ministries, 'exercised not only executive functions

---

1. Don Juan de Zúñiga Avellanada y Cárdenas, sixth conde de Miranda del Castanar, was governor of Catalonia (1585) and then viceroy of Naples (1586–95). Philip III appointed him to the councils of state and war.

2. Conde de Fícalo y de Mayalde, son of S. Francisco de Borja.

3. *Relazioni:Spagna*, eds. Barozzi and Berchet, p. 251. He was chosen, as were all Philip's confessors, by Lerma. Cf. *R.E.*, xviii (1871), 165.

4. 'The council of state . . . was a purely consultative body. Its duty was merely to give an opinion on matters submitted by the king. They (*sic*) had no further competence.' Davies, *Golden Century of Spain*, p. 125.

5. *Los consejos no eran simplemente órganos de asesoramiento pues tenían tambien el carácter de órganos superiores de la administración, y sus miembros el de altos funcionarios o ministros.* Aguado Bleye, *Historia de España*, ii. 692.

but also legislative and judicial ones'.[1] Cordero-Torres, on the other hand, who insists on the executive as well as consultative functions of the councils, argues against Ballesteros y Beretta and Gounon-Loubens that the council of state was an indispensable instrument of government since it was the council of the king and not of the vast number of heterogeneous provinces that it represented with him, whose problems only the councillors out of their special knowledge could lay before him.[2]

This is not to say that the council of state *was* the government, and yet in the final analysis Cordero-Torres agrees with Carter, and for essentially the same reason, in allotting the reality of power to the council of state. For Carter the council of state was made up of those who by birth or ability or experience were the best entitled to conduct the affairs of the Spanish empire. These men formed an élite corps, whose experience and knowledge extended to all the Spanish kingdoms. Any problem of government could be delegated to a small committee of councillors, augmented if needs be by experts from outside, which, when it had resolved the intricacies of the problem, placed it before the council of state for a decision. Thus the effective government of Spain was the council of state in particular rather than the councils in general.

This solution, which has the virtue of neatness, has much to be said in its favour. The various councils had grown so slow-moving and cumbersome as to be unable to transact affairs in any businesslike manner. The council of state found an escape for Spain from this dangerous impasse by reserving to itself all matters of high policy. Adopting the principle of the 'council of night', the council of state referred important matters to small juntas which could be expanded, dissolved, or revived in accordance with the need of the moment. In this way the council of state ensured that there would be a continuity of policy in regard to individual questions—by making each the province of a particular junta—and that (since a junta could be set up to meet each case) no pressing matter would be neglected.

The handling of the expedition to Ireland will serve to illustrate the mode of procedure of the council. When, early in 1601, the decision was taken to send the expedition a junta of three, Fray Gaspar and the

1. Lynch, *Spain under the Habsburgs*, i. 182.

2. Cordero-Torres, *El consejo de estado*, ch. VIII; Ballesteros y Beretta, *Historia de España*, vol. iv, pt. II, ch. I; Gounon-Loubens, *Essais sur l'administration*, ch. V.

secretaries of state and war, was appointed to see to the assembly of men and necessities required. The junta in no way removed the direction of the enterprise from the council of state; nor did it seek to. Its appointment was simply a matter of convenience, a result of the council of state's desire to expedite the preparation of the expedition. The council continued as before to supervise the preparations and the junta, once its specific task was accomplished, simply ceased to exist.

To take another example: in the summer of 1601 Hugh O'Neill's eldest son, resident in Spain, decided to become a Franciscan. This decision embarrassed the Spanish government, who were afraid that if they allowed him to do so his father would regard it as a breach of trust on their part, since the young prince would in due course be expected to succeed to his father's lordship. The matter was referred for advice first to a junta of Salamanca theologians, then to the Valladolid theologians, and finally to a special junta of councillors of state headed by Cardinal Guevara. Other matters as they cropped up were referred to yet other juntas. These were purely *ad hoc* committees and once they had disposed of the problem of the moment they ceased to be.

This analysis of the functioning of the council reveals its indispensability and also the secret of its success as an organ of government. It does not, however, establish beyond dispute that power was located in its hands rather than in those of Lerma. Far from it. In the first place the leading councillors were, as has been stated, the duke's creatures. He thus exercised a considerable, if indirect, control on the workings of the council. Furthermore, Lerma was indolent, his direction of affairs wavering and uncertain; and a number of energetic Spanish diplomats and governors, with no clear guidance from above and concerned with maintaining the greatness of Spain, were led to developing their own policies independently of either Lerma or the councils. The results were spectacular but in the long run disastrous for Spain and for Europe.[1]

Yet Lerma retained the initiative regarding what matters were discussed in council, and when it suited him he also acted independently of the conciliar structure. Whoever, like the Irish leaders and their friends, wished to see Spain embark on a particular policy sought above all to gain the ear of the duke. The documents in the Simancas archives reveal that twice there was a divergence between the king

1. Cf. Mattingly, *Renaisssance diplomacy*, pp. 224–5, 256, 266–8.

and his council over the desirability of sending an expedition to Ireland. First the king was in favour of it, the council against; later, while
the council pressed for it, the king shilly-shallied. On both occasions
there was an impasse. But when Lerma determined to launch the
expedition he acted in complete independence of the council. The
decision was his, not theirs. The corollary of this is that without Lerma's
decision the expedition would never have sailed.

This is not to deny that in fact the council was concerned from first
to last in the direction of the expedition. The invasion at each succes-
sive stage, from the first proposals to launch it until the end of the
inquiry that resulted from it, was the subject of conciliar debate and
advice. Time and again the advice remitted by the council was not
acted upon, but each fresh proposal, each new consideration was sent to
the council of state (or war) for its opinion, to be given in the light of the
councillors' knowledge, both of the Irish problem and of the whole
complex of administrative problems of Spain. When decisions were
taken they were generally—but not always—arrived at in the light of
the considerations presented by the council. The history of the Irish expedition, in short, would tend to reveal the council, in the time of Lerma
at least, as an indispensable organ of government, but would also indicate that Lerma and not the council occupied the central seat of power.

If one wishes for a clearer understanding not only of how the government of Spain worked but also of the relations between the council of
state, the favourite, and the king, one requires more detailed knowledge of conciliar procedure, already touched upon.

Council meetings might deal with one or several matters of interest.
The number of members present at a meeting varied with the number of councillors in attendance at court, the number appointed to a
junta, and so on. The record of proceedings, drawn up from minutes
made by a secretary, went to the king in the form of a *consulta*, the
expression of the council's opinion. For the period under review here
the secretary of state who handled northern affairs (including Irish)
was Andrés de Prada, while the secretary of war was Esteban de
Ibarra. Pedro Franqueza y Esteve, Lerma's protégé, became secretary
of state for Italian affairs in 1600, displacing Francisco de Idiáquez, and
in 1603 took over the entire secretariat, Prada going to the council of
war. Franqueza committed northern affairs to Antonio de Arostegui.[1]

1. Juderías y Loyot, 'Don Pedro Franqueza', in *R.A.B.M.*, 3ª época, vol. xix (1908), II.
319–22; *D.H.E.*, i. 1180.

Consultas were of two kinds, *de oficio*, 'of office', which dealt with matters of state, in this case relations with England, Ireland, Scotland, and other countries, and *de partes*, i.e. decisions on memorials submitted by and about private individuals.

The *consultas* always began with a summary of the document or documents sent for deliberation to the council or junta, perhaps a request for help from O'Neill and O'Donnell, perhaps a memorial on the Irish situation or a problem raised by the king or the favourite. Then the councillors gave their opinion. Often enough a minority view was expressed.

If the council had reached a consensus, and if the king (advised of course by Lerma) approved of it, he signified his agreement in the margin: *está bien* or *como parece*.[1] The formula *no hay que ver*[2] showed that he had decided that no action was required. The secretary then made out a document in the sense indicated by the marginal notation. This was signed by the king *yo el rey*[3] and countersigned by the secretary *refrendaba*.[4] Dispatches were accordingly sent out, letters it might be to the Irish leaders or to Archduke Albert, or instructions to Sessa, the king's ambassador at Rome, Castel-Rodrigo, Caracena (the viceroy of Galicia), or some other servant of the crown.

Policy-making was of course affected by delays in communication. Dispatches might reach Lisbon within a week, Brussels within a fortnight, and Rome within anything from three to six weeks. By the time they had arrived the march of events might have made the dispatches out of date. This was even more true of letters sent to Ireland. Though a fast patache with favourable wind and tide could make the sailing between Galicia and an Irish port in as little as four days, often, owing to delay in securing both licence to depart and shipping, a courier might find weeks or perhaps even months slipping by before he could deliver his documents to the Irish leaders.

In cases where the king did not accept the suggestion of the council or where the council itself advised against action the *consulta* was filed away in the Irish *legajos* or bundles, to await resurrection when the council, inspired by some fresh order, reconsidered the Irish situation. It often proved useful in refreshing the memory of the councillors; sometimes, on the other hand, it merely interfered with the effective-

1. 'Very well' or 'As it appears'.   2. 'Action is unnecessary.'
3. 'I the king.'   4. '(He) countersigned.'

ness of their decision, because it referred to conditions that had since changed.

The invasion of Ireland must be viewed in the general context of Spanish policy, which at the time was one of disengagement. Philip III ratified the treaty of Vervins in 1601, made peace with England in 1604, and signed a truce with the Dutch in 1609.[1] He did nothing to upset the truce, in being since 1578, with the Turk in the Mediterranean (appearances in 1601 notwithstanding), and sought alliance with Persia to contain the Ottoman threat to the Empire and to the Portuguese colonies in Asia. The intervention in Ireland was a last attempt to gain an advantage over his English opponent. The king wished by invading Ireland—as also by encouraging Federico Spínola's project to occupy a port in England—to exert pressure on Elizabeth and make her come to a serious discussion of peace terms. Ultimately, he hoped, the invasions of Ireland and England would help him to gain the succession to the English throne for his own candidate.

Peace between England and Spain was not, however, to be achieved until after James I had in 1603 succeeded Elizabeth on the English throne. James took as his motto the text, 'Blessed are the peacemakers'. He was conscious of the futility of war and conscious too of England's need for peace to build herself up. But he was not the only one in high position who for one reason or another sought an easing of international relations.[2] Pope Clement VIII's desire to effect a reconciliation between the Habsburgs and the French and to write *finis* to the anti-Protestant war has already been mentioned. On Clement's initiative negotiations opened in 1601 for a marriage treaty between the prince of Asturias (later Philip IV) and Elizabeth of Bourbon, daughter of Henry IV. In the Netherlands Archduke Albert and his chief advisers,[3] foremost among them the remarkable Ambrosio Spínola who became captain-general of the army of Flanders, all wished to see an end to the war with the Dutch, so that Albert might be enabled to impose his authority, restore the economy, and perhaps win back the Northern Provinces. Lerma himself was the

1. Abreu, *Tratados de paz*, i. 82: oath by Philip III, 27 May 1601, binding himself to keep treaty of Vervins; i. 243: treaty of London, 28 Aug. 1604, between Philip III and the archdukes on the one hand, and James I on the other; i. 458: twelve years' truce, Antwerp, 9 Apr. 1609; i. 484: commercial treaty, Antwerp, 9 Apr. 1609.

2. Carter, *Secret diplomacy of the Habsburgs*, pp. 11–16.

3. Cf. the initiative taken by Richardot, president of the council of state, and other Walloon aristocrats in 1598–9 to end the war with the Estates-General. Loomie, *Spanish Elizabethans*, pp. 77–80.

disciple of Ruy Gomez de Silva, prince of Éboli, who in the time of Philip II had been the advocate of conciliation towards the Netherlands.

There were many considerations urging Spain to seek a disengagement. Spain, in spite of the reverses suffered by her at the hands of the English, Dutch, and French, and in spite of clear evidence of decline, was still regarded as the foremost European power. Her king ruled over the Iberian peninsula and the Americas. He claimed for himself exclusive rights to the trade and navigation of Africa and the Indies, although it was becoming increasingly difficult for him to maintain these claims against English, Dutch, and French interlopers. In Italy he still ruled Milan, Naples, and Sicily, and his control of the Balearics, Corsica, and Sardinia made him lord of the western Mediterranean. He was head of the Habsburg house, whose junior branch ruled the empire and was his faithful ally. His sister and her husband governed the Netherlands, with effective control over the southern provinces and Franche-Comté and with hopes of yet regaining the rebel north.

But with the death of Philip II Spain's great days were over, although the fact was barely recognized as yet. Politically and economically the giant that had been Spain was shrunken in stature. Politically Habsburg Spain had failed in her bid to control the direction of French affairs and in her efforts to make the Dutch return to what she considered their 'proper' allegiance. She had not only failed to conquer England but had been unable to prevent the English from giving aid to the Dutch; she had had to look on, helpless, while the English and Dutch broke into the trade of 'her' Indies. Still the acknowledged leader of the Catholic world, her cherished dream of restoring Catholic unity was shattered. She had no real power even to alleviate the sufferings of persecuted Catholics who appealed to her with tales of intolerable grievances.

Spain had found it impossible to impose her will on Europe, and now her helm of state was taken over by indolent and incapable hands. As Spain grew progressively weaker France, now at peace and engaged in reconstruction, grew stronger, and Henry IV's hostility towards Spain remained undiminished. Henry still pursued the French secular aim of breaking out from Habsburg encirclement; and the eldest daughter of the Church found her natural allies against the Catholic king in the enemies of Catholicism and even of Christendom. There was danger that France might combine with the Turk in an attack upon Spain, or might, allied with some of the west German states, resume the war against Spain on the side of the Dutch and English. Or Henry IV might attack Milan, which was also eyed greedily by Venice and Savoy. Finally, since the treaty of Vervins had left certain matters in dispute between France and Savoy, Henry might attack Savoy. If he did, Spain would be forced to go to the defence of Savoy in order to protect the Milanese. Everywhere she looked Spain saw danger.

If the political situation made it advisable for Spain to make peace with her enemies, the state of the treasury made it imperative for her to do so. The crown was in desperate financial straits, its resources alienated or mortgaged to bankers. From about 1519–20 prices had begun to rise in Spain, partly at least as a result of the increase in bullion, imported from Mexico and Peru, in relation to other goods. The price-rise was maintained throughout the century, so that goods fetched five times in 1600 what they had in 1501.

Charles V had commanded that all traffic with his possessions over-seas should flow through Seville. In examining the registers of bullion imports at Seville, Professor Earl J. Hamilton, the American economic historian, observed what seemed to him a significant correlation be-tween the volume of the precious metals, chiefly silver, imported into Spain and the price inflation, and was led to conclude that there was a direct relation between the two. The increase in prices, Hamilton endeavoured to show, coincided with the increase in imports of bullion; while both increases were significant in the first part of the century, both reached their peak in the second part. The increase in silver, it seemed obvious, had a powerful effect on the Spanish economy and was the chief cause of the price revolution.

It is agreed among scholars that there was an expansion in Spanish industrial production in the first half of the sixteenth century but that in the second half this expansion halted and production went into decline. Hamilton argued that since the immediate effect of the in-crease in treasure imports in the early part of the century was to raise prices, wages began to lag behind prices, thus providing industrialists with an incentive towards increased production. But after the middle of the century wages caught up with prices, whereas in England and France they did not. In fact, whereas the price-rise was now being felt in these and other countries, it was to a much less harmful extent than in Spain. Spanish industry therefore lost its incentive and began to go into decline at the same time that it was faced with the competition, both in the home and American markets, of cheap foreign goods. For Hamilton, then, there was a direct correlation between the influx of treasure and not only price inflation but also the fluctuation first upwards and then downwards of the Spanish economy in the sixteenth century.[1] The Spanish economy suffered from a surfeit of bullion.

More recent studies, however, have suggested that the case was not so simple. Both Hamilton's figures for the quantity of silver entering Spain and his assumption that the bullion entering was all injected into the Spanish economy have been questioned; furthermore, it seems established that the price-rise was proportionately greater in the first rather than (as Hamilton thought) the second half of the century, even if prices continued to rise until they reached their maximum at the end of the century.[2]

The question has thus been raised whether the influx of treasure from the Indies is alone sufficient to account for the inflation in sixteenth-century Spain. Pierre Chaunu, the French scholar, has therefore sought to establish a correlation between the price-rise and the volume of trade between Seville and America.[3] But it seems likely that a convincing explanation for the price-rise and the decline in the economy following upon this inflation will have to take account of a multiplicity of factors, somewhat as follows.

Throughout the sixteenth century Spain, which with its seven and a half million people as compared with France's sixteen million was indeed under-populated, saw a slight increase in population.[4] At the same time that her home market expanded, Spain was faced with an increasing demand for her textiles and agricultural produce in the Low Countries and Italy and found a new market in the Americas. The increase in specie caused prices to mount, while at the same time Spanish production, both agricultural and industrial, was too back-

1. Hamilton, *American treasure and the price revolution in Spain 1501–1650*; 'American treasure and the rise of capitalism 1500–1700', in *Economica*, ix (1929), 338–57; 'The decline of Spain', in *Econ. Hist. Rev.*, viii (1938), 177–9.

2. Elliott, *Imperial Spain 1469–1716*, pp. 184–5; Lynch, *Spain under the Habsburgs*, i. 124.

3. Chaunu, *Séville et l'Atlantique 1504–1650*, viii. II. 18–25.

4. Carande, *Carlos V y sus banqueros*, vol. i, ch. III, placed the apogee of Spanish population between 1530 and 1570, when according to him the figures for Spain were seven and a half million. Chaunu, *Seville et l'Atlantique 1504–1650*, viii. I. 245–6, suggests that the population at the middle of the sixteenth century was somewhat less than seven and a half million rising to that figure or something over at the end of the century. The population of Castile, he suggests, rose during the same period from something under to something over six and a half million.

ward to meet the increased demand, thus aggravating the revolution
in prices. By the middle of the century the price inflation and increase
in costs were making themselves sharply felt. The Spanish administration, faced with the fact that foreign goods were cheaper than those
produced at home, decided that Spain was exporting too much,
especially to America.[1] Because of this erroneous diagnosis the government forbade the export of goods from the country. The contraction
of markets on top of the high costs of production proved too much for
Spanish industry. It became unable to stand up to foreign competition even on the home market, and went into decline.

Other inflationary factors were at work to aggravate the situation.
Charles V had issued *juros*, or credit bonds, to finance his borrowings,
and he and Philip II mortgaged the American bullion in advance (as
they did the European revenues of the Habsburg house) to pay the
foreign bankers who financed their wars. The inflationary extent of
these two practices cannot be estimated precisely, but at least a great
deal of the crown revenues went to pay the bankers. The American
bullion was thus eaten up or else was used unproductively by the
aristocracy, on the construction of grandiose buildings or on the pur-
chase of luxury goods, clothes, and jewellery, instead of being acquired
by industrialists as capital for investment. Thus it came about that
from the middle of the sixteenth century, what with the adverse
balance of trade, heavy taxation, the unproductive use of wealth, and
the expense of foreign wars, the Spanish budget was in a chronic state
of imbalance.

The decline in industry, trade, and agriculture was attributable,
therefore, among other things to price inflation, the imperialism of
Philip II, the extravagance of the court, wasteful expenditure, and the
drain in manpower through war, emigration to America, the rise in
membership of the religious orders, and the elimination by the
Inquisition of many productive subjects. And this decline had caused
a great decrease in revenue and had left the crown greatly in debt.
The young Philip III succeeded to a throne burdened by his father's
debts to the tune of at least 20,000,000 ducats.[2] In 1598, the floating
debt apart, the consolidated debt stood at the huge sum of 76,540,000
ducats, while the best revenues of the crown were engaged for years
to come to Genoese, Florentine, and native bankers. Income from the
plate fleets, owing, it is fair to say, to the vigilance of Lerma, remained

1. *New Camb. mod. hist.* i. 454.   2 Lynch, *Spain under the Habsburgs*, i. 128.

high; after 1601 it was declining, but there was no marked drop before 1630.[1] But this income amounted by 1598 to only a quarter at most of the crown's annual revenues; the rest was borrowed or came from taxes. The traditional taxes were augmented by a new tax of the type called *millones* (sales taxes) in 1590. This latter tax was increased in 1596 and again in 1600, when the Cortes of Castile were forced to vote to the king, for the support of Archduke Albert, the enormous sum of 18,000,000 ducats, to be paid at the rate of 3,000,000 a year for six years. But revenue still fell far below expenditure, which was estimated at 12,000,000 a year by the mid-1590s. While the crown was put to the most extraordinary shifts, such as debasing coinage[2] to raise money, Philip showered immense gifts of money on Lerma and Lerma's friends.

There was no significant inflation in the decade following 1606; but with a debt of 12,000,000 ducats on hand again in 1607 the crown suspended payments to the bankers yet again. Philip II had resorted to this device three times, the last time being in 1596. Just as that last bankruptcy had shattered Philip II's dream of crushing the Protestant powers of the north and had been a major factor in forcing him to make the treaty of Vervins with the French, so that of 1607 ended the Spanish attempt to subdue the Dutch and contributed towards making Philip III conclude the twelve years' truce of 1609.

In a country denuded of men by the war in Flanders and in a state of perpetual financial embarrassment, the decision to send an army of 6,000 troops to Ireland at a cost of 300,000 ducats was not to be lightly taken. The men might be raised at the cost of great efforts, and ships might be found in which to transport them. The money too might be raised; it was of little enough account in comparison with the large amounts squandered on grandiose buildings and displays of pomp by the crown and nobility, or with the sums with which the favourite enriched himself (by 1602 Lerma's annual income stood at 200,000 ducats). But the raising of the expedition placed one more burden on the strained resources of Spain and could only be justified by the expectation of solid political gain.

And in spite of the many considerations that urged Philip towards disengagement there was at least an arguable case for carrying the war into Elizabeth's territory. On the one hand peace would help to restore the credit of the crown and benefit the Spanish economy. It

1. Hamilton, *American treasure and the price revolution*, p. 34.   2. Ibid., pp. 75–9.

4

would, as Albert strongly pleaded, be of economic and political benefit to the Netherlands. On the other hand, it was urged, a strong attack on Elizabeth would force her to give up helping the Dutch and draw off English attacks on the Indies and the plate fleets. In any case, even if Spain did make peace with England, that would not prevent the English from aiding the Dutch secretly. An attack on Ireland would expose Elizabeth's weakness; the war in Ireland had meant a frightful drain on England in men and money, so that England in fact needed peace to draw breath and recuperate. More, England herself would easily be conquered from Ireland. For with Spain in control of Irish harbours it would be an easy matter for her veterans to cross over and land in England. Such an attack on England would prove decisive for making the English politiques, who, Philip was assured, occupied most influential positions in the government, declare themselves openly in favour of the Infanta Isabel as successor to Elizabeth. Thus at one stroke Philip would redeem his father's promise of 1596 to the Irish, demonstrate that Spain was a champion to whose aid hard-pressed Catholics need not resort in vain, impress the king of France and other monarchs with the reality of Spanish might, and prevent any possible alliance between England, France, and the Turk against Spain.

These were strong arguments for making Spain carry the war to England, and when chance provided the nucleus of an invasion army at Lisbon they were to prove irresistible.

IV · O'NEILL

I saw Mark Antony offer him a crown; yet 'twas not a crown
neither, 'twas one of those coronets.
                                  Shakespeare, *Julius Caesar*, Act I, Sc. ii

ROBERT DEVEREUX, second earl of Essex, arrived in Dublin on 25
April 1599 to take up office as lord lieutenant. He had left London with
the cheers of the citizens ringing in his ears. His enemies on the council,
led by the second Cecil, had less love than the populace for the haughty
and difficult earl. But the situation in Ireland was desperate, and Essex,
if he exercised the statesmanship and the military quality of which he
was certainly possessed, might be just the man to restore Ireland to
order. His absence would at least relieve the Cecilian faction of his
opposition in the council, and should he fail they might be rid of him.
Elizabeth, however insupportable she might have found his insolence
in the past, had enough confidence in his abilities to agree to the
appointment. And so it was with high hopes of returning, bringing
rebellion 'broached on his sword', that the new Henry V, to whom
Shakespeare in the prologue to his latest play clearly alluded, came to
Ireland.

But the task before him would test the qualities of even the bril-
liant, arrogant favourite. Hugh O'Neill, after his great victory of the
previous 24 August at the Yellow Ford, the greatest defeat the English
had ever sustained in Ireland, might have been expected to go on to
attack Dublin, the citadel of English rule in Ireland. Yet to the terrified
Dublin council's plea that he spare the remnant of their army, the
last life-line of the English now walled up in the towns, he acceded.
There were various reasons for this restraint, remarkable as it was.
O'Neill knew that Elizabeth would not yield easily, and he would
have difficulty in keeping his allies together for a sustained offensive.
The Irish besides were short of arms, powder, and armour. These war
supplies were obtained from Scotland or from the merchants of the

towns, who bought them in England and sold them to the chieftains at exorbitant prices: six beeves for a sword, a headpiece, or a musket. Again, O'Neill had no siege-cannon. He was also fearful just now lest an English force should land at his rear at Loch Foyle.[1]

Hugh realized that for ultimate victory foreign help was essential. His present military superiority belied very real weaknesses in his position, and his forbearance after the Yellow Ford showed wisdom; it was a card he could play in case he should find himself at some later date brought to sue for pardon from the queen. But scenting victory he now set himself a threefold goal, towards the realization of which he directed all his considerable talent and energy: he attempted in the first place to rally all Ireland to his cause; he tried secondly to build up a modern army capable of meeting an enemy in the field; and he sought finally the outside support, military and political, without which his efforts at home could scarcely hope to succeed.

In O'Neill Gaelic society had found its greatest leader. He had natural gifts for generalship and for diplomacy, and these were allied in him with a flexibility of purpose and a patience that were truly remarkable in an Irishman. The old traditional values of his race appealed to everything that was native in him, the more so as the years went on, and he could give a truly Celtic display of emotion which never at the same time clouded his brain. He had formed a certain detached view of the Irish way of life, although this can hardly, as was once thought, be altogether ascribed to his residence in England, where he had lived between the ages of twelve and eighteen.[2] It was rather his own political sagacity that made him see the weakness of the Gaelic system and its need to change, to adapt itself to meet the challenge from a new order of things. He had a sound understanding of political reality in Europe and was conscious of the effort needed to turn the balance of forces in his own favour. He had the ability to set himself a goal and to work towards its attainment with steady, painstaking purpose. O'Neill was in fact the most formidable adversary that the English crown had ever encountered in Ireland.

By now the conflict known as the 'nine years' war' had hardened into a struggle whose explicit aims were the restoration of the Catholic

1. Maxwell, *Irish history 1509–1610*, pp. 42, 191.
2. Cf. J. K. Graham, 'The birth-date of Hugh O'Neill, second earl of Tyrone', in *I.H.S.*, i (1938), 58–9.

religion and the complete liberty of action of the subject,[1] and O'Neill stood out among his confederates as the champion both of national autonomy and Catholicism. Yet that calculating brain of his never allowed him to take a chance without weighing the consequences, and as his aims were never extreme, but modified by circumstances, he always allowed himself a line of retreat.

The basis of confederate strength lay in the north—in the alliance of O'Neill, O'Donnell, and, until his untimely death in March 1600, Maguire. The northern chiefs, however, needed the support of the lords and towns of the south. The southern lords could supply men and the rich lands of the south provision them, and provision too the hoped-for invasion force; the towns could provide arms, ammunition, and money. If O'Neill had command of the ports he could utilize their commercial strength to fill his war-chest and could control entry into Ireland. The south, however, would not accept Hugh's pre-eminence in Ireland, and this he was prepared to sacrifice. He would ask some foreign prince on whom common agreement could be reached to accept the throne of Ireland.

Although unable there and then to press home the advantage gained at the Yellow Ford, O'Neill had achieved much. He had saved Ulster from invasion and driven the enemy to take refuge within the Pale and within the cities. During the following months through his lieutenants he had set Leinster and Munster aflame, and Munster had not stirred since the Desmond wars. James Fitzthomas, nephew of Gerald the 'rebel' earl, who had been disappointed by Elizabeth in his hopes of gaining the earldom, was set up as earl of Desmond by O'Neill. The Geraldines rallied to their new and handsome leader, who cleared the undertakers, including Edmund Spenser, wholesale out of much of Limerick, Cork, and Kerry and was soon master of almost all the territory from Dunquin to the Suir. The English, in impotent rage, spitefully labelled this creation of O'Neill's the 'sugan' or strawrope earl. Sir George Carew fell back on Mallow, Norris on Cork, and the earl of Ormonde retreated to the defence of Kilkenny and Tipperary. A number of Munster gentlemen, the White Knight (Edmund Fitzgibbon), Patrick Condon, Lord Barry's brother John, and Lord Roche's son David joined the Irish, as also did Lords Mountgarret and Cahir.

1. Cf. demands by O'Neill in 1595 and in 1599–1600 in Maxwell, *Irish history 1509–1610*, p. 182.

In Leinster the O'Mores took Philipstown and Athy; and on the Shannon Redmond Burke, O'Neill's captain, took one of Ormonde's castles, Druminagh, as a base from which to attack Clanricarde.

Clerics, among whom the Jesuit Father Archer was the most prominent, were at work rallying the southern lords to O'Neill's side. Father Archer wrote for James Fitzthomas to Philip III, advising the king that Fitzthomas had taken the field for the restoration of the Catholic faith and for the maintenance of his right to the Desmond earldom. He asked for cannon and powder to assail the planters who had taken refuge in 'his towns and cities'—while Spenser had escaped with his wife to England other 'undertakers', as the planters were called, had fled to the safety of Youghal and other towns—and for soldiers to lodge in the cities.

Red Hugh O'Donnell, O'Neill's dashing ally, kept up from Tyrconnell a constant attack on English rule in Connacht. He again set up in Mayo Theobald Burke as MacWilliam, took Ballymote castle, and aiming to open a way through Connacht into Munster raided Clanricarde and even Thomond's county of Clare. North of Thomond only the garrisons of Boyle, Tulsk, and Roscommon and the castle of Sligo held out against him.[1]

Up to the present the strategy employed by the two Hughs, O'Neill and O'Donnell, had been purely defensive; they had sought to keep the English out of Ulster, to prevent, by frequent raids southwards, their enemies from massing any attack on them, and to keep the road to Munster open, in case the Spaniards should land in that province. They had avoided pitched battles but had lured the enemy into positions where the odds were altogether in their own favour and where they might always disengage their forces if victory were not falling to them. Generally victory had been theirs.

But until O'Neill could establish his superiority in the field he had no hope of ultimate victory. He therefore created the trappings of a disciplined army with which to oppose the national militia of the queen. He did so by taking over elements of the English system, organizing his forces into separate companies, composed largely of musketeers, calivermen, and pikemen, and by transforming the mercenary *buannachadha*, the service of billeted men. His soldiers were

1. *A.F.M., ad an.* 1598; *Cal. S.P. Ire.,* 1598–9, pp. 501–2; Ó Domhnaill, 'Warfare in sixteenth century Ireland', in *I.H.S.,* v (1946), 48–53; Bagwell, *Tudors,* iii. 301–7; Falls, in *The Irish at war,* ed. Hayes-McCoy, pp. 35–46.

trained in the use of firearms and his army combined squares of pike-men, musketeers, and cavalry in the accepted manner of the age.[1]

O'Neill and his allies were able to infuse a certain professional stiffening into the ranks of their enthusiastic but raw levies. A number of Spaniards from the *tercios* of the Armada had remained in their service since 1588, and Irish veterans of the wars in Europe had come home to take service with the northern armies. Amongst these were such as Captain Richard Owen, O'Neill's kinsman, who had twelve years of active campaigning in Flanders behind him and who was now put in command of O'Neill's infantry; Captain Hugh Mostyn or Mostian, an English veteran of the wars in France, Flanders, and Ireland, who had been won over to the Irish cause by Father Archer; and Alexander Walshe, who after four years' service in Brittany came to Ireland with the archbishop of Dublin and Don Martín de la Cerdá, after which he served four years under O'Neill.[2] O'Neill hoped to secure the services of more of these veterans. The confederates were also able out of their scanty resources to hire Scottish 'redshank' mercenaries for periods.

Hugh O'Neill by his 'assumption of the forms designed for open warfare' had created a 'modernized' army. Yet he was hampered by shortage of supplies and by a lack of officers, and the main body of his followers was without the hardening resulting from frequent battle-testing. The Irish cavalry arm in particular was weak, although under Maguire's leadership it had done well at the Yellow Ford. The horses, Don Juan del Águila was to note, were small animals and their riders wore no armour and fought with half-pikes from saddles without stirrups.

O'Neill and O'Donnell had at this time under their command prob-ably 20,000 fighting men in all, but not even half that number, the late Seán Ó Domhnaill (a good authority) estimated, were even moderately well-armed. Red Hugh had after the Yellow Ford sent his dark and indomitable mother to Scotland to hire a thousand Scots from her kinsmen. Hugh Boy MacDavitt and Edmund Birmingham went off to Spain to carry the news of the victory to Philip II and to beg him for the help required to follow up the success.

O'Neill, despite numerous disappointments suffered by him during

---

1. Hayes-McCoy, 'Strategy and tactics in Irish warfare 1593–1601', in *I.H.S.*, ii (1941); 'The tide of victory and defeat', in *Studies*, xxxviii (1949).
2. AGS, Estado 1745: Memorandum, Walshe to Prada, 17 Feb. 1603.

the reign of Philip II, placed in Spain his main hope of help. A sufficiently strong Spanish army could, united with his own forces, be relied
on to clear the English out of Ireland. Here again, in the international
field as in the national, Hugh had to walk warily to maintain balance
among conflicting interests. In Ireland the Catholics in general would
not accept the northern chief's leadership, while abroad the landing
of a Spanish army in Ireland would be calculated to arouse the fears
of France and the Papacy. O'Neill desperately required papal support
in order that he might be accepted as leader by all the Catholics of
Ireland. But the Papacy, whose main effort under Clement VIII was
directed towards the maintaining of peace between France and the
Habsburgs, would fear that a Spanish invasion of Ireland must make
France uneasy and upset the precarious peace. Hugh sought to man-
œuvre the Papacy into declaring the Irish war a crusade and giving
its blessing to the dispatch of an army by Spain to Ireland. This, as will
appear, was the aim towards which his agents at Madrid, Rome, and
Brussels were working.

Next to Spain O'Neill looked to Scotland for outside help. James VI,
Hugh calculated, would support him in revenge for his mother's
execution by Elizabeth. James was anxious to succeed to the English
throne and (until Cecil became his ally in 1601) sought and welcomed
encouragement from every source, Catholic and Protestant. A yearning
for the throne of England and not revenge for a mother slain was the
passion that inspired this northern ruler's actions, and he was therefore
very careful not to encourage Elizabeth's displeasure by openly traffick-
ing with her enemies. Realizing, however, that O'Neill's friendship
might be invaluable in the event of Elizabeth's death, he secretly
welcomed the Irish leader's offers of service and winked at his hiring
of Scottish mercenaries. But for the queen of England's benefit James
formally forbade his subjects to serve O'Neill or to trade with him.[1]

The two Irish agents MacDavitt and Birmingham, on their arrival
in Spain in October 1598, found Philip II already dead, but they pleaded
with the new government for an army of 6,000 men, with arms and
ammunition, to be sent to Ireland in 1599. MacDavitt was careful to
conceal the intent of his negotiations from the English Catholic exiles,
who wished rather for an attack on England.[2]

1. Willson, *James VI and I*, pp. 138–48; Gardiner, *History of England*, i. 80; Ó Ceallaigh,
Gleanings from Ulster history, pp. 101–2.
2. Loomie, *The Spanish Elizabethans*, p. 146.

This army, it seemed, could come none too soon to be of service to O'Neill. For when Essex arrived in Ireland, he had at his disposal an army of 16,000 foot and 1,300 horse. His aim was the establishment of a base at Loch Foyle to take O'Neill in the rear. But as a result of differences between him and the Cecilian party in the privy council he was left without the necessary carriage-horses and ships to enable him to establish this base.

Left, then, without the required support from England, Essex and the council of Ireland formed a new plan. They decided that the lord lieutenant should march southwards through Leinster to Waterford in order to prevent the complete defection of Munster, so much of which had recently rebelled, and in order to guard against the Spanish landing which they anticipated in the south. Essex therefore went on this campaign, which lasted from May to July.

As recent research has demonstrated, the censorious attitude of the older historians towards Essex's conduct of his lieutenancy is thus seen to be unjustified. It was once the accepted view that the earl squandered time and a great army in Munster and neglected the attack on Ulster to which he had previously been pledged. 'An army and a summer had been wasted', says Bagwell tartly, 'and nothing had been done.' Such strictures take no account either of the fact that Essex was prevented by his enemies on the privy council from setting up his planned base at Loch Foyle or of the fears of a Spanish invasion of Munster entertained by the government. True, the invasion did not materialize (and, as will directly appear, was never intended), but the threat was not one that could have been ignored. Essex did squander an army and a summer, but by showing his strength on the return journey from Limerick through Cork to Waterford he had done the government what could be considered valuable service; there were besides other useful gains to show, in the capture of Cahir (possession of which was necessary for any force operating westwards from the Suir) and in the reduction to obedience of Lords Mountgarret and Cahir.[1]

The English government were convinced that a Spanish invasion of Ireland or England was imminent, but they did not know where the

1. Cf. Henry, 'The earl of Essex and Ireland 1599', in *Inst. Hist. Res. Bull.*, xxxii (1959), 1–23; 'Contemporary sources for Essex's lieutenancy in Ireland 1599', in *I.H.S.*, xi (1958), 8–17. Hicks had already ('Sir Robert Cecil Father Persons and the succession 1600–1', in *Archiv. Hist. Soc. Iesu*, xxiv (1955), 100–1) indicated the importance of the denial by the Cecilian party to Essex of the 200 carriage-horses he asked for.

point of attack might be. And so while Essex sought to guard against an invasion of Munster there was also a great mobilization of ships at the Medway to meet a possible attack on England.[1] Since the attack never came, earning for the expected Spanish armada the description 'invisible', it has been suggested that Philip III was deterred from an invasion of Ireland or England by the putting to sea of the queen's ships and chiefly by the presence in Ireland of the man who had sacked Cadiz.[2]

In reality, and in spite of contemporary convictions, which were so strong as to deceive even modern scholars,[3] Philip III was not in 1599 planning any attack on Ireland or any major attack on England. The projected 'invasion' of England amounted to this. At the end of 1598 Philip had agreed in principle to the scheme proposed by the Genoese adventurer Federico Spínola that he (Spínola) should with a fleet of six galleys attack and take some port in England, to hold it as a bridge-head for further landings. Federico, who was then active in the war in Flanders, had originally made this proposal to Philip II in 1597, namely that at the command of some galleys carrying 5,000 men and a de-tachment of horse,

he would cross over to England and take some place, which when he had fortified it all England would not storm. . . . He would then transport to that stronghold all his army. He would feed and maintain this army by exactions on the country round about, and would support it with his galleys . . . .

Philip II died before deciding upon this proposal. But at the end of 1598 Philip III, when the suggestion was placed before him, accepted it. 'He ordered', said Spínola, 'that an agreement be made with me according to which I should be given the six galleys which were at Santander and had served on the Breton coast, together with 1,000 Italian infantry who were there . . . .' The king agreed that Spínola could as well embargo ships in Dunkirk and raise 1,000 Walloons and 1,000 horse in Flanders, with twenty pieces of artillery and munitions, provided that Archduke Albert agreed. Favouring this plan, Philip therefore rejected the somewhat similar scheme which Sir William Stanley and Father Joseph Creswell, S.J., urged repeatedly from 1597

1. Cf. *Elizabethan government and society*, p. 360.
2. Cf. Tenison, *Elizabethan England*, vol. xi: *1599–1601*, p. 161.
3. Henry, in *Inst. Hist. Res. Bull.*, xxxii, 15 n. 3. Cf. the pertinent remarks by Pollard, *History of England 1547–1603*, p. 437.

to 1602. Stanley offered, at the head of an expeditionary force of English exiles, to seize and hold some positions in England.[1]

Fedérico at the beginning of 1599 secured Albert's agreement to the proposal, and in June at the court at Barcelona Philip III made a financial settlement with the Genoese. The latter took ten galleys with him from Santander to Flanders, but then Albert (who had come back to Brussels in September) would not spare him the men and artillery, so that for the time being the project fell through.[2]

Far from contemplating an attack on Ireland or England in 1599, Philip was himself fearful of English aggression against Spain. Given the existing enmity between the two countries, it was to be expected that each should be suspicious and distrustful of the other. In the spring Spain was full of rumours that Elizabeth was preparing a great expedition. This, it was learned, was to be made up of 8,000 foot and 600 horse and was to go to Ireland. Later it was the talk that this army, under cover of going to Ireland, really meant to land in Portugal. Then on 11 June a fleet of an estimated sixty English sail was sighted off Corunna. This fleet went on to attack Great Canary Island on 26 June. The English occupied Las Palmas and demanded tribute before leaving. The Adelantado left Corunna towards the end of July in pursuit, but when he arrived at the Canaries the enemy was gone.[3]

Philip, although more concerned in 1599 to defend himself against attack than to take the offensive himself, did nevertheless encourage O'Neill and O'Donnell to hope for some support from him. MacDavitt was provided with a cargo of 1,000 arquebuses, 1,000 pikes, 150 quintals of powder, and 100 each of lead and match. Don Fernando de Barrionuevo, sergeant-major, was sent with him as special envoy to the Irish leaders from Philip, and the cargo was carried in three zabras commanded by General Marcos de Aramburu. Barrionuevo's instructions were threefold: he was ordered to encourage the Irish chiefs to continue their struggle, to assure them that the king would do what he could to assist them, and to report on their harbours and country from a military viewpoint.

1. Loomie, *The Spanish Elizabethans*, pp. 158–75.
2. AGS, Estado 621 (Rodríguez Villa, *Ambrosio Spínola*, p. 30; summary, *Correspondance*, eds. Lonchay and Cuvelier, i. 97): Memorial by F. Spínola, undated. Lonchay and Cuvelier summarize another document of the same tenor, dated, Vallid., 21 Feb. 1602. The two documents must be about the same date. Cf. Rodríguez Villa, op. cit., pp. 23–5; Cabrera, *Relaciones 1599–1614*, p. 2.
3. Cabrera, *Relaciones*, pp. 17–49, *passim*.

On 29 June Aramburu put in at Killybegs, 'one of the best ports of Ireland', Barrionuevo noted, 'able to take any large armada', and capable of being easily fortified against attack. That same day the sergeant-major went with O'Donnell to Donegal Friary, where the following day O'Neill joined them. Theobald Burke, O'Donnell's MacWilliam, was also there.

Cheered by the hospitality of the friars and with no more warlike sound to disturb them than the midsummer lapping of the waters against the shores of Donegal Bay, the chiefs and their guests sat down to confer. Don Fernando showed himself to be accommodating and subtle.

Don Fernando expressed regret for the failure of Philip II to succour the Irish in spite of the late king's best intentions, which had been foiled most notably when the weather destroyed Padilla's army of 1596, and he assured them of Philip III's resolution to stand by them. Comforted by this reassurance, the two Hughs swore to remain loyal to the king of Spain and not to enter into any treaty or agreement with Essex before the end of November.

Barrionuevo decided that these oaths could readily be accepted, for by November the campaigning season would be over. There would be time for Spain to send some help before the following spring or summer saw pressure mounted on the confederates to submit. Mac-William, to whose independence Barrionuevo testified by referring to him as *señor libre*—'independent lord'—swore without any limitation in time. Don Fernando soon grasped the underlying tensions which the conflicting claims, territorial or jurisdictional, created between the different lords, and was quick to bring home to them the need for presenting a united front, particularly if they looked to Spain for support. The chiefs took the hint and agreed to lay aside disputes about precedence for the duration of the war.[1]

Barrionuevo was a good diplomatist; of that there could be no doubt. Young Brian O'Rourke would not accept O'Donnell's claims to dominion over Brefni O'Rourke, and so stayed away from the conference at Donegal. Barrionuevo hearing of the trouble set out to soothe the prickly young chief, and wrote to him. O'Rourke was easily mollified by the courtesy of the envoy of Spain. O'Donnell in turn was

1. *Trató de confederarlos y lo hizó con que fuessen amigos verdaderos y las causas de su pre-heminencia se dexassen y suspendiessen por el tiempo que durasse la guerra* (He sought to make them allies and was so far successful that they became real friends, leaving aside and suspending their disputes about pre-eminence for the duration of the war).

persuaded to go to Strabane to meet Brian, and there they made peace, exchanging hostages, and O'Rourke took the same oath as the others.[1] The fruit of Barrionuevo's diplomacy was seen later in the support given by O'Rourke to Red Hugh at the battle of the Curlews in the month of August.

Don Fernando finally divided his cargo of arms equally between the two Hughs and went back to Spain to report.[2]

Whatever then may have been Essex's fears of a Spanish landing in Munster they were unfounded, as Barrionuevo's mission showed. After his return to Dublin the lord lieutenant went into Offaly in the last week of July. Here he relieved Maryborough and Philipstown and went on to confer with Clifford, the governor of Connacht. The latter, by agreement with Essex, took the offensive in the west, moving against O'Donnell. But in an encounter with Red Hugh and O'Rourke on 15 August at the pass of Bellaghboy in the Curlews he was defeated and killed. Thereupon O'Conor Sligo submitted to Red Hugh, surrendering Collooney castle to him. By this victory O'Donnell secured his grip on Connacht and greatly strengthened the Ulster defences.

Essex, although now reduced to 4,000 men, finally set out against O'Neill, but was induced to hold three parleys with the chief near Louth town. The outcome of the parleying was that by verbal agreement Essex and O'Neill agreed on a cessation to last in periods of six weeks until May, either side being free to break it on fourteen days' notice. If any of O'Neill's confederates refused their assent, Essex was at liberty to attack them.[3] From the evidence of Irish sources O'Neill, it can be gathered, made at the first and famous secret parley, when Essex and he met alone for half an hour in midstream, a tentative offer of the kingdom of Ireland to the Englishman. If Philip of Spain or James of Scotland would not take the crown of Ireland, perhaps Essex would; his great name would draw in the Anglo-Irish and he would be acceptable to all the Irish as king. Had Essex agreed, the course of history might have been different; but he did not, either because he feared that Philip would not forgive him for his sack of Cadiz, as Archbishop Oviedo learned, or because he would not trust

---

1. Ó Clérigh's laudatory biography of Red Hugh has no mention of this dispute.
2. AGS, Guerra Antigua 3143. Barrionuevo died on 17 Oct., but his report later came into the hands of the council of war; cf. Ó Clérigh, *Beatha Aodha Ruaidh*, i. 210.
3. Tenison, *Elizabethan England*, vol. xi: *1599–1601*, p. 196.

himself to the Irish, as Peter Lombard believed; or perhaps because his loyalty would not allow him.[1]

But the truce was quite a victory for O'Neill, as its dating 18 September 'in the new style' underlined. O'Neill, O'Donnell and Maguire had been observing the new Gregorian calendar from 1584; its observance symbolized both their Catholic orthodoxy and their defiance of government. O'Neill might not have gained Essex, but he had won sufficient breathing-space until the army promised by Barrionuevo should come to ensure certain victory. Hugh was left with the hope that this army would come before Christmas,[2] a hope which, the reader will remember, Barrionuevo saw no point in disabusing him of. Meanwhile, there were in the Irish regiment in Flanders veterans in plenty who might be enticed home to add a professional element to the raw native forces. To the Archduke Albert, O'Neill now turned, reminding him that in keeping Essex's army occupied in Ireland he had relieved the Netherlands of English pressure, and asking him to allow all the Irish soldiers resident in the Low Countries to come to Ireland.

But eight months were to pass before a reply came from Albert, and even then it was non-committal. The moment was not indeed favourable for an Irish approach to the archduke. After his resumption of rule in Brussels, in September 1599, the situation had been going from bad to worse. Though the rebels had lost the French alliance after Vervins, Elizabeth continued to support their war with Spain. In March 1599 the archduke had already sent his agent, Jerome de Coemans, to England to prepare the way for peace negotiations. Philip supported this move. If the archdukes were childless, the sovereignty of the Low Countries would in time revert to Spain: Philip therefore was anxious to have Elizabeth withdraw her support from the Dutch so that their revolt might collapse. The king of Spain was also concerned, in view of the now failing state of Elizabeth's health, to ensure that James VI did not secure the succession to the English throne, which he wanted for the Archduchess Isabel, his sister,

1. AGS, Estado 840, f. 79; Estado 185 (Cal. S.P. Spain, 1587–1603, p. 656): Oviedo to Philip III, Donegal, 24 Apr. 1600; Lombard, Commentarius, pp. 174–5. (Mr. Henry is quite wrong in regarding the Commentarius as embodying 'the Irish oral tradition of nearly a generation later' than 1599. Cf. I.H.S., xi (1946), 16. It was written in 1600.) For another suggestion that Essex had been in treasonable complicity with O'Neill cf. Hume, Treason and plot, p. 416. (For the Fr. Bluet and Dr. Bagshawe mentioned here, cf. Elizabethan government and society, pp. 383, 386.)

2. Lombard, Commentarius, p. 174.

or for himself.[1] It is in the context of these considerations that Philip's dispatch of Barrionuevo to Ireland must be considered. However much Barrionuevo might stress Spanish interest in Ireland that country was in reality but a pawn on the chessboard. If the pawn must be sacrificed to gain the greater piece of England, then it would be.

Given the situation existing in the Netherlands, it is not to be wondered at that Archduke Albert did little to help Ireland. Albert had much correspondence with the Spanish court and with the duke of Lerma, but the student will search his letters in vain for mention of the Irish struggle.[2]

Undoubtedly some gesture from the archduke would have been of great assistance to O'Neill as he played for time, for he was finding it difficult to persuade his fiery young ally O'Donnell of the wisdom of this policy. It was with much ado that O'Neill got the younger chieftain to agree to the cessation. O'Donnell's recollection of O'Neill's promise not to make peace without licence from Spain was in the circumstances inconvenient.[3]

After the departure of Essex from Ireland in October, and in accordance with his instructions, Sir William Warren went northwards on three occasions to negotiate with O'Neill for an extension of the cessation. The truce, indeed, continued until the end of the year. But it was uneasy. O'Neill's attitude, owing largely to O'Donnell's intransigence, was now hardening, and he was standing strongly on religion, demanding complete freedom for Catholicism in Ireland. In spite of the cessation Father Henry Fitzsimon, S.J., the famous controversialist and kinsman of Ussher, was imprisoned in December. O'Neill demanded his release from Warren.[4] The Jesuit, who had a great influence

---

1. Cf. Hume, *Treason and plot*, pp. 419–26. The memoranda on the succession question prepared by Fr. Persons, S.J., then rector of the English college, Rome, are dealt with by Hicks in *Archiv. Hist. Soc. Iesu*, xxiv (1955), where he argues the case for Cecil's support of Isabel's claims. This argument is shown to be less than convincing by Hurstfield in *Elizabethan government and society*, pp. 374–9.

2. AGS, Estado 2023 (*Correspondance*, eds. Lonchay and Cuvelier, i. 103): *consulta*, Vallid., 18 May 1602; VA, Borghese III, vol. 98 C, pp. 102–4; AGS, Estado 617 (*Archiv. Hib.*, iii (1914), 235–7, and xxiv (1961), 58–9): O'Neill to Albert, Dungannon, 27 Feb. 1599, and James MacDonnell to same, 'Ndunlibhsi' (Dunluce), 13 Oct. 1599. It seems to have been Albert's letter that Frangipani, internuncio in Brussels, sent to the cardinal secretary of state, 24 June 1600. Frangipani also sent copies of two letters that O'Neill had written to Albert. VA, Borghese III, vol. 98 C, f. 93v (*Archiv. Hib.*, iii. 240 and xxiv. 58).

3. Cf. *Cal Carew MSS. 1589–1600*, p. 269: O'Neill to Philip, July 1597, which letter had contained such a promise.

4. Gilbert, *Facsimiles of national MSS of Ireland*, pt. iv, I, p. 116 (*Cal. S.P. Ire., 1599–1600*, p. 327): O'Neill to Warren, Dungannon, 25 Dec 1599. Cf. *Cal.*, cit., pp. 279–81; *Cal. Carew MSS. 1589–1600*, pp. 348–9; O'Clery, *Life of Hugh Roe*, pp. cvii–cix; Ó Domhnaill, 'History

within the Pale, remained aloof from the rebellion, as did his superior, Father Richard de la Field. Fitzsimon's release, therefore, if O'Neill could secure it, would help to strengthen Hugh's position as the Catholic champion. Still anxious for veterans from Flanders, Hugh in another scarcely veiled hint told Albert at the end of December that he had cancelled the truce, as the English were minded to send their soldiers in Ireland to the Low Countries.[1]

But Albert was in no position to help O'Neill. At the beginning of 1600 mutiny for lack of pay among his troops had led to Maurice's gaining successes in Guelderland. The estates assembled in Brussels refused to support the archdukes with an extraordinary grant, and Albert was forced to negotiate with the rebel states. But a conference at Bergen-op-Zoom proved abortive.[2] In these circumstances Albert was as little inclined to support an expedition to Ireland as he was to provide Spínola with men and artillery for an attack on England.

1. *Cal. S.P. Ire., 1599–1600*, p. 338: O'Neill to Albert, Dungannon, 31 Dec. 1599.
2. Blok, *History of the people of the Netherlands*, pt. III: *The war with Spain*, p. 284.

of Tír Conaill in the sixteenth century', pp. 321–4; *Cal. Carew MSS. 1589–1600*, pp. 349–50: O'Neill to Philip, Dungannon, 31 Dec. 1599.

V · DIPLOMACY

He who would England win
Must with Ireland begin.
Sixteenth-century proverb

O'NEILL HAD SURVIVED the attack on him by Essex, but however he might boast to Archduke Albert he well knew that the queen could not relinquish her effort to conquer Ireland. In the new year he went down to Munster in order (by his presence there) to undo the work of Essex in the south. As in 1599 the nobles again rallied to his side, and only the towns held out against him. To reduce them he sent to Spain for artillery.[1]

Side by side with his use of force at home Hugh waged a diplomatic campaign abroad. The object of this campaign was to secure support for his war against the queen, military support from Spain and moral from the pope.

Father Edmund MacDonnell, dean of Armagh in exile, was Hugh's personal representative in Spain. It was MacDonnell who briefed Fray Mateo de Oviedo with arguments to convince the Spanish government that they should intervene effectively in Ireland. Fray Mateo, ever since his selection twenty years previously by Bishop Sega, then papal nuncio to Spain, to further James Fitzmaurice's cause, had worked tirelessly to promote an invasion of Ireland. In recognition of his usefulness O'Neill gained his appointment to the see of Dublin in May 1599.[2] Dr. Peter Lombard of Waterford, commissary of the university of Louvain at Rome, was from about 1599[3] O'Neill's special agent at the Holy See.[4] Lombard in his efforts to influence Cardinal Mathei, the

1. *Cal. S.P. Ire., 1599–1600*, p. 416: Thorton to Ormonde, 30 Dec. 1599, old style; *Cal. cit.*, p. 473: Information from Fenton, 14 Feb. 1600, old style. Cf. Kelso, *Die Spanier in Irland 1588–1603*, pp. 53–4.
2. *Archiv. Hib.*, xviii (1955), 84.
3. Cf. Ibid., ii (1913), 283–4.
4. Cf. *Wadding papers 1614–38*, ed. Jennings, p. 2; Reusens, *Éléments de paléographie*, pp. 353–4: University of Louvain to Lombard, 25 July 1601.

protector of Ireland, Cardinal Aldobrandini, the secretary of state, the duke of Sessa, the Spanish ambassador at Rome, and above all Clement VIII, was able to recruit the services of Father Persons, S.J., the celebrated rector of the English college at Rome. Besides Oviedo, Lombard, and Persons, O'Neill had other advocates of his cause on the continent, so that he had in fact the elements of a diplomatic service.

But operating against the success of O'Neill's diplomacy was the division among Irish Catholics. Elizabeth, out of motives of policy, allowed a good deal of latitude to Catholics, even in those parts of the country under her control. In Munster, the Pale, and the towns Catholicism had grown in strength in the decade (1583–93) between the Desmond war and the war of the two Hughs. Its increase owed most to the 'Jesuits and seminaries', or priests, secular and regular, who had been trained on the continent and had since about 1570 been returning home in ever-increasing numbers to work in Ireland.

By about 1590 Protestantism was a lost cause among the old English, who were now firmly established in their Catholicism. O'Neill's victories against the government encouraged them to make ever more open profession of their faith. In spite of this, they remained unwavering in their loyalty to the crown. Their priests encouraged this loyalty and maintained that a good Catholic need not meddle in matters of state. The Bull excommunicating Elizabeth was not a problem for these Catholics. Irish loyalists had been quick to point out that Pius V had not deprived Elizabeth of Ireland but only of England. In any case, after 1580 a declaration by Pope Gregory XIII allowed Catholics to accept the queen as their head in the temporal order.[1] In the Desmond wars the corporate towns and the Pale lords had for the most part remained unshakeably loyal, and the Munster lords had learned from the ferocious penalty exacted from them after that war how unwise it was to oppose the crown. The towns, the strongholds and foundation of English rule in Ireland, and the lords of the Pale and of Munster, both old English and old Irish, supplied the government armies with many troops. Of course such troops often deserted, but the supply increased as the nine years' war went on.[2]

The more clear-sighted English officials like Carew admitted the reality of the distinction which the old English themselves made be-

---

1. Ronan, *Reformation in Ireland*, pp. 313–15; Pollen, *English Catholics in the reign of Elizabeth*, pp. 283–5.
2. Falls, *Elizabeth's Irish wars*, pp. 41, 342–3.

tween their spiritual and temporal allegiances. Lacking sympathy for O'Neill, whom they considered as bent only on establishing his own supremacy in Ireland, the old English maintained their loyalty to the queen, and with Lord Barry claimed that she was indifferent to their exercise of their religion.

The desire of the Anglo-Irish to dissociate themselves from the northern rebellion was made plain to the internuncio at Brussels,[1] to the Jesuit general Aquaviva, and to Pope Clement. Against the voices of the old English Peter Lombard raised his in an effort to convince the pope that their loyalty was misplaced and that O'Neill was the champion of Catholic freedom in Ireland. Instructed by O'Neill, Lombard sought from Clement an excommunication, such as had been issued by Gregory XIII during the Geraldine war, against Catholics who favoured the queen; he sought also the crusade indulgence for O'Neill's supporters, the filling of all ecclesiastical appointments in Ireland only on O'Neill's nomination, and some temporal help.[2] Ten days after the truce with Essex O'Neill wrote to Clement directly to appeal for a subsidy. He had been offered very good terms, he maintained, but neither he nor his allies would accept them until their enemies granted the same freedom of religion in the rest of Ireland as they did in the territories subject to the northern confederation. Hugh insisted that he would make no peace that did not secure the complete freedom of the Catholic religion.[3]

Peter Lombard completed by 1600 a work, *De regno Hiberniae sanctorum insula commentarius*, in which he sought to convince the Papacy of the justice of Hugh O'Neill's recourse to arms. He argued that England had by her misgovernment of Ireland lost her right— based as it was on papal grant—to dominion over Ireland. The Ulster chiefs had been forced to take up arms against the queen for the defence of their religion, and their leader, Hugh O'Neill, was by birth, education, personal qualities, and zeal the man most fitting for leadership of that struggle. In delaying to take up arms himself until he was ready O'Neill had exhibited great foresight and prudence. For he had long foreseen that the English were determined on the destruction of all Ireland, and he had with great patience set about preparing for an effective resistance to this aim.

1. Cf. *Archiv. Hib.*, iii (1914), 242.
2. Ibid., ii (1913), 280–1, 283–4, 286–92; iii. 235–8.
3. VA, Borghese III, vol. 124 C, f. 9 (*Archiv. Hib.*, ii. 286–7): O'Neill to Clement VIII, *Cal. S.P. Ire.*, *1599–1600*, pp. 337–8: O'Neill to Philip, Dungannon, 31 Dec. 1599.

During the late sixteenth century a succession of English writers, Campion, Camden, Hooker, Derricke, and others, following the earlier model of Giraldus Cambrensis, wrote in uncomplimentary terms of the native Irish. Richard Stanihurst, the Dublin friend of Campion and Hooker, showed in his historical works how he, a Palesman, shared their prejudices. The image of Ireland created by these writers, an image which could indeed receive strength from an unsympathetic reading of the Irish court poets writing in their traditional modes, was one of a society that was barbarous and inflexible, ignorantly superstitious and fickle. Whether the image was a true one is another question. Eoin MacNeill believed that the members of the Irish patrician class, although brave, intelligent, and energetic, were rendered incapable by one radical defect from 'using their intelligence to profit with the times'. This fatal defect, he argued, was pride of caste and it made the chiefs 'conservative, inadaptable, unproviding'. The great Celtic scholar's conclusions find an echo in Seán O'Faolain's strictures on the inflexibility, the inactivity of brain, of the Irish system.[1]

Yet MacNeill himself admitted that we have no real history of the Irish people, based on their own records, from the fifteenth century onwards. The fragmentary remaining Irish records are sufficient to assure us of the grace, emotional appeal, and felicity of Gaelic literature, of the stability of Gaelic society, and of its development and purpose.[2] Until such an history as MacNeill desired comes to be written the historian must reserve judgement.

At all events, the harm done by the creation of this unflattering view of Ireland was apparent to O'Neill. His attempt to lay the ghost of James Fitzmaurice, to whose clarion-call of religion he had been deaf, is apparent now in all his attempts to make himself the Catholic champion, while Lombard's concern to lay the different ghost of Giraldus gives a particular urgency to the classical diction of the *Commentarius*.[3]

O'Neill's diplomacy as exercised at Rome could record some successes. Fray Mateo's appointment to Dublin had been a gain for him; it was another when on 18 April 1600 Clement VIII granted a Bull of indulgence to all who assisted him and appointed him captain-general

1. MacNeill, *Phases of Irish history*, pp. 354–5; O'Faolain, *The great O'Neill*, pp. 17–33.
2. Cf. Ó Ceallaigh, *Gleanings from Ulster history*, pp. 93–118.
3. Lombard, *Commentarius*, ed. Moran, pp. 149–78.

of the Catholic army in Ireland.[1] This was a typically Clementine compromise, for O'Neill's greater desires remained unsatisfied.

In Spain Oviedo, acting for O'Neill, sought to induce Philip III to send an expedition to Ireland and to put pressure on the pope to give his official blessing to this expedition and to the war being waged by the two Hughs. But in spite of the urgency of the pleas made to him the only help that Philip was as yet prepared to send was of a minor nature. The war in Flanders, as a correspondent of O'Neill's pointed out,[2] had drained Spain of men. Philip merely consented to Oviedo's accompanying Don Martín de la Cerdá with a shipment of arms to Ireland. The archbishop was refused permission to take Dean Mac-Donnell with him.

Captain Martín de la Cerdá had qualities something out of the ordinary. He was informed, discreet, and capable of intelligent execution of his orders: *que es soldado y tiene noticia de muchas cosas y hombre querdo y inteligente para executar con cuydado lo que se ordenará.* A patriotic Spaniard, he became a wholehearted advocate of the Irish cause and was soon a valued intermediary between Spain and the northern confederates.

As well as sending a shipment of arms to O'Neill Philip agreed to accept Henry, the chief's eldest son, as his father's pledge. The king, lastly, took the Irish Catholics under his protection, but without exacting any oath from them lest that embarrass them.[3] The proposal not to exact an oath is interesting, not for the reason given but because an oath such as that taken in Barrionuevo's presence must prove rather an embarrassment to Spain, should she not be able to send help before O'Neill's time-limit had expired.

Finally, after many delays, early in April 1600 Cerdá sailed with his shipment, two or three small boats in all. Don Martín had with him a sum of one hundred ducats, to provide for the expenses of Henry O'Neill's return journey with him to Spain. He had in his cargo 1,000 arquebuses with their powder-flasks and horns and other equipment,

1. Cf. *Cal. Carew MSS. 1589–1600*, p. 523.
2. HMC, MSS. Hatfield, part x, p. 16: Sinnote to O'Neill, 'The Grin' (Corunna), 4 Feb. 1600.
3. AGS, Guerra Antigua 3143 (*Rep. Nov.*, i. 94–5): Martín de Idiáquez to (?) E. de Ibarra, 2 Oct. 1599; Guerra Antigua 3143 (*Rep. Nov.*, i. 96, 98–9): Oviedo to Philip 28 Oct. and *consulta* on Oviedo's proposals; Guerra Antigua 539: *consulta* by council of war, Madrid, 28 Oct.; Estado 839 (O'Clery, *Life of Hugh Roe*, p. cxxi): Philip to O'Neill, Madrid, 24 Dec.; Estado 840, f. 4 (*Cal. S.P. Spain, 1587–1603*, pp. 653, 658): Abp. of Santiago to Philip, 18 May 1600.

100 quintals of powder, 100 of lead, and 100 of fuse. In command of the vessels was Ensign Pedro de Sandoval.[1]

Archbishop-elect Oviedo went as envoy from both Clement VIII and Philip, although, in spite of O'Neill's desires, he had to be content with something less than legatine accreditation from the one and ambassadorial from the other. Clement in a message to O'Neill congratulated him on his victories and exhorted him to persevere in his glorious struggle, so that Ireland might not be subject to heresy. Shortly afterwards, in further token of how successfully O'Neill and Lombard had gained the ear of the pontiff, Clement on 18 April granted a Bull of indulgence to all who assisted O'Neill, whom he appointed captain-general of the Catholic army in Ireland, in the war that the chieftains had undertaken to recover and preserve the liberty of the people of Ireland.[2]

Lombard had found a sympathizer at Rome who was above all things an Englishman. This was Father Robert Persons, S.J., rector of the English college, Rome, between 1588 and 1589 and again from 1598 until his death in 1610. Even better, O'Neill's agent could now avail himself of the support of Don Antonio Fernández de Córdoba, fifth duke of Sessa and Spanish ambassador at Rome.

Persons held the belief that there was a party in the English council in favour of an approach to Philip III, with a view to securing the succession to the English throne of Philip's half-sister, the Infanta Isabel. Persons's authority for this belief was an unnamed English correspondent[3] who maintained that this party of councillors was composed of Cecil, Charles Howard, earl of Nottingham, the lord high admiral, and Lord Buckhurst, the treasurer. The concern of this group of 'politiques', the correspondent maintained, was to prevent James VI from gaining the English crown; James was supported by Cecil's great rival Essex, and Cecil and his friends feared—and this was what really made them take the position that they did—that the king of Scotland would hold them responsible for his mother's death. If Philip would declare the infanta his candidate for the throne, they were ready to

1. AGS, Estado 187, Guerra Antigua 3143 (*Rep. Nov.*, i. 355): Royal schedule, Vallid., 31 Dec. 1601.

2. O'Clery, *Life of Hugh Roe*, p. cxvi; Lambeth MS. 608 (*Cal. Carew MSS, 1589–1600*, p. 523).

3. Richard Verstegan kept Persons informed of events in England from Antwerp. Verstegan had correspondents in England, among them Fr. Henry Garnet, S.J., and others who wrote more openly than Garnet. Unfortunately Verstegan's extant dispatches to Persons cover only the period 1591–5. Cf. *Letters and despatches of Verstegan* (CRS., LII), pp. xvii–xviii; Loomie, *The Spanish Elizabethans*, pp. 57–8.

support her claim. But immediate declaration by Philip was essential, for only thus could they be assured of effective military support from Flanders for Isabel's claims when the time came. Besides, the English Catholics, now leaderless, must be given a cause and a champion, otherwise James would succeed without opposition.

The story that Cecil and part of the privy council supported the infanta's claims[1] was apparently without any substance. Yet it is an odd fact that no less a person than the lord treasurer's son was to turn up in Rome early in 1603 to tell Sessa the same story.[2] At any rate, Persons believed it, and he wished to go to Flanders to arouse the infanta's interest, and through her Philip's, in the proposal. Sessa, although prudently refusing Persons leave to go to Flanders, was yet excited enough by the Jesuit's story to urge on the king a Spanish attack on Ireland; he agreed with Lombard that this would now be most opportune, as it would arouse the wavering English politiques to give more practical support to Philip. After listening to Lombard and Persons, Sessa was thoroughly convinced that no expedition directed against Elizabeth could be easier for Philip or of more benefit to him than the one that Lombard sought.[3]

The ambassador's dispatches came more and more to re-echo the arguments of Lombard and Persons for an Irish enterprise. The king should act, urged Sessa, for (according to Father Persons) the death of Elizabeth was imminent. Philip should not desert the Irish Catholics but should aid them in secret as Elizabeth did the Dutch rebels. The parallel between Ireland and the Netherlands was indeed striking, and Hugh O'Neill, as was soon to be made even clearer, was not failing to draw it.

Had Philip, Sessa went on to argue, aided the Irish in the past, Queen Elizabeth would now be very humble indeed. But seeing that he had not and was not even now preparing to do so, the queen was making a mockery of the peace negotiations. The king of France, too, was asserting that he would not allow any attack on Elizabeth while he lived. But the Irish did not care for France, but only for Spain. Ireland was very necessary to Spain for the conservation of the Indies

1. Hicks, 'Sir Robert Cecil, Father Persons and the succession 1600–1', in *Archiv. Hist. Soc. Iesu*, xxiv (1953), 111–17. The first letter from Persons's correspondent that Fr. Hicks considers is dated 25 Apr. 1600. But that Persons had heard from his correspondent in the sense in which he later wrote, before 19 Apr. is clear from Sessa's report.

2. Loomie, *The Spanish Elizabethans*, p. 174; cf. *English government and society*, p. 377.

3. AGS, Estado 972: Sessa to Philip III, Rome, 19 Apr. 1600.

—another point to be further developed by O'Neill before long. Philip, Ambassador Sessa ended, if he did not wish to hold Ireland for himself, could appoint O'Neill as its lord; the latter would pay some tribute and recognize his dependence upon the crown of Spain.[1]

O'Neill's arguments—as these substantially were—would, however, have no effect unless they appealed to the duke of Lerma, the real power in Spain. And O'Neill's diplomacy now seemed to be telling at last on the lethargic favourite. What impressed Lerma was firstly that in answering O'Neill's appeals Spain would be relieved at the least possible cost of English attacks, as the major part of England's strength would then be engaged in Ireland; and secondly, that to sustain the war would be to improve the peace conditions for Spain and meantime to encourage the English Catholics to persevere.

Something then would have to be done for O'Neill. The king needed little prompting from his favourite. He wrote to promise O'Neill and his allies the patronage and protection of Spain; even now, he said, a force was being prepared in Spain to go to their aid and to restore them to full liberty.

The king by taking the Irish under his protection had now given such a guarantee as his more politically experienced and circumspect father had never done. But Philip had responded over-enthusiastically to his favourite's suggestions. The duke was not preparing an expedition to go to Ireland; he merely ordered that a sum of 20,000 ducats be raised. This together with 4,000 quintals of biscuit and a quantity of arms and ammunition would be dispatched to Ireland when ready. The decision whether to send the Irishmen O'Neill wanted from Flanders was to be left to the Archduke Albert[2]—which meant that they would not be sent.

The truth was that negotiations for peace were now in train between England and Spain. Elizabeth had at length agreed to a congress to discuss the possibility of a settlement. Boulogne was chosen as the location for the conference and the envoys of Spain, England, and the archdukes arrived there at the end of May. However, neither side was in earnest. Philip wished (the more so as he had reason to believe that certain Walloon nobles, advisers of the archdukes, were

---

1. AGS, Estado 972: Sessa to Philip, 11 May 1600.
2. AGS, Estado 840, f. 104, Estado 2511 (*Cal. S.P. Spain, 1587–1603*, pp. 657–8): council of state to Philip, Madrid, 4 May 1600; VA, Borghese III, vol. 98 C, f. 92 (*Archiv. Hib.*, iii (1914), 237–8; xxiv (1961), 58): Philip to O'Neill, 17 Apr.; AGS, Estado 185: Sec. Prada to Sec. Ibarra, Madrid, 10 May.

offering the queen of England a peace that would exclude Spain) to keep Elizabeth at the conference table and away from meddling in the Netherlands. Cecil, on the other hand, was merely concerned to deter James VI from intriguing with Essex, the pope—the guileful James had since 1599 been giving Clement hopes that he might be converted—and various foreign powers.[1]

Negotiations at Boulogne therefore dragged on between May and July. These negotiations were not concerned with the serious matters at issue—the retention of the security towns by the queen, free trade, and the navigation of the Channel—but on questions of precedence. This was not of course altogether without point, for precedence was a vital matter in the diplomacy of the age. Spain insisted that the Dutch were rebels, without belligerent status, and insisted on her trading monopoly 'beyond the line', a monopoly that included everything westward of the Azores and southward of the Tropic of Cancer. To establish her precedence, therefore, at the conference table would be for her to go half-way towards vindicating these claims. England, which did not grant the Spanish claims, was well aware of this, and therefore refused to admit Spanish precedence. When stalemate was reached the English delegates were recalled by an order dated 26 July.[2]

With peace between England and Spain still too remote a possibility for serious discussion it behoved the Spaniards to keep alive, at the least cost to themselves, the war in Ireland. It was for that reason that Lerma dispatched Cerdá to Ireland.

Don Martín with his companions put into Donegal Bay in April. Again the friars at Donegal made their convent available for a conference, which a large gathering of sixty or more of the confederate leaders, anxious to hear what help they might expect from Spain, attended.

The two Hughs had already waited over six months beyond the time undertaken in their oath to Barrionuevo. O'Neill's presence in Munster had given heart to his allies, notably James Fitzmaurice and Florence MacCarthy (whom he had made MacCarthy More), and he had bound other lords to him by exacting hostages from them. With Munster as loyal as he could make it he had slipped home, leaving a

---

1. Willson, *King James VI and I*, pp. 142–59; cf. Loomie, *The Spanish Elizabethans*, pp. 77–8.

2. AGS, Estado 2511; Hamy, 'Conférence pour la paix entre l'Angleterre et l'Espagne tenue à Boulogne en 1600', in *Societé Académique de Boulogne-sur-mer Bulletin*, vii (1906), 434–60; *Cal. S.P. Venice, 1592–1603*, pp. xxv–xxvii.

force of up to 2,000 bonnachts behind, under Richard Tyrrell, to hold the province. Now, instead of the Spanish force that would make victory in Ireland certain, there was yet another embassy with its promises! This was maddening when victory at the cost of very little Spanish effort lay so near; and there were clouds on the horizon, for a new lord deputy, Lord Mountjoy, and a new lord president of Munster, Sir George Carew, had arrived in Dublin before O'Neill's return from Munster, and O'Neill waited in daily expectation and dread of a landing by the enemy at his rear on Loch Foyle.

Thus the new embassy found the Irish in more impatient mood than had Barrionuevo. The Irishmen reminded the Spanish envoys that they had been prevented from making an advantageous peace in 1596 only by the clear offer of help which Philip II had then sent by his emissary Alonso Cobos. 'Continue the fight to expel the English', the then king had said, 'and you can be sure of my help'.[1] To this reminder Archbishop Oviedo replied with truth indeed that it was bad luck rather than lack of intention that had prevented Philip II from landing an invasion force in Ireland. Oviedo's patent honesty made O'Neill agree to continue the war for another five months in expectation of an army from Spain; this was the furthest extent to which O'Neill and O'Donnell could guarantee to pay their men and to which they could hope to hold their none-too-firm allies.[2]

Vastly relieved to find that the Irish in spite of their disappointment were agreeing to continue the struggle, Cerdá moved on to a discussion of tactics. O'Neill and O'Donnell assured Cerdá that Limerick was the most suitable port for an army of three or four thousand men to land at, if the intention were to effect a speedy junction with the Irish and to strike a quick blow with the united forces before Elizabeth had time to prepare. If the forces from Spain were of 6,000 men or upwards, Waterford or Cork would be best, but if only of 2,000 or less it should come to Killybegs. This was tactically sound; a weak Spanish force should go where the rebellion was strongest, whereas a strong invading army should aim to gain possession of the southern towns at once. Traces and harness were wanted for the Irish hill horses so that

1. . . . *si vero . . . eodem animo in posterum Dei hostes ex ditionibus vestris omnino expellandos curabitis . . . non est cur minora vobis inde bona promitatis quam ex Alphonso Cobos qui isthuc a me mit[t]itur cognoscetis, cui integram fidem adhibebitis.* AGS, Estado 2604: Philip II to Irish Catholic lords, 14 Aug. 1596. Cf. Estado 840, f. 3 and Estado 839 (*Cal. S.P. Spain, 1587–1603*, p. 619): testimony by Cobos, Lifford, 15 May 1596.

2. AGS, Estado 840, f. 79 (*Cal. S.P. Spain, 1587–1603*, p. 656): O'Neill and O'Donnell to Philip III, Donegal, 26 Apr. 1600.

they could transport artillery; there were no carts but plenty of beasts of burden and mounts for cavalrymen.[1]

The meeting finally decided to send Cerdá back to Spain to present the Irish appeal for help to be sent within five months. Archbishop-elect Oviedo remained in Ireland. Cerdá with Henry O'Neill was back in Santiago by mid May and the king received him in Segovia early in June. Henry O'Neill was given a house in Madrid.[2]

Cerdá's new appraisal of the Irish situation was accorded but leisurely attention, for the peace negotiations had just begun at Boulogne. The conference there, however, soon reached stalemate on the point of precedence. On 1 July a junta of councillors, Borja, Idiáquez, Guevara, and the cardinal-archbishop of Toledo, reported to the king on the memorials presented by Cerdá. The latter presented in addition to the other documents a memorial on his own account. It is of interest as giving one of the clearest statements of the motives which induced the court of Philip III finally to send the expedition which came to Kinsale.[3] O'Neill together with Oviedo and Cerdá had gone to great pains to set out the strongest case possible for Spanish help.

At present, said the memorial, the plate fleets were forced to ply out of due season in order to avoid the attention of the enemy. This placed a strain upon the royal navy and exposed the ships to risk from storm. Now an expedition sent to Ireland would set free the coasts of the Spanish empire from attack; the money heretofore spent on the defences of these coasts could be used to attack England from Ireland; commerce would increase, thus, among other benefits, contenting the Portuguese; and Elizabeth could no more indulge in 'piracy'.

Spain was not now in a position, the argument continued, to conduct an offensive war against England; a diversion in Ireland was the safest, as it was the cheapest and most effective, entry into England. If Spain did not answer the Irish pleas, the Irish would be forced to accept

---

1. AGS, Estado 840, f. 74, Estado 185 (Cal., cit., pp. 656–7): Oviedo to Philip III, 1600; Guerra Antigua 3144, Estado 185 (Cal., cit., p. 663): Answers by O'Neill and O'Donnell to Cerdá's questions (the copy in Archiv. Hib., xvii (1953), 40–1, is rather faulty.)

2. AGS, Estado 840, f. 4: Abp. Sanclemente to Philip, Santiago, 18 May; Estado 840: Lerma to (?) Prada, 8 June.

3. AGS, Estado 2511 (calendared very briefly and indeed inadequately in Cal. S.P. Spain, 1587–1603, pp. 680–1, where it is wrongly dated 1601): council of state to Philip, Madrid, 1 July 1600. RAH, Col. Salazar, L 24, ff. 61–5v: P. López de Soto, 'Causas divinas y humanas que obligan a amparar a Yrlanda', is quoted by Fernández Duro, Armada española, iii. 218, as stating the arguments which motivated the expedition to Kinsale. But López wrote this *after* the defeat at Kinsale.

terms and would thus be added to Spain's enemies. Elizabeth well knew the value of creating diversions in Philip's territories; thus she sent out a fleet every year to keep Philip's forces occupied and away from her kingdom. Philip by invading Ireland could impose restrictions, impress the northern rulers (Henry IV and James VI), and force the return of Holland and Zeeland to their proper obedience. An army sent to Ireland need consist of only six or seven thousand men: 20,000 Irishmen, most of them armed, said the memorial optimistically, would be ready to join the Spaniards; no resistance would be offered. Finally, the sea off the Irish coast was free from rocky shoals.

An old proverb ran current in England, *Qui Angliam vincere vellet ab Ybernia incipere debet*:

> He who would England win
> Must with Ireland begin.[1]

This proverb had acquired a profound significance, since the Irish war had cost Elizabeth the loss of 40,000 of her men and her best captains. The same reasons of state counselled the sending by Spain of men to Ireland as to Brittany; indeed, they applied in greater force, since the enemy there was greater and the queen and the world would have to know that those who attacked Spain must pay.

The queen, in spite of holding all the chief towns and strongholds of Ireland, made such great efforts to gain the inferior parts of the country held by the Catholics as to demonstrate how valuable possession of these parts would be to her. Philip in holding Ireland would have a strong bargaining counter in the peace negotiations. It was a like motive that had decided Elizabeth against the advice of many in her council to take the Dutch (in the treaty of Nonsuch) under her protection.

If France broke the peace, as she was like to do, Cerdá's discourse went on, she would make an expedition to Ireland very difficult. Now was the time to act before England came to agreement with France. If France did break the peace and the Turks descended on the coasts of the Spanish empire, England would be prevented from joining forces with Frenchman and Turk, provided that Spain already held her engaged in Ireland. English interference in Flanders, the king should remember, had enabled Philip's rebellious vassals to thwart the greatest expeditions.

1 This couplet was much in vogue at the time in England. Cf. Froude, *England: Wolsey to Elizabeth*, x. 480; Ronan, *Reformation in Ireland*, pp. 487, 501.

The Irish Catholics were constant to Spain and in Ireland the king would gain friends, soldiers, sailors, and timber for his navy and deprive the queen of all these. But if Philip did not decide on the Irish enterprise, Cerdá (faithful beyond doubt to O'Neill's briefing) concluded, he must on no account pay the Irish soldiery, but rather pay their leaders very well and let them pay their troops.[1] So O'Neill and O'Donnell sought to guarantee their independence of the Spaniards, should they indeed invade Ireland.

This memorial, presented by Cerdá and inspired, if not dictated, by O'Neill, was a shrewd compound of reasons of state, commercial motives, and prospective military gains, all urging the profit to be derived by Spain from an attack on Ireland. Not the least important consideration in the case presented was the benefit to be gained by Philip from an increase in Hispano-Irish commerce.

The Gaelic resurgence of the fifteenth century had brought with it a development in Irish commerce, and trade had continued to flourish throughout the first part of the sixteenth century. The trade with the continent was more important than that with England. Ireland's exports were mainly of raw materials: fish, hides and leather, woollen and linen cloth, tallow, salt beef, grain, pipestaves, and boards for shipbuilding. Spain, England, and other countries were in eager competition for these products, in return for which Ireland imported salt, wine, iron, and in increasing degree various luxuries.

Ireland's main trading partner was Spain; with that country and with France, Portugal, and Flanders she conducted trade through the ports of the west and southwest: O'Donnell's ports and Galway, Limerick, Dingle, and Kinsale among others. In 1569 it was reported that two hundred sail came annually to the south-west coast, fished there, and carried away (besides fish) two thousand beeves, hides, and tallow.[2] The ports of the south and east traded mainly with the English west country, exporting fish, hides, and cloth, although they traded with the continent as well.

In the second part of the sixteenth century the Tudors, for commercial reasons, sought to transfer the profits of the Irish trade to Anglo-Irish and English hands, and for political reasons sought to divert the Irish trade with Spain to England. The effect of this interference, however, an effect that was aided by the devastation of war, by the

1. AGS, Estado 185 and Estado 840, f. 80 (abbreviated version): Discourse by Cerdá (1600).
2. Longfield, *Anglo-Irish trade in the sixteenth century*, p. 105.

devaluation of the currency, and the attraction of European fisher-
men to the richer fisheries of the Newfoundland banks, was rather to
injure the trade: industry (linen cloth and friezes) and exports
both declined. An Irish carrying trade with the colonies began and
new towns, which exported raw linen yarn and wool-fells to Liverpool
and Chester, arose north of Dublin. At the same time the smuggling
trade in meat, butter, and corn became significant. But none of these
developments compensated for the decline in the fishing trade, in
finished products, and in provisions.[1]

As Cerdá reported to the council of state, an Hispano-Irish victory
in Ireland would bring with it among other things important commercial advantages to Spain and would seriously injure Elizabeth, by
diverting the produce of the south and east of Ireland from England
to Spain. Spain would once again receive from Ireland abundant
supplies of fish, provisions, and corn, and from the vast Irish forests—
now at the beginning of their exploitation by Sir Richard Boyle,
Raleigh, Petty, and others[2]—pipestaves and timber for her galleys;
for these naval supplies Spain was now dangerously dependent upon
the Baltic trade.[3] She would win back again the valuable export of
wines to Ireland, which because of Elizabeth's imposts she was now
losing to France,[4] and would find in Ireland a ready market for iron,
salt, spices, and luxury goods. Finally, as Cerdá said, Spain would have
in Ireland a recruiting ground for soldiers and sailors.

1. The foregoing paragraphs have for basis Miss Longfield's invaluable work.
2. McCracken, 'The woodlands of Ireland circa 1600', in *I.H.S.*, xi (1959), 280–1.
3. *New Camb. mod. hist.*, i. 456.
4. Kearney, 'The Irish wine-trade 1614–15', in *I.H.S.*, ix (1955), 400–42.

VI · CHANCE

This expedition and enterprise is so important for the peace of
Spain and the preservation of the Indies and the reduction of
the States.

Oviedo to Lerma, 26 January 1602[1]

CERDÁ'S ELOQUENT PLEA for an invasion of Ireland was given a
hearing, but without effect. Lerma would not go beyond the order
given in May to send money, food, and arms to the Irish to encourage
them to continue the war. The council, taking into consideration that
an armada could not now sail before mid September, which would
expose it to risk of storm, that the money required to finance it (estimated at 150,000 ducats) could not be raised in time, and that an effort
was already being made to mobilize four thousand men for service in
Flanders, agreed with the duke in disregarding Cerdá's appeal.

King Philip, however, did not; he wanted to send an armada to
Ireland, and in 1600. The king, rarely concerned about affairs of state,
grew quite obstinate in this, and he and the council found themselves
at variance. Philip showed himself obdurate, and the council had to
yield and agree to try to raise the Irish expedition in 1600. The king's
final argument was that he would pay the expedition's cost out of his
own pocket:

This enterprise [he wrote] must so further God's service, and the earnestness
and zeal shown by the council for it must so animate those entrusted with its
execution as to overcome all the difficulties foreseen. I myself will see that the
money is provided, even at the expense of what is necessary for my personal
state—*aunque sea quitándole de lo necessario para mi persona*. The expedition must
go this year; to that end the council will put all in order with the utmost
speed . . . .[2]

1. *Si esta jornada y impresa importa tanto a la quietud de España y conservación de las Indias y
redución de los Estados.* AGS, Guerra Antigua 3145.
2. AGS, Estado 840, f. 107 (*Cal. S.P. Spain, 1587–1603*, p. 663), Estado 840, f. 4, Estado 2511:
consulta by council of state, 1 July 1600; Estado 187: Philip to Adelantado, Madrid, 10 July;
Estado 2511 and 840, f. 105 (*Cal.*, cit., pp. 666–7): *consulta*, 13 July; Estado 2511 and 840, f. 106
(*Cal.* cit., pp. 666–7): *consulta* 23 July; Estado 2511: *consulta*, 29 July; Estado 2023: *consulta*,
5 Aug.

But although Philip might wish to invade Ireland, he was not yet prepared to name the Archduchess Isabel as his candidate to succeed Elizabeth on the English throne. This was what Lombard, Persons, and Sessa now wished him to do. They warned him that James VI was mobilizing the support of the English and other Catholics for his succession to Elizabeth. They wished Philip to try to win the pope's support for the infanta. They urged him to spend what was needed on the army in the Netherlands and the fleet in Spain and to send an army of 6,000 men to Ireland, so that the day Elizabeth died Isabel's succession might be backed up without delay both from the Low Countries and from Ireland. On the other hand, they suggested, should Philip decide to make peace with England, Ireland should be exempted from the treaty terms so that she might be covertly aided to continue the war against Elizabeth.[1]

These schemes won the council of state's approval more readily than Philip's. It was true that if the infanta became queen of England, that would not necessarily make England a Spanish dependency. Indeed, it was no part of Father Persons's intention to make England subject to Spain. He simply wanted a Catholic successor to Elizabeth and his support of the archduchess was motivated by his realization that without Spanish backing no candidate could hope to succeed against James.[2] But of course any threat to disturb the balance of power by placing Philip's half-sister, the sovereign of the Netherlands, on the English throne must alarm France and the pope. Clement VIII, the Aldobrandini pope, who had in 1595 absolved Henry IV despite the best efforts of Sessa to prevent him, was in reality more affected towards France than Spain; and during Archbishop Gennasio's tenure of office as nuncio in Madrid (February 1600–June 1605) there was continuous friction between the Holy See and the court of Philip III.

In regard to the English succession the pope was undecided. He was in two minds whether to support Cardinal Farnese—whose claim was derived through his mother, the Infanta Maria of Portugal, from Edward III—or to be satisfied with any Catholic who might be likely to make his claim succeed.[3]

---

1. AGS, Estado 840, f. 82 (*Cal. S.P. Spain, 1587–1603*, pp. 663–5): *consulta* of 11 July; Estado 972: letters from Sessa, 19 Apr. and 11 May. Cf. Hume, *Treason and plot*, pp. 411–14.

2. Cf. *Cal. S.P. Spain, 1587–1603*, p. 665, no. 686; AGS, Estado 840, f. 81 (*Cal.*, cit., pp. 682–3): council of state to Philip, Madrid, 1 Feb. 1601. Cf. Meyer, *England and the Catholic church under Elizabeth*, p. 382.

3. Cf. Pollen, 'The accession of James I', in *Month*, ci (1903), 573–5.

PHILIP III OF SPAIN
By Diego Rodríguez de Silva y Velázquez and an anonymous painter

PROBABLE LIKENESS
OF HUGH O'NEILL,
SECOND EARL OF TYRONE.
Enlarged detail of an engraving
from Primo Damaschino, *La spada
d'Orione stellata nel cielo di marte* (Rome, 1680)

FRANCISCO GÓMEZ DE SANDO-
VAL Y ROJAS, DUKE OF LERMA.
Detail of the painting by Sir
Peter Paul Rubens, 1603

To attempt then to secure the English throne, as Lombard, Persons, and Sessa suggested, would be a serious step for Spain to take in view of the international implications. There was time enough yet, Philip realized, to name the infanta as his candidate.

While Philip was insisting that a major expedition go to Ireland in 1600, and while the council of state pressed him to make public his support of the archduchess's claims, the sending to O'Neill of the help agreed on in May was delayed. Neither army nor guns had come from Spain; and the pope still withheld plenipotentiary powers from Oviedo.

Denied help from Spain, O'Neill was in straits. In May 1600 Sir Henry Docwra had landed at Culmore on Loch Foyle behind O'Donnell's back; he won over Sir Arthur MacHenry O'Neill and later Sir Arthur's son, Turloch, Niall Garbh O'Donnell, who felt, and with some justice, that he had a better right to the chieftaincy of Tyrconnell than Red Hugh and Rory O'Cahan. 'Woe to the country and fair land', wrote a chronicler of these events in the stereotyped, academic style, 'woe to the territory and district in which ill-luck permitted relatives and kinsmen to hew and destroy each other . . .'[1] Docwra set up three garrisons along Loch Foyle, obliging O'Donnell to maintain three encampments opposite them. And in September O'Neill was obliged to go to the Moyry to meet an attack by the lord deputy, who commanded three thousand men. Of course, for Philip's benefit O'Neill made the number of the opposing forces much larger, all of seven thousand men. But he could hardly be blamed for painting a black picture. He had neither food for his own men nor money for payment, and his allies were deserting him for Elizabeth. Mountjoy's strategy in attacking O'Neill front and rear was having results.[2]

Hugh might have felt less overwhelmed with troubles had he known that at last the king of Spain and his council had agreed to send an army to his aid. To ensure secrecy the men were to be levied on the pretext that they were going to Italy (whither it had already been decided to send infantry), and the ships to carry them, with the munitions and arms necessary, were to be got ready on the excuse that they were bound for the Indies. The council planned that a total force of

1. Ó Clérigh, *Beatha Aodha Ruaidh*, i. 272.
2. O'Clery, *Life of Hugh Roe*, p. cxvii: O'Neill to Philip, the Catholic camp, 3 Aug. 1600; pp. cxix–x: same to same, 17 Sept.; pp. cxx–xxi: Oviedo to (?) Lerma and to Philip, 18 Sept. Cf. Bagwell, *Tudors*, iii. 372, and *infra*, pp. 88–9; Falls, 'España e Irlanda', in *Segundo curso de metodología y crítica históricas*, p. 335.

10,000 men was to be embarked for Ireland: 6,000 infantry to land,
1,500 to guard the ships, and 2,500 seamen. Philip accepted these plans
and agreed to give Don Antonio de Zúñiga command of the army and
Brochero, admiral-general of the Atlantic fleet, command at sea. The
ships must return as soon as they had disembarked the men; if they
remained in Ireland, the council believed, nothing would be gained
beyond the consumption of victuals by the seamen. Besides, the Irish
had defended themselves so well against England without anyone's
help that they would need only the Spanish infantry to support them;
it would be unnecessary for the fleet to remain. This line of argu-
mentation was unfortunate, as events were to show. Shipping to a
grand total of 14,780 tons was to be prepared to carry the expedition,
the total cost of which was estimated at 601,700 ducats.[1]

O'Neill had sent his son to Spain as a pledge of his placing his person, territories, and state at Philip's command. The king now, in view
of Cerdá's imminent return to Ireland, wrote to O'Neill to express his
joy at Henry's arrival. At O'Neill's request he agreed in principle that
only those Irish ships which carried passports from O'Neill and the archbishop of Dublin would be allowed into Spanish ports. This move was
designed to bring pressure to bear on the towns through the merchant
class to come over to Hugh's side. Counting the smuggling trade there
was, as has been seen, still a considerable commerce between Ireland
and Spain. It was not, however, before the following spring that
Philip gave final orders to embargo Irish vessels which did not carry
the required passport, and the embargo had little effect on the war.
O'Neill also wished Maurice, son of John Og Fitzgerald,[2] to come from
Lisbon with the expedition to Ireland. Though a rival of James Fitzthomas for the Desmond earldom, Hugh hoped that he would not
press his claims and that his coming with the expedition would
strengthen the confederate side by encouraging Maurice's kinsmen
to come over.

As the war went on, there were signs that the English of the Pale
were coming to have more belief in O'Neill. Fathers de la Field and
Fitzsimon were by the end of 1599 coming round to the view that
victory by Hugh would mean the re-establishment of Catholicism,
and at Douay at the same time the young gentlemen of the Pale, who
formed the majority of the student body in the college, were (at least

---

1. AGS, Estado 2053 (two copies): council of state on help to Flanders and Ireland,
Madrid, 5 Aug. 1601, with Philip's autograph reply.   2. Cf. I.E.R., ser. 5, xcii (1959), 289.

by report) coming to identify themselves with the national struggle now being carried on at home.[1] At the same time, however, Nuncio Frangipani, who at his sounding-post in the Netherlands heard the views of many Catholic exiles, was coming to distrust the purity of O'Neill's motives.[2]

From Rome, Sessa, urged on by Dr. Lombard, continued to plead the Irish cause with Philip. Through Lombard, O'Neill sought to get Pope Clement to order public prayers in Rome for a happy outcome of the struggle, to send an excommunication against all who carried arms against the Catholic belligerents, and to restore to O'Neill the *juspatronatus*, the patronage of benefices, held by his ancestors. Hugh also asked that to subsidize the war there might be given all the ecclesiastical income from places vacant; and he sought Oviedo's appointment, with wide faculties, as papal nuncio. His grand design was that the pope would grant investiture of Ireland in Philip, who would then send a force from Spain to liberate the country.[3]

While Lombard won Sessa's support for these aims, he made little progress with the pope. O'Neill therefore sent Father Archer off to plead with Clement. The Jesuit went by way of France to Rome, where he arrived in November, after a six-week journey from Ireland. He was armed with credentials not only from O'Neill but also from Florence MacCarthy, Edmund Fitzgibbon (the White Knight), Cormac MacDermot of Muskerry, and the O'Sullivans.[4]

Father Archer insisted in Rome that all the Irish Catholics either openly or secretly opposed Elizabeth; all that was required to make her secret opponents publicly declare themselves was the express announcement by the pope of a religious war and the support of a Spanish army sufficiently strong to free Ireland. Following his instructions, Archer went on to say that although the Irish recognized the pope as their lord they saw the need for Philip's help for their release from servitude. The forces of the pope, he pointed out, were far away and besides were too weak at sea. He asked Clement therefore to use his authority with Philip to send a Spanish army and to agree with

1. Cf. Hogan, *Ibernia Ignatiana*, pp. 50–1, 68; *Distinguished Irishmen*, pp. 167–71; J. Brady, in *Measgra Mhichíl Uí Chléirigh*, ed. O'Brien, p. 101. There is an interesting statement made by Richard Stanihurst in 1601 that he was then acting as O'Neill's agent at Brussels. Cf. Loomie, 'Richard Stanyhurst in Spain', in *Huntingdon Library Quarterly*, xxviii (1965), 147.

2. Edwards, *Church and state*, p. 290.

3. Cf. VA, Borghese III, vol. 124 C, f. 57 (*Archiv. Hib.*, ii (1913), 297–300, xxiv (1916), 79): memorial to the pope; *Archiv. Hib.*, ii. 287–97: letters of date 1600; AGS, Estado 972: Sessa to Philip, Rome, 2 Aug. and 12 Sept. 1600.   4. Cf. *Cal. S.P. Ire.*, 1601–3, p. 160.

Philip on a king whom the Irish would all obey, or else to give Ireland as a fief to Spain.[1]

Unfortunately for the success of Archer's mission he was the bearer of a message of a very different tenor to Rome. This was a letter from his superior, Father de la Field, to the General Aquaviva. De la Field, even if his sympathy for O'Neill might be growing, was yet mindful of his general's monition not to let his spiritual mission be damaged by his becoming too involved in political matters. He therefore wrote to assure Aquaviva of the existence of Irish Catholics who did not support O'Neill. He advised the general that a re-issue of the Bull of excommunication—as O'Neill desired—would have no other effect than to create difficulties for these Catholics. If they heeded such a Bull, de la Field argued, they would have their property confiscated and their persons condemned for high treason; if they did not, they would incur the Church's censures and be deprived of the sacraments and the mass.[2]

Because of the division between old Irish and old English in Irish Catholicism, therefore, Father Archer's mission was not successful. Relations in any case between the Papacy and Spain continued to be glacial. Outstanding were the papal grievances against the viceroy of Naples, Lemos. Clement claimed that Lemos was seeking to damage the trade of Benevento, which belonged to the papal states. This matter and other disputes which had resulted from infringement of ecclesiastical jurisdiction were not settled until 1601.[3]

While O'Neill's diplomacy gained little in Rome, the preparation in Spain of the proposed expedition hung fire. Lack of money was the main cause; there was no reserve to draw on. So little had been done by November 1600 that king and council agreed to postpone the expedition for the current year and to concentrate on sending help to Flanders. In vain did Richard Owen, infantry commander in his cousin O'Neill's army, warn that unless Spain shortly sent help O'Neill would do as he was urged by James of Scotland and accept the generous terms being offered by the queen.[4] Philip had lapsed into indifference about the fate of Ireland. Ironically, the council of state

1. AGS, Estado 972: Sessa to Philip, 27 Nov. 1600.
2. Hogan, *Ibernia Ignatiana*, p. 68; *Distinguished Irishmen*, pp. 170–1.
3. Pastor, *History of the popes*, xxiii. 217–18.
4. AGS, Estado 840, f. 89 (*Cal. S.P. Spain, 1587–1603*, pp. 673–4); memorial by Owen, Madrid, 20 Nov. 1600; Estado 840, f. 90, Estado 2511 (*Cal.*, cit., p. 673): council of state to Philip, 28 Nov. 1600. For James's letter and O'Neill's answer cf. Gardiner, *England from the accession of James I*, i. 80.

was now pleading with him to take the Irish expedition in hand. Heretofore the king's determination to aid Ireland had contrasted with the council's lukewarm reception of his plans. Now that the expedition had been agreed on the council sought to go forward with it, while Philip's interest began to fail. In this the capriciousness of Philip III appeared. The men who were now being levied, said the council, must go to Italy; the council of war should then be ordered to choose more captains, with a view to raising men for Ireland. Philip, though pressed further, now showed himself rather in favour of following up the peace negotiations and seeking a suspension of arms. Nor would the king yet commit himself to the proposal of the English Catholics and Jesuits that he should have an invasion force ready to back up the claims of the Infanta Isabel (or some other candidate) to the English throne when Elizabeth died.[1]

Like O'Neill, Fedérico Spínola was called upon to exercise a good deal of patience. Fedérico, when in 1599 Archduke Albert had refused him the artillery he needed for his proposed expedition to England, had had perforce to remain in Flanders, where with his galleys he caused havoc to Dutch shipping. Now in August 1600 when the peace negotiations broke off Philip again showed interest in Fedérico's project. It was decided to give Spínola six new galleys, so that if peace were not made he would then have twelve for his expedition. Philip wrote to Albert in October saying that Spínola—saving the peace negotiations, which were the primary thing—should get the help that he wanted.[2] But after that months were to go by before anything more was done.

At last Philip took the step of proclaiming the infanta as successor to Elizabeth and wrote to secure the pope's approval and aid. It was not until later that Philip advised the archdukes of his decision. When he did so Albert showed no enthusiasm for pressing his wife's claim. For the safety of the States, Albert desired nothing better than peace with England.[3] And even the council of state in time came to see the hopelessness of trying to establish Isabel on the English throne.

1. AGS, Estado 2023 and 840, f. 101: council of state to Philip, 12 Dec.; Estado 2023: same to same, 19 Dec.; Estado 840 (*Cal. S.P. Spain, 1587–1603*, pp. 674–6. Cf. Estado 840, ff. 95 and 135 and Hume, *Treason and plot*, pp. 415–17): memorandum from Fr. Creswell, S.J., 2 Dec., and report thereon by council of state.

2. AGS, Estado 617: *consulta*, 5 Oct. 1600; Estado 2224: Philip to Albert, 13 Oct. 1600; Estado 621 (Rodríguez Villa, *Ambrosio Spínola*, p. 25): undated memorial by Fedérico Spínola.

3. AGS, Estado 187: Philip to Sessa, 24 Jan. 1601. Cf. *Cal. S.P. Spain, 1587–1603*, pp. 649, 660, 663–5, 669, 675, 650–3, 668; Pollen, articles in *Month*, c (1902), ci (1903); *Dodd's church history of England*, ed. Tierney, iii. 30 n., lxx–lxxii.

But that was in the future, and at this juncture, as Father Persons warned that James of Scotland was intriguing with the pope, the council urged Philip to declare publicly his support of Isabel's candidature. This would forestall James, whom the council thought to be playing a double game in order to gain the English councillors (Nottingham, Buckhurst, and Cecil) whom Persons reported to be favourable towards choice of the infanta. Sessa, while seeking to win over the pope in the matter, should, the council recommended, keep continually before Clement the question of investiture of Ireland in Philip. Every effort should be made to persevere in the Irish business until the decision taken to send an army of 6,000 men to Ireland had been carried out.[1]

While the king and his council argued over the question of aid to Ireland, Cerdá, who was eager to return to O'Neill with definite assurance of an army to follow, had to kick his heels in Spain. Eventually, early in December, he was allowed to leave Corunna, in command of two pataches and bound for Killybegs. But although he did not come empty-handed, he bore with him no news of an intended expedition. Storm drove him into Broadhaven, on the Mayo coast, but finally he made Teelin and unloaded his cargo of 2,000 arquebuses and 150 quintals each of powder, lead, and fuse. He had also brought a sum of 20,000 ducats for division between the Irish leaders. O'Neill and O'Donnell arrived and divided the munitions between them, each apportioning his share among his sub-chiefs, who were also present. Dean Edmund MacDonnell divided the money according to the terms of the royal schedule.[2]

The chiefs, after their long wait, were bitterly disappointed at receiving only such inconsiderable help, and their disappointment was not alleviated by letters from Philip which only urged them to continue the struggle and gave no definite promise of major support. O'Neill pointed out to the Spaniards that he had not the munitions or infantry with which to oppose the superior English forces. At length Cerdá prevailed on the Irish to wait until the feast of St. James, 25 July

---

1. AGS, Estado 840, f. 81 (*Cal. S.P. Spain, 1587–1603*, pp. 682–3): *consulta* by council of state, 1 Feb. 1601.

2. AGS, Estado 186: statement by Ensigns Cuenca and Trigo and Sergeant Niebla to Governor Caracena, sent with dispatch, Caracena to Philip III, Corunna, 28 Jan. 1601; Ó Clérigh, *Beatha Aodha Ruaidh*, i. 280–4; A.F.M.; Docwra, 'Narration', in *Celtic Soc. Misc.*, ed. O'Donovan, p. 247; AGS, Estado 1743: 'Ermundo Donaldino's' testimony, Donegal, 5 Jan. 1600 (*recte* 1601). Ó Clérigh says the Spaniards unloaded cargo at Killybegs, but Teelin is more likely. Cf. Silke, 'Where was "Obemdub"?', in *Ir. Sword*, vi (1964), 276–81.

1601; if an expedition had not come by then, O'Neill would be free to follow his best interest, even if that entailed making peace. Archbishop Oviedo, for his part, pledged his word that in May, if Spain were not going to support the chiefs, he himself would come to inform them. And so Cerdá, accompanied by the archbishop and Father Chamberlain, O'Neill's confessor, returned again to Spain at the end of January to beg Philip once more to send the Irish the help they needed.[1]

It says not a little for O'Neill's constancy, a year and a half after the original undertaking given by Barrionuevo, that he was still prepared to yield to the Spanish envoys' request that he continue the war. For he had already abandoned hope; with France and Savoy at war, he thought (as Cerdá's discourse made clear) that Philip's armies would be engaged on the side of Savoy and that therefore the Spanish king would have no men to spare that year. Hugh was a great realist, but his fidelity to his country's cause was just now surviving a great test.

Still exercised about the port of disembarkation of the expedition, Hugh advised the archbishop that if it were small, it should go where the ships carrying messages (de aviso) went; if it consisted of 6,000 men or more, it should go to Munster. What O'Neill meant by the place where the ships de aviso went is without doubt Donegal Bay, and more particularly the port of Teelin or Killybegs. What he had in mind was this: Munster offered more prizes to an invading army and was easier to operate in and live off than Connacht or Ulster; but only a large army could maintain itself and hold the initiative there until O'Neill had come south to effect a junction with it. A small force then, if only such arrived, should come to Donegal Bay, where O'Donnell had all the ports at his command now, from Teelin to Broadhaven, and where the Spaniards could easily unite with the Irish armies.

Besides the north and south there was a third choice, the east, and of all Irish ports Drogheda was in O'Neill's opinion the best for the landing. Disembarking there would bring the Spaniards right away into contact with the enemy, while O'Neill himself could be there inside a day and a half. Artillery could easily be moved in the level country round about. But the way to Drogheda by Connacht round Loch Foyle meant a long journey, exposing the fleet to the peril of storms, while entry by St. George's Channel was dangerous too. And

1. AGS, Estado 619: Zúñiga to Philip, 12 July 1601; Estado 186: Caracena to Philip, 28 Jan. 1601; Estado 187: royal schedule, Vallid., 31 Jan.

also the queen held two adjacent ports—Dundalk and Carlingford—
with garrisons of foot and horse.

While O'Neill preferred the southern ports, all things considered, to
the northern, he preferred Cork to all of them. To one side of Cork
lay Clancarty, which, in so far as the setting up of Florence MacCarthy
as MacCarthy More, could effect it, was loyal to O'Neill; to the other
lay the lands of the earl of Desmond and of the Barrys. Although the
Barrys were now subject to the queen, it was, O'Neill claimed without
much regard to truth, perforce. MacCarthy and Desmond would be
at Cork to join the Spaniards within two days and O'Neill himself
within ten. There was plenty of food available in the vicinity.[1]

The Irish confederates begged Spain for an army of 5,000 men. They
told of most severe damage inflicted on them by Elizabeth the preceding summer, by land and sea, with 16,000 foot and 2,000 horse.[2]

O'Neill was indeed very much on the defensive. He was shut in on
all sides, was short of cattle, and lacking in corn, bread, and butter.
The English force on Loch Foyle held Inishowen and established Niall
Garbh at Lifford. Meanwhile, Mountjoy had during 1600 forced the
submission of Conor Roe Maguire—one of the rival claimants to the
Fermanagh chieftainship—ravaged Laois and Offaly, killed Owen
MacRory O'More, and in February dispersed Tyrrell's troops. Be-
tween October and November 1600 he had hemmed in O'Neill north
of the Moyry, razed the defences there, and established the fort of
Mountnorris, eight miles north of the Newry.

Bad as was all this, there was worse to come. Keeping up the campaign throughout the winter, a departure that came as a shock to the
Irish, accustomed heretofore to a breathing-space when their enemies
had retired to winter quarters, Mountjoy early in January 1601 des-
poiled Wicklow, and in March Felim MacFeagh submitted. The lord
deputy placed garrisons in Tullagh and Wicklow; in March he received
the submission of Ever MacCooley, lord of Farney, in Monaghan.
O'Neill's communications with Munster were cut off, and he was
rendered unable to go to the assistance of James Fitzthomas.

Dermot O'Conor Don, Desmond's captain of bonnachts, had been
driven back into Connacht, and there on 3 November 1600 he was
murdered by Tibbot na Long. Carew drove James Fitzthomas into

---

1. AGS, Guerra Antigua 3144: Archbishop of Dublin on choice of port, 1600.
2. AGS, Estado 840, f. 38: *consulta* by junta of councillors, Simancas, 9 Feb. 1601. Elizabeth
had by July consented to raise the establishment to 16,000 men. Cf. Falls, *Mountjoy*, p. 136.

the woods and intimidated Florence MacCarthy. By the end of the year 1600 not a castle in Munster remained in rebel hands.

But while in Ireland O'Neill's cause declined, at last there seemed promise of real help from Spain. By the treaty of Lyons in January 1601 France made peace with Savoy. The peace was favourable to Savoy, so that Spain was relieved from the likelihood of being called to go to the aid of the Savoyards. For once fortune smiled on the Irish, for it was at this juncture that Oviedo and Cerdá arrived at the court to remind King Philip of his father's and his own promises to the Irish, and to lay before the king the memoranda with which O'Neill and his fellow leaders had supplied them.[1] The council of state was not at the time with the king, who therefore appointed a junta of court councillors, the marquis of Velada, Don Juan de Idiáquez, Fray Gaspar, Franqueza, and Esteban de Ibarra, to hear the archbishop and Cerdá.

The peace between France and Savoy altered the international situation in favour of Ireland. The shrewd O'Neill had grasped the fact that as long as Savoy was threatened by attack from France Spain would not be in a position to send an army to Ireland. Savoy and the Netherlands were of more importance to Spain than was Ireland. Encouraged by the failure of Archduke Albert to make headway at the conference table, either at Bergen-op-Zoom or Boulogne, the States had sent Maurice with an army into Flanders. Near Nieuport Maurice found himself cut off by Albert from his base at Ostend. He therefore stood to fight on the sands of the Dunes. In the battle of the Dunes (2 July 1600), in which the Irish regiment fought in Albert's rearguard, Maurice inflicted a very serious defeat on the archduke. Albert lost over a hundred infantry companies, 6,000 men, and appealed to Spain for troops. Philip did not let the archduke's appeal go unheard, and 2,000 men were levied in Spain. In the state of relations between France and Savoy it was not considered safe to send this army by the landward route through Milan to Flanders; consequently they were embarked in ships at Lisbon, with a view to sending them by sea.

But with the treaty of Lyons, it became unnecessary to send them. The treaty of Vervins, embracing in its terms France, Spain, and Savoy, had left unsettled the claims of Duke Charles Emmanuel of Savoy or Piedmont to the marquisate of Saluzzo. At Lyons the duke was allowed to keep Saluzzo, while he ceded to France the less important territories of Bresse, Bugey, Valromey, and Gex. The treaty really

1. Cf. *supra*, p. 75.

showed diplomatic wisdom on the part of Henry IV; Savoy controlled the passage of troops from the Rhône valley into Milan, or vice versa. A friendly Savoy was a real asset to France, as it was to Spain.[1]

The danger to Piedmont had now receded, and Spain could afford to send to Flanders some of the men the count of Fuentes had taken to the Milanese. Besides, the winter was now advanced, and an expedition from Lisbon at this time of the year would run a grave risk at sea. The 2,000 infantry were therefore held in reserve at Lisbon for further calls; meanwhile they were set to guard the Portuguese coast.[2]

With this nucleus of men and ships at the ready Spain was at last in a position to prepare an army for Ireland. Lerma decided to send an army of 6,000 men, and Philip gave orders for the raising of this force; to the 2,000 infantry at Lisbon were to be added 4,000 other soldiers, made up of recruits then being raised in Spain, 1,200 veterans from Terceira, in the Azores, and other veterans from Galicia.

Orders were given for the making of biscuit in the ovens at Corunna and Lisbon; 10,000 quintals would be embarked, 4,500 as food for the two month's voyage provided for, and 5,500 to be disembarked in Ireland; while 10,000 must remain in Lisbon as food for the men in the ships there, in Andalusia, and elsewhere.[3]

Plans were formed for providing storehouses in Corunna, which was the most convenient place from which to provision the men in Ireland as well as the ships continually coming and going with news and reconnoitring in the English Channel, and for providing artillery and arms.

A summary of the estimates was as follows. The 2,000 infantry in Lisbon, together with the crews of the transport ships, had already been provided with everything necessary for a stay of two months in Lisbon. Next, there were the costs of raising and sending to Ireland a further 4,000 soldiers and 500 seamen:

	Ducats
Embarkation and maintenance of 4,500 men for two months	40,000
One wage for the 4,000 new recruits	20,000
Two wages for the veterans for the garrisons in Galicia and Portugal	12,000
Shipping for and maintenance of the men from Terceira	17,000
Two wages for the infantry from Terceira	16,000
Money to be taken to Ireland for payment of the men and other needs	200,000
Total	305,000

1. Petrie, *Earlier diplomatic history 1492–1713*, p. 104.   2. AGS, Estado 840, f. 276; Estado 961 (*Cal. S.P. Spain, 1587–1603*, p. 676): *consulta* by council of state, Vallid., 4 Aug. 1601.

3. The quintal was the equivalent of four arrobas, each of twenty-five libras. The libra was somewhat heavier than the avoirdupois pound, or 1·014 lb. avoirdupois. The quintal therefore weighed 101·4 lb. avoirdupois.

The 'wage' mentioned in the estimates was a subsistence. Soldiers in Spanish as in English armies knew to their cost that it was not always forthcoming.[1] Out of the grand total of 305,000 ducats the council expected a sum of 200,000 that the king had lent for the maintenance of the Indies' fleet, to be already available at Lisbon.[2]

1. Cf. the system of payment in the English army, described by Neale, *Essays in Elizabethan history*, p. 181.

2. AGS, Estado 840. ff. 41–6 (*Cal. S.P. Spain, 1587–1603*, p. 685): estimates of expenses of Irish expedition.

VII · PREPARATION

Señor, conozca V.M. a un hombre que nació sin miedo (Don
Fernando de Toledo introduces Águila to Philip II).

González Dávila, Felipe tercero

THE COUNCIL OF STATE's hope that the expedition would be ready
to sail by the feast of St. James (25 July) was not realized. Speed and
secrecy in preparation would give the expedition the advantage of
surprise over the enemy. In April 1601 an embargo was imposed by
Philip on Irish ships entering Spanish ports without a passport from
O'Neill and O'Donnell. This was a year after the chiefs had first recommended the step. It failed either to ensure secrecy, since Elizabeth's
spies were already reporting to her (in wildly exaggerated terms it is
true) on Spanish preparations for an invasion of England, or to provide
sailors and pilots for the expedition, since the few poor little craft
embargoed had not many to offer.[1]

Don Diego de Brochero y Añaya was appointed naval commander
of the expedition and about the beginning of March presented himself
for orders at Lisbon. By mid April there was some progress to report
in the raising of the expedition. Twenty-five companies of recruits
were being raised in Castile and would soon be on their way to Lisbon,
while nine companies whose numbers had gone down had left that
capital to return on being re-formed into a lesser number of companies. There were in the sixteenth-century company nine officer
ranks or 'places': captain, ensign, sergeant (to keep accounts), cor-
porals, quarter-master, drummers and fifers, colour-sergeant, and (a

1. AGS, Guerra Antigua, 3143 (*Rep. Nov.*, i. 352): Oviedo to Lerma, Madrid, 4 Apr.; Estado
188: letters from Thomas Charli to Elizabeth, Cecil, and others, Feb. 1601 (intercepted and
sent to Philip, 3 Apr.; Estado 2511: O'Neill and O'Donnell to Philip, Donegal, 24 Apr. 1600;
Estado 186: Adelantado to Philip, 7 Jan. 1601; junta to Philip, 9 Feb.; Estado 187: Philip to
Adelantado, Vallid., 31 Jan. and to Adelantado and others, 8 Apr.; Estado 186: Cerdá to
Philip, undated, with covering note by Lerma. Five craft were embargoed in Cadiz and
Puerto de Santa María. Estado 186: Adelantado to Philip, Cadiz, 2 May; abstracts by Notary
Molina of the processes heard in Cadiz, Pto. de Sta. María, 7 and 15 July.

tribute to his importance) baker. This re-forming therefore would mean some saving in expenses. Three companies of veterans as well, comprising four hundred men, were due to leave the garrisons of Galicia for Portugal. Castel-Rodrigo, the viceroy of Portugal, was sent some money, and promised more, to provide for the needs of these soldiers. But the money arrived in driblets only and the promises were slow in honouring, and in the garrisons, in Galicia as in Lisbon, there was great distress.[1]

A levy of seamen was ordered in the ports of Guipúzcoa, Biscay, and Quatro Villas. The incidence of plague and the bad treatment of the men in earlier levies made it difficult, however, to raise sailors. But by degrees and with many injunctions from the king to speedy action and many complaints from his ministers of insufficient funds, with ever-recurring delays and not a little rancorous exchange among those charged with the mobilization, the little force began to assemble at Lisbon.[2] Don Antonio de Zúñiga de Gimiel de Mercado, who at the end of April had been appointed land commander, made such difficulties, however, that it was decided to replace him by a new captain-general.[3]

Brochero, who came to Lisbon on 31 May, this time to take up his command, devoted himself with the energy he always displayed to the securing of everything that was necessary to making the expedition a success: money, an embargo of foreign ships, equipment, pilots, and hospital facilities. But he was at loggerheads with the viceroy, who resented having anyone to share with him the direction of the preparations. Differences such as these were to affect the success of the expedition greatly.[4]

With the preparations for the Irish expedition in train, Philip sought again to give impetus to the Spínola scheme, which appealed to him so much. At his order Fedérico came to Spain in April 1601, while

1. AGS, Guerra Antigua 3145 (*Rep. Nov.*, i, 352): Oviedo to Lerma, Madrid, 10 Apr.; Guerra Antigua 3144: estimate of troops, 18 Apr.; junta to Castel-Rodrigo, Vallid., 18 Apr.; Lerma to same, 18 Apr.; Guerra Antigua 587: Castel-Rodrigo to Philip and to E. de Ibarra, 29 Mar.; Caracena to Philip, 23 Apr.

2. AGS, Guerra Antigua 3144: junta to president of Casa de Contratación and to Adelantado, 29 May; Philip to Castel-Rodrigo, 4 Apr.; estimate by Ibarra; Guerra Antigua 587: Carlos de Amezola to Philip, Bilbao, 12 May; F. de la Riva Herrera to same, Santander, 13 May; Francisco de Fuica to same, Bilbao, 12 May; Verastegui and others to same, Portuagalete, 17 May.

3. AGS, Guerra Antigua 3144: Castel-Rodrigo to Philip, 26 May.

4. AGS, Guerra Antigua 3144: Castel-Rodrigo to Philip, Lisbon, 4 June; Guerra Antigua 3145: Brochero to Philip, 4 June.

Philip secured the council of war's agreement to an attack on England. Difficulty with the archduke, the council suggested, would be avoided if the army were raised not in Flanders but in Italy. Philip therefore ordered Fuentes to give Fedérico Spanish and Italian veterans and to allow him to levy other men up to a total of 6,000; these 6,000 would be taken to Flanders, where 2,000 of them would be mounted. Ambrosio Spínola would be *maestre de campo*. Fedérico would take four hundred Turks for the galleys from Hungary by way of Genoa, Barcelona, and Santander to Flanders, while Albert would help with the mounting of the men and their equipment in Flanders and would send twenty pieces of artillery to Sluys. Of this great undertaking Fedérico would provide the costs.[1]

Such was the plan. Philip was now bent on carrying the war to Elizabeth; he would attack her on two fronts, in Ireland and in England. If his plans succeeded, England would soon be faced with the grim threat of conquest.

But if O'Neill had at last gained one of his objectives, namely an army—or at least the promise of one—from Spain, he had been less successful in gaining the other, the co-operation of Pope Clement in the enterprise of Ireland. The pope, after consultation with Cardinals Bellarmine and Mathei and the Jesuit general Aquaviva, appointed by brief of 17 May 1601 Father Ludovico Mansoni, S.J., as his legate *a latere* to Ireland. While Clement did not choose Oviedo, or even a Spaniard, as O'Neill desired, Mansoni had for many years been provincial of his order in Sicily, which was, of course, under Spanish domination, and had acted in a confidential capacity to Philip II. The pope was thus going some of the way towards satisfying the Spanish king in the choice of a legate.[2]

He did not, however, satisfy the two Hughs. O'Neill and O'Donnell were disappointed that Clement had listened to the representations of the old English at Rome and had appointed not Oviedo but Mansoni as his legate. Although the appointment of a papal representative was a gain for their cause, Oviedo would have identified himself much more clearly with their interests. The Irish leaders sought to play on Spanish antagonism for Italians in order to make Philip inter-

---

1. Rodríguez Villa, *Ambrosio Spínola*, pp. 25–7, 29–30; Cerrolaza, *Spínola*, pp. 36–7.

2. Cf. *Archiv. Hib.*, xvii (1953), i. 18, 52–60; HMC, *rep.* 10, app. v, p. 346: Bellarmine to Aquaviva, 3 Nov. 1600; AGS, Estado 972; Sessa to Philip, 14 Nov. 1600. The first part of this dispatch (dealing with the succession to England) is translated in *Archiv. Hist. Soc. Iesu*, xxiv. 126–8.

vene to have Mansoni replaced by Fray Mateo. Philip, however, afraid
of offending the pope, contented himself with seeking to persuade
Clement not to send any nuncio until Ireland was reduced to a better
state and in the interim to commit to the archbishop of Dublin the
dispatch of necessary business. In this he was unsuccessful.[1]

Suddenly there was a new problem. Henry O'Neill, surety for the
good faith of his father and uncle (Henry's mother was Siobhán
O'Donnell, Red Hugh's sister), took the dramatic but unwelcome
step of entering the Franciscan noviciate at Salamanca. This decision
of O'Neill's eldest son to renounce the world posed an awkward
problem for his protectors, in whom O'Neill was likely to feel his
trust misplaced. Oviedo, who in fulfilment of his promise to the Irish
chief was trying anxiously to get Lerma to send news of the intended
invasion to Ireland, had in May to go to Salamanca at the duke's
request to try to get the troublesome affair put to rights.

At the beginning of June Archbishop Mateo was back, armed with a
theological opinion from the university of Salamanca, which was to the
effect that in becoming a friar Henry would sin mortally and that the
best course for Philip to follow was to secure an order from the nuncio
for the boy to give up the habit. The worried Lerma did not accept
this opinion until it was confirmed by the Valladolid theologians and
then by a special junta headed by Cardinal Guevara and appointed by
the favourite to decide the matter. Still the patache to warn O'Neill
was not sent, and with the feast of St. James, the deadline set by
O'Neill for the arrival of the Spanish army, only twenty days away
Oviedo fretted that Hugh would retire from the war and that the
armada would consequently suffer the common fate of Spanish
expeditions, failure.[2]

But now infantry and sailors were coming steadily into Lisbon, and
there was embarkation for 8,000 men there, many more ships than
were needed. Eight hundred effectives from Terceira landed at Lisbon
on 6 June.[3] A total of nine Irish ships had been embargoed on the

1. AGS, Estado 840, ff. 285–6 (Cal. S.P. Spain, 1587–1603, p. 683 n., where the proper date
does not appear) and Estado 2511: consulta by council of state, 19 May; Estado 187: Philip to
Sessa, 21 June; Estado 972: consulta, 19 June.

2. AGS, Guerra Antigua 3144 (Rep. Nov., i. 352): Oviedo to Lerma, Madrid, 4 Apr.; Guerra
Antigua 387: Oviedo to Philip, Vallid., 3 May; Guerra Antigua 3143 (Rep. Nov., i. 353–8):
Oviedo to Ibarra 7 May, 5 and 12 June; Oviedo to Lerma, 12 June; Estado 2511:
Guevara to Philip, 19 June. Cf. Walsh, The O'Neills in Spain, pp. 5–7; Walsh, The will and
family of Hugh O'Neill, p. 30.

3. AGS, Guerra Antigua 3144: Castel-Rodrigo to Philip, 6 June; Brochero to Philip, 6 and
10 June.

Andalusian coast, and three at Bilbao. They were all small vessels, and hopes that they might provide seamen and pilots were disappointed; these little craft carried no skilled seamen and their sailors showed no desire to serve with the expedition.[1]

General Pedro de Zubiaur arrived on 11 July with eleven ships sent by the Adelantado from Andalusia. These ships carried a total personnel of 415, nine or ten of whom were down with plague. Twelve out of the twenty-five companies of recruits from Castile had arrived from Alcántara by that day, and the three companies of veterans, led by Captain Juan de Albornoz, had come from Galicia. Sailors were coming from Bilbao and San Sebastian—unwillingly enough, for past experience taught them to expect poor treatment. In order to keep the men who had arrived from running away they were being fed on the food set apart for the voyage. Unfortunate as this might be it was a necessity, because there was no money to buy other provisions. By 2 August the twenty-five companies from Castile were all in Lisbon and embarked in their ships. But so far only 2,000 men had been found in the garrisons of Portugal.[2]

The *maestre de campo* Don Juan del Águila was the man chosen to replace Zúñiga as captain-general. With the appointment, announced by royal schedule of 2 July, went a delimitation of the commands of Águila and Brochero. The latter was supreme in all that belonged to the navigation, ships, sailors, and seamen, and the former was made land commander in Ireland. Each was forbidden to interfere in the other's sphere. This was a clumsy arrangement and an appeal by the king for the two commanders to work in harmony went largely unheeded; it soon became clear that co-operation between them was sadly lacking.

Águila was born in Barraco in the province of Avila and had his military formation first under Sancho Dávila in Flanders and then under Don García de Toledo against the Turk in the Mediterranean theatre. He returned to Flanders under Alexander Farnese, duke of Parma, and had distinguished service, rising from the rank of infantry

1. AGS, Guerra Antigua 587: Lic. Verastegui, corregidor of Biscay, to junta of war, 25 June; Irabién, purveyor of Biscay, to Philip, 6 July; Guerra Antigua 3144: junta to Verastegui, to Irabién and to Padilla, 28 June.
2. AGS, Guerra Antigua 3144 (cf. *Epistolario de Zubiaur*, p. 140): Report on Zubiaur's ships, forwarded by Ibarra to Castel-Rodrigo, 25 May; Castel-Rodrigo to Philip, 5 and 11 July; Guerra Antigua 3145: Brochero to Philip, 5 and 10 July; Guerra Antigua 587: Irabién to junta and Verastegui to same, 2 July; Castel-Rodrigo to Philip and to Ibarra, 2 Aug.

CHARLES BLOUNT, LORD MOUNTJOY

From a contemporary engraving by C. Cockson

THE INFANTA ISABEL OF SPAIN
Wife of Albert, and joint ruler of the Spanish

ALBERT VII OF HABSBURG, ARCHDUKE OF AUSTRIA
Joint ruler, with his wife Isabel, of the Spanish Netherlands.

captain to that of *maestre de campo*, commander or colonel of a regiment.

Águila returned to Spain after twenty-four years' soldiering and after some home service was in 1590 sent as captain-general by land and sea to Brittany to help the French Catholics, who were led by the duke of Mercouer. In France, where he was supported by Admiral Brochero, by dint of hard fighting he gained for a time mastery of Brittany. But, owing to dissensions between the Spanish commanders and Mercoeur and the bad state of the Catholic troops, the advantage gained was lost even before Vervins. Already in June 1597 the forces in Brittany, whose lot was most miserable, had taken their captain-general and his captains prisoner and informed Philip II that they could no longer bear Águila's extreme harshness. They had had seven years of misery, they said, without food or clothes. Other grave charges were soon laid against Don Juan, and on 27 May 1600 he, his wife, and the paymaster of his army were lodged in prison on information that they had benefited over-much from the royal treasury. When the decision was taken to appoint him to the Irish command he was released from gaol.[1]

This was the man chosen to lead the Spanish troops in Ireland, a very seasoned campaigner in different theatres of war and a commander with considerable success to his credit, even though he might not have earned the eulogium of his fellow Avilan González that he was one of the greatest luminaries that war gave birth to in his age. But although some of the charges against him must be considered in the light of the circumstances in which Spanish armies of the time fought, without sufficient equipment or money, with their supply-lines often cut and with an administration ill-organized, his was without doubt a difficult temperament, stern and bleak as the landscape of his native province. But even if Águila had been of one mind with the others responsible for the conduct of the war in Ireland, the task before him was indeed formidable: forced to fight in a theatre of war so far removed from Spain, with not enough troops, with inadequate supplies, he was asked to embark on an undertaking whose success would almost have demanded a miracle. There was every possibility,

---

1. González Dávila, *Felipe tercero*, p. 246; A[bilio] B[Arbero], in *D.H.E.*; Fernández Duro, *Armada española*, iii. 67–77, 83–93, 168–70, 218; Lavisse, *Histoire de France*, vi. 405; Hauser, *La prépondérance espagnole, 1559–1600*, p. 159. The Venetian ambassador reports on Aguila's command in Brittany in *Cal. S.P. Venice, 1592–1603*, pp. 149, 164, 227. Cf. also Cabrera, *Relaciones*, p. 70.

indeed that the armada might not even make a landfall in Ireland.[1]

Águila arrived in Lisbon on 18 or 19 July. Orders now issued from Valladolid said that the viceroy was to bring up the number of effectives sailing to 6,000 and that Archbishop Oviedo was to be in charge of the hospital with the army. Águila was ordered to avail himself of his and Cerdá's mediation with the two Hughs and of their experience of Ireland, and to take with him also Bishop Thady Farrell, O.P., of Clonfert. Father Archer, S.J., was also appointed to go as adviser with Águila, and Bishop O'Mulrian of Killaloe was to go as well. The expedition must be off by the beginning of August.[2]

Brochero had this order from Philip on 26 July and finding nothing in it about the port of disembarkation consulted with Águila. In doing so he started off a great controversy. At the conference in Donegal friary, in 1600, it will be recalled, O'Neill had laid down the principle that the port of landing must be determined by the size of the army sent. If it were of 6,000 men or larger, it should land at Waterford or Cork; if between 3,000 and 4,000 at Limerick; but if only 2,000 or under it should come to Killybegs or Teelin. To Cerdá at the turn of the year he reiterated the principle; an army 6,000 or more in size should go to Munster, preferably to Cork, but a small force must come to a port in Tyrconnell or perhaps in Connacht.

Such was O'Neill's thinking on the port of disembarkation. An invading army of 6,000 men would be strong enough to take the initiative without immediate help from the confederate Irish. Strategy then demanded that it should aim to take the key Munster towns. The army could move its siege-cannon readily in the level country of Munster and it would have abundant supply of food in that fertile province. Florence MacCarthy and the sugan earl would rally west Munster to the Spaniards at once, and the northern armies would come to join it in good time. For reasons of both strategy and logistics, therefore, an army of 6,000 men should come to Cork, or else Waterford.

If the Spaniards numbered only 4,000 men and were therefore too weak to take the offensive in Munster, they should come to Limerick.

1. Olagüe, La decadencia española, i. 355.
2. AGS, Guerra Antigua 3144 (cf. Rep. Nov., i. 368): Royal schedules to Girón, Padilla and Castel-Rodrigo, Vallid., 7 June; to Oviedo, Águila, and Castel-Rodrigo, 20 July; to Aguila, 31 July; Guerra Antigua 3145: Royal schedule to Brochero, 12 July; Brochero to Philip, 23 July; Guerra Antigua 3143 (Rep. Nov., i. 359–60); Oviedo to (?) Ibarra, Vallid., 10 July and Tordesillas, 16 July; Guerra Antigua 3144: junta to Castel-Rodrigo, to Aguila, and to Brochero, Vallid., 20 July; to Águila, to Bp. O'Mulrian, and to Castel-Rodrigo, Vallid., 31 July.

O'Neill and O'Donnell could join them more quickly at Limerick than at Cork and until the northern chiefs came they would be seconded by O'Donnell's western client, Theobald Burke. From Limerick the united armies would be well enough placed to strike hard at Elizabeth before the English had time to concentrate their forces.

Only if the Spaniards were too weak to take the initiative or even to defend themselves, O'Neill contended, should they land in or near the northern stronghold of rebellion. The north was inhospitable country, unable to provide food for the invaders and unsuitable for the transport of artillery. The voyage there was, besides, long and inconvenient for both the square-rigged ships and high-sided galleons,[1] and the north was too far removed from strategic objectives. Drogheda was central; it lay between O'Neill and the seat of government power, Dublin, and therefore had great strategic advantages, but a landing there would run too many risks. The queen held Dundalk and Carlingford and, while a voyage by way of Loch Foyle was perilous because of storm, entry by way of the shallow St. George's Channel was dangerous too. Once they had entered the ships too could easily be prevented from leaving the Channel again by the enemy, who could also prevent supplies and reinforcements from reaching the men. For these reasons O'Neill rejected Drogheda and also Carlingford, Richard Owen's choice. Owen favoured Carlingford because he believed that Dublin, not Munster, was the key to Ireland.[2]

These principles were noted and understood by the royal council at Valladolid. Since the army was to be 6,000 strong, Cork therefore should have been designated as the port of disembarkation. But at Lisbon, between Águila on the one hand and Oviedo, Cerdá, and Brochero on the other, a bitter argument developed which lasted for over a month. The argument really was between Oviedo and Águila, two men of strong personality. But whereas the friar was more passionately committed to what he regarded as best for Ireland, the general took a calmer, more objective view of the military issues involved.

In the discussion of 26 July, Águila wanted the landing to be in St. George's Channel, where he might occupy the ports facing England

1. AGS, Estado 840, f. 276; also Estado 961 (cf. Ir. Sword, ii (1954), 29): council of state on expedition to Ireland, Vallid., 4 Aug. 1601.

2. AGS, Estado 840, f. 89 (Cal. S.P. Spain, 1587–1603, pp. 673–4): memorial by R. Owen, Madrid, 20 Nov. 1600.

in preparation for an attack on that country. Brochero, on the other hand, felt that the Channel was too dangerous (it was shallow and had treacherous currents, the ports were in enemy hands, and English ships could prevent the Spaniards from either retiring or being reinforced). Don Diego therefore wanted to go to the north, to 'Obemdub' (a code-word for Donegal Bay), so as to join forces with the Irish at once. Agreement between the two commanders proving impossible, Marcos Hernández, Brochero's admiral in 1600, was sent off to Valladolid to inform King Philip of the divergence in view and secure his decision.[1]

The following day Ensign Pedro de Sandoval sailed from Corunna for Ireland. He carried news of the impending invasion to O'Neill and O'Donnell and was commissioned to find out their views on where the fleet should land.[2] A few days later, and before Hernández had arrived at court, the council of war sent instructions to Castel-Rodrigo, Águila, and Brochero to agree on a choice of port. The council laid down four conditions which the port should satisfy: it must be abundant in food, the terrain round about must be level for carriage-transport, it must be the port to which O'Neill and O'Donnell could come most swiftly, and it must be situated most advantageously for seeking out the enemy and fighting with him:

Siempre que se ha platicado donde será bien que se desembarque el socorro para Yrlanda se ha tenido por la parte más conveniente aquella que fuese más abundante y más tratable para el carruaje y donde con más breuedad puedan venir las fuerças de los condes Onel y Odonel y la más acomodada para buscar al enemigo y pelear con el.

Águila, the council said, should bear two things in mind, what was best from the viewpoint first of receiving support from his Irish allies and second of carrying the offensive to the enemy:

... que el sitio de la desenbarcación sea aquel que más se ajustará con su [Águila's] intención y con la comodidad de la gente y para que quede en la parte que más a la mano estuvyere para ser favorescida de los amygos y hazer ofensivo a los enemygos ...[3]

On 4 August the council of state learned from Captain Hernández of the divergence of views at Lisbon. The council advised the king that no precise order on the disembarkation could be given from Valla-

---

1. AGS, Guerra Antigua 3145: Brochero to Philip; Moura to same; Guerra Antigua 3144: same to Ibarra; all 26 July. Cf. Silke, 'Where was "Obemdub"?', in *Ir. Sword*, vi (1964), 281.
2. AGS, Guerra Antigua 3144: junta of war's commission, 14 July.
3. AGS, Guerra Antigua 3145: Schedules to Moura, to Águila, and to Brochero, Vallid., 31 July.

dolid. Águila and Brochero must decide between them, Águila to have the final choice. Lerma accepted this opinion and urged Águila to come to an agreement with the Irish on the matter.[1] To aid the captain-general's choice the council of war issued an *aide-memoire* on the risks of landing in the north (which, the council said, could not victual the Spaniards and from which the march to meet the enemy must encounter many rivers and other natural obstacles) or in the Channel.[2]

As soon as Castel-Rodrigo received the junta's instructions of 31 July he called together Águila and Brochero, the fleet's pilots, and Richard Owen to a meeting. 'Obemduff' (Donegal Bay) was the choice of this meeting.

At this point, however, Archbishop Oviedo and Don Martín de la Cerdá arrived in Lisbon. Learning of the discussion they, relying on the advice that they had received from O'Neill and O'Donnell, pressed the claims of Cork or Limerick. They persuaded Brochero that the choice lay between these two ports, but Águila maintained his preference for Donegal Bay. The order that Águila must make the final decision failed to satisfy the opposition, now led by Oviedo, and each side again presented its case by means of memoranda to Valladolid. Águila's objections to the south were stronger than ever. If he landed at Donegal Bay, he declared, he would be joined within ten days by O'Neill and O'Donnell and would have time to train his raw men and take some of the eastern ports before reinforcements came from Spain. Help would come from Spain, said Águila, more easily to Donegal Bay than to the south. If he landed on the east coast, the Irish would find it difficult to join him. But if he landed in the south, they would, he reasoned, find it impossible to get through an enemy deploying 8,000 foot and 1,500 horse to bar his way. Even if they did break through it must take them a month and they would arrive without food. The south, contrary to Oviedo's opinion, would never rally to him. There was news, said Águila, that the lords of the south had made peace with the queen. O'Neill too, he declared, had lately been unable to get his forces together to go to the aid of the south. Águila believed that if he were to land in Munster, the southern lords would flee with their cattle and wagons to their fastnesses, and he would be forced to dig himself in, to his great disadvantage.

1. AGS, Estado 840, f. 276; also Estado 961 and 2511 (cf. *Ir. Sword*, ii (1954), 29–30): *consulta* by council of state, Vallid., 4 Aug.; Estado 187: Lerma to Ibarra, Vallid., 8 Aug.

2. AGS, Guerra Antigua 3144: junta of war to Castel-Rodrigo, 14 Aug.

These arguments were not admitted by Oviedo. He claimed to be spokesman for O'Neill and O'Donnell, and, maintaining that the choice was reduced to one of the three ports Limerick, Waterford, or Cork, he insisted that the southern Irish would declare for the Spaniards once they had landed in Munster.[1]

The memoranda embodying these different opinions came to the war council on 26 August, and that very night the council dispatched an answer to say that if Sandoval had not returned before the armada sailed, bringing directions from the two Hughs, then the armada must go wherever directed by Oviedo and Cerdá, who spoke for the two chiefs.[2]

While the dispute over the port of disembarkation raged, Zubiaur was trying to get the order revised which said that the transports must return immediately after disembarking the soldiers. Don Pedro felt strongly that the ships should remain in Ireland throughout the winter until Águila was seen to be well placed. But neither the king nor Águila would listen to him, and Zubiaur was excluded from the conferences among the high command at Lisbon.[3]

Sandoval landed at Sligo apparently, for O'Donnell came to meet him there on 10 August. O'Neill was unable to get through Mount-joy's garrisons, which now ringed his territory. But from Dungannon he sent a message giving Sandoval his opinion on where the Spaniards should land. Since Florence MacCarthy and James Fitzthomas, as O'Donnell and O'Neill now advised, were prisoners in English hands and the English had fortified Waterford and Cork, the Spaniards ought to make for Limerick; in the event of mishap they could come to any port between Limerick and Loch Foyle.[4]

The northern leaders therefore no longer thought, as they had given Oviedo to understand, that Cork and Waterford were the most suitable ports to land at. Unfortunately Sandoval did not return with

1. AGS, Guerra Antigua 3144, 3145 (*Rep. Nov.*, i., 360–1, 366–7): memorials by Águila, Brochero, and Oviedo, forwarded 18 Aug. by Castel-Rodrigo to Philip; Guerra Antigua 3145 (*Rep. Nov.*, i. 361–2): Oviedo to Philip, 17 Aug.; Guerra Antigua 3144, 3145: Oviedo to Castel-Rodrigo, 16 Aug., Brochero to Philip, 16 Aug; Castel-Rodrigo to Philip, 18 Aug., with copies of three preceding letters; Guerra Antigua 3144: Castel-Rodrigo to Ibarra, 18 Aug.

2. AGS, Guerra Antigua 3144: junta to Moura, 26 Aug.

3. AGS, Guerra Antigua 3145: Zubiaur to Philip, Luarca, 15 Jan. 1602.

4. AGS, Guerra Antigua 3144: junta to Caracena, Vallid., 17 July; Guerra Antigua 587: O'Neill and O'Donnell to Philip, Sligo, 17 Aug.; Guerra Antigua 3144: junta's commission, approved and corrected by Philip, to Sandoval, 14 July; Guerra Antigua 587: Sandoval to junta, Corunna, 27 July; Caracena to Philip, Santiago, 7 July, and Corunna, 1 Oct.; O'Don-nell to Philip, Sligo, 17 and 26 Aug.; O'Neill to Philip, Dungannon, 17 Aug.

this message until after the fleet had sailed. Detained by contrary winds, he did not reach Corunna until 1 October.[1]

On receiving the order of 26 August from Valladolid, the viceroy on 1 September communicated its contents to Águila, Brochero, and Oviedo. Águila protested strongly against going to the south, and in particular objected to Cork, since it was fortified. The sole concession he could win from Oviedo was that the armada might go to Kinsale (although that port had not been mentioned by O'Neill and O'Donnell) rather than to Cork. And so in this conference of 1 September the decision to land at Kinsale or Cork was arrived at, although the archbishop maintained his preference for Cork. Afterwards Oviedo gave Castel-Rodrigo, at the latter's insistence, official confirmation of this decision, for which he thus accepted responsibility.

To sum up. The position now in regard to the port of disembarkation was that Oviedo had decided that it should be Kinsale or, failing that, Cork (which port he himself would prefer). When Moura later heard from Brochero of the landing at Kinsale he expressed satisfaction that it had been made at one of the ports determined on, and the one which had been most considered.[2]

Sandoval's main mission to Ireland was to inform O'Neill and his allies of the imminence of the invasion. He also reported to O'Neill the matter of Henry's taking the Franciscan habit and of the king's command that he leave the order again. Despite what had been feared in Spain, Henry's father made no complaint about this. O'Neill was much more concerned about the appointment of Mansoni as nuncio; he maintained that this appointment had been at the instance of an Irish Jesuit who falsely represented that Mansoni was the choice of O'Neill and O'Donnell. By this Jesuit he probably meant Fr. de la Field, or possibly Fr. William Bathe.[3] Nothing could be further from the truth, said the two chiefs; their choice had always been Oviedo, who had worked so hard on behalf of Ireland and knew and loved them so well. O'Neill again asked Philip to request Oviedo's appointment as nuncio. The nuncio must be a Spaniard in order to secure that in their spiritual and temporal affairs O'Neill and O'Donnell got fair and impartial treatment.[4]

1. AGS, Guerra Antigua 587: Caracena to Philip, 1 Oct.
2. AGS, Guerra Antigua 3144: Castel-Rodrigo to Philip, 6 Nov. 1601.
3. See p. 107, *infra*.
4. AGS, Guerra Antigua 587: letters from O'Neill, Dungannon, and O'Donnell, Sligo, to Philip, 17 Aug.

On 28 August the armada for Ireland was brought down to the bar of Lisbon at Belém. Pedro López de Soto arrived that day to take up his duties as *veedor* (inspector) and paymaster to the troops. His post was more or less equivalent to that of quartermaster-general. López during twenty-five years' service in Spain, Italy, and Flanders had acted as secretary to four captains-general. Energetic and assertive in the discharge of his duties, López showed himself of a meddlesome, not to say fractious, disposition and became much involved in controversy over the conduct of the expedition.[1]

The armada set sail from Belém on Monday, 3 September 1601, between 6 and 7 a.m., and crossed the bar at 10 a.m.[2] The number of ships was thirty-three, of which twenty belonged to the king and thirteen were privately owned. The number of effectives, 4,432, fell considerably below the stipulated 6,000. They were distributed in forty-three companies, Spanish and Italian. Besides the infantrymen there were 1,383 others, made up of sailors, ship-boys, cabin-boys, and artillerymen.[3] Brochero was ordered, as soon as the infantry were landed in Ireland, to dismiss the private vessels, whether hired or embargoed, and to return with the king's ships, these latter manned with armed sailors. The special guard of infantry he had repeatedly requested for this return voyage could not be spared; the sailors would have to do, and he was reminded that the enemy trusted in his artillery and fearing to come to close quarters with the Spaniards refused to board their ships.[4]

Fortunately Brochero was not called on to put this belief to the test. For lack of seamen he was using all the English prisoners he could. He had also taken men from German hookers and French ships in Lisbon. The Frenchmen and Germans had shown a reluctance that was likely to be shared by their princes. It was bad, felt Don Diego, to

1. AGS, Guerra Antigua 3144: Castel-Rodrigo to Esteban de Ibarra, Lisbon, 28 Aug., and to Philip, 5 Sept.; schedules appointing López de Soto, 13 Aug.; Guerra Antigua 591: five memorials by López, with covering letter from Don Rodrigo de Calderón to Ibarra, Vallid., 4 Mar. Cf. *Cal. S.P. Spain, 1587–1603*, p. 646 n. 1.

2. AGS, Guerra Antigua 3144: Castel-Rodrigo to Philip, 5 Sept.: Guerra Antigua 587: Caracena to Philip, 14 Sept.

3. Muster by Juan de la Peña Zorilla, 30 Aug. AGS, Guerra Antigua, 587: inventory by Peña Zorilla, 1 Sept.; Peña Zorilla to Philip, 4 Sept. Juan de Pedrosso's account gave 4,464 infantry and 1,052 sailors, with some others. Guerra Antigua 3144: inventory by Pedrosso, with letter, Castel-Rodrigo to Philip, 8 Nov. But the difference seems to be one of classification only, and is negligible (Castel-Rodrigo gave 45 companies). Seventy men remained behind in the hospital.

4. AGS, Guerra Antigua 3145: Brochero to junta, 18 July; Guerra Antigua 3144: junta to Brochero, Vallid., 31 July.

have to be more wary of one's own seamen than of the enemy. But Brochero had nothing but praise for the service given by the Germans.[1]

Velasco, the constable of Castile,[2] had thought that an army of 6,000 men was only half the size required for the invasion of Ireland, since too many troops would be needed to garrison whatever places were taken so that the others could be operational. The king had to agree with him, but accepted the view of the rest of the council that the overriding consideration was to make the Irish retain confidence in Spain; and so he agreed to the departure of the armada as it stood. He promised the constable that reinforcements would be sent in fast vessels to supplement these. But since the number of effectives fell so far below the expected 6,000, where were the reinforcements to come from?[3]

Centeno commanded one of the two *tercios* into which the infantry were divided; the other went without its *maestre de campo*, for Don Francisco de Padilla lay ill at Estremoz. The thirty companies of recruits had been re-formed into sixteen, to save money on 'dead' places. Diego Ruiz de Salazar, paymaster of the expedition, carried with him a sum of 164,681 escudos, in contemporary values some £45,000. This was the famous 'treasure' carried by Águila, which increased so much in the telling. Reports put it anywhere between 500,000 and 8,000,000 ducats.[4] Juan de Pedrosso had put on board 13,000 quintals of biscuits, so he said, 7,000 for 7,000 men for the journey, and 6,000 for 6,000 men disembarking in Ireland.[5] Of the food López complained that there had been such deception in the provisioning of the armada with victuals for its two months in Lisbon that only the biscuit lasted for that time, and not in all the ships either.

1. AGS, Guerra Antigua 3145: Brochero to Philip, 7 and 17 Nov.

2. The constable of Castile was captain-general of the land armies, the equivalent of the admiral-general at sea. Under Ferdinand and Isabella the title became honorary. Juan Fernández de Velasco was constable from 1585, was a grandee of Spain, and was governor of Milan at different periods. He was made president of the council of Italy and belonged to the councils of state and war.

3. AGS, Estado 840, f. 276; Estado 961 and 2511: council of state on expedition, 4 Aug. 1601, with Philip's holograph. Estado 187: Lerma to Esteban de Ibarra, Vallid., 8 Aug.

4. AGS, Guerra Antigua 3144: Peña Zorilla to Philip, 4 Sept.; Castel-Rodrigo to Philip, 5 Sept. In contemporary values the escudo stood at 5s. 6d. (Loomie, *Spanish Elizabethans*, p. 240 n. 1), the ducat at about 6s. 3d. In a report that 2,000 marks had been set (by Mountjoy; cf. Bagwell, *Tudors*, iii. 372) on O'Neill's head dead and £2,000 alive, a marginal note gives the value of 2,000 marks as 5,333 ducats and some pesetas over (AGS, Estado 620: news from London, 29 Feb. 1602, old style).

5. AGS, Guerra Antigua 3144: account by Pedrosso, sent with letter, Castel-Rodrigo to Philip, 8 Nov.

The meat had ended at the first month or before, the cheese also; the wine had been put on half-ration and even that had been cut after a month. Águila had had only one pipe of wine from Pedrosso to take with him.

While Brochero complained of the shortage of seamen (many had fled) and of food, Águila wrote as his galleon the *San Andrés* was already leaving the gulf to complain that he was short in everything, money, clothes, munitions, men, and food. Practically all his men were naked and barefoot too.[1] The 600 suits made in Lisbon, added López, were little good for 4,500 men. (By Pedrosso's account, the most naked of the men from Terceira had 1,100 suits divided among them and 300 other suits were taken for the most needy men in Ireland.)[2]

Supplies on board for the army included six battery pieces, 600 quintals of powder, 600 of match, and 300 of lead, with spare armour, saddles, bridles, and a large number of swords and lances for the Irish, picks, shovels, spades, and so on. That the army went short-supplied there can be no doubt, but López perhaps exaggerates short-comings. For instance, he declared that Águila had with him only a hundred pine boards from Flanders for building fortifications; whereas the official account gave 1,500.[3]

Aboard the flagship *San Andrés* were Brochero and Águila, with Archbishop Oviedo and the bishop of Clonfert. The bishop of Killaloe did not arrive in time to sail, and Cerdá in the moist Portuguese air had contracted malaria, a 'double tertian', a few days before and so was unable to travel on the expedition he had worked so long to foster.[4] The admiral vessel *San Felipe*, a galleon of 960 tons, carried Zubiaur, López de Soto, Centeno, and Sebastián de Oleaga, paymaster and inspector-general of the fleet. Father Archer went as Águila's chaplain. The Jesuit had selected Brother Dominic Collins, S.J., as a companion. There were also a Dominican friar and many other Spanish friars and priests, as well as nuns and other women. Richard Owen was with the expedition, as were Captains Raymond Lavin,

1. AGS, Guerra Antigua 3145: Brochero to Philip, 2 Sept.; Guerra Antigua 587: Águila to Philip, 3 Sept. Cf. Guerra Antigua 3144: junta to corregidores and officials of Guipúzcoa, Biscay, and Quatro Villas on the seamen who had run away.

2. AGS, Guerra Antigua 3144: López to Philip, El Ferrol, 26 Oct., and Corunna, 11 Nov.

3. AGS, Estado 840, f. 157 (*Cal. S.P. Spain, 1587–1603*, p. 692).

4. Cerdá was able to write after about ten days, after he had been blooded six times. He had been advised to take the Castile air, and sought leave to go there. He also sought back pay and office somewhere. AGS, Guerra Antigua 587: Cerdá to Philip and to E. de Ibarra, 14 Sept.

Andrew Butler, Darby or Dermot MacCarthy, Cormac MacFinnin MacCarthy, Maurice Fitzgerald, Walter Lea of Waterford, married in Spain, and a number of other Irishmen and Englishmen. Lambert Gould, said English reports, was chief pilot and among the other pilots was Captain Upton.[1]

Father Mansoni was not with the expedition. He did not leave Rome until the autumn, and reached Valladolid only in December; Father William Bathe, S.J., who belonged to the county Dublin gentry, travelled with him. The nuncio was still in Valladolid, having failed to get shipping for Ireland, in August 1603. He was then preparing to return to Rome. O'Neill did not want him in Ireland, and the rout at Kinsale and return of the Spaniards put paid to any last hopes he had of going there.[2]

One who was glad to see the expedition leave was the viceroy, the marquis of Castel-Rodrigo. Don Cristóbal unburdened his feelings on Águila and Brochero in a frank letter to Secretary Ibarra. What an amount of work it had been, he said, to send off that armada under two different heads, two men besides so opposite in their humours. One wanted to go to the north, the other to the south, while both, alleged Moura, rested as much as they could. And yet there was no end to the demands they made.

Never, the viceroy urged Ibarra, never advise the king to divide a command so equally between two leaders, neither of whom had any respect for the other. Castel-Rodrigo hoped that a certain soldier's gloomy prognostication would not be realized. This soldier had said that four 'good' things lay in front of his comrades and himself—*buenas quatro cosas llevamos*—winter, Ireland, Centeno, and Pedro López de Soto.[3]

1. AGS, Guerra Antigua 587: Caracena to Philip, with memorial by López, 24 Apr. 1601; Hogan, *Distinguished Irishmen*, pp. 91, 339, *Pac. Hib.*, ii. 67; *Cal. S.P. Ire.*, 1601–3, pp. 85, 87, 129; MacCarthy (Glas), *Florence MacCarthy*, p. 347.
2. *Archiv. Hib.*, xvii. 36–9; Hogan, *Distinguished Irishmen*, p. 379.
3. AGS, Guerra Antigua 3144: Castel-Rodrigo to Ibarra, 5 Sept. He had originally written Don Juan del Águila's name before that of Centeno, but stroked it out, substituting López's name.

VIII · LANDFALL

El invierno, que haze largas y mal siguras las cossas de la mar . . .
Secretary Ibarra, 22 December 1601

WITH WHATEVER FOREBODING the rank and file might regard their future, at first all seemed to go well. The little armada went off with a fair wind, and a week out from Lisbon stood thirty leagues from Ireland. Now a further and final consultation took place on where it should land. It was on Brochero's initiative that this staff-meeting took place, and taking part in it on board the flagship *San Andrés* were Brochero himself, Águila, Archbishop Oviedo, General Zubiaur, and López de Soto. The conference got off to a bad start, the regimental commander Centeno refusing to attend. Águila and he were on bad terms, for Centeno, spurning recruits, had against Don Juan's wishes taken with him only veterans in his galleon, the *San Felipe*.

Brochero had excuse for calling the conference. The chance of encountering Sandoval had enabled Águila to maintain a stubborn opposition to Kinsale or Cork, but now that chance was certainly gone. An added reason for Brochero's wishing to have the thorny question of disembarkation settled once and for all was most likely the fact that the fleet was running into foul weather; for it took another three weeks for it to reach the Irish coast. 'The winds', says *Pacata Hibernia* at 27 September, 'were *still* contrary (to ships coming from Spain) and the weather very stormy and tempestuous.' Oviedo spoke of the storms, *malos temporales y tempestas*, which kept the armada so long at sea on the way.[1]

Some master pilots and men familiar with the Irish coast were called to attend the meeting. Águila again voiced his preference for

---

1. *Pac. Hib.*, i. 275. Italics present writer's; cf. *Rep. Nov.*, i (1956), 365. Dermot MacCarthy gave as a reason for the conference that the Spaniards had heard of the apprehension of the sugan earl and Florence MacCarthy. But they did not apparently learn of this until after arrival in Kinsale. Cf. *Cal. S.P. Ire.*, 1601–3, pp. 160, 84; *Pac. Hib.*, i. 290.

sailing to the north, but Oviedo, although none too clear-headed from sickness, insisted that the landing must be in the south, and gained the majority decision in his favour. By agreement of the meeting Brochero therefore gave an order in writing to each ship's captain that the vessels if separated should rendezvous at Kinsale, or if that were impossible at Castlehaven.

Another issue which apparently came up at this meeting was the desire expressed by some that Brochero should remain with his ships to support the land army. Don Diego, however, pleaded that he was ordered, once he had disembarked the army, to send the embargoed vessels away and return home with the king's ships. The order could not be gainsaid, but Oviedo could see that it satisfied nobody. He therefore offered his plate and all that he had or might be possessed of to pay the sailors. Zubiaur, not to be outdone, supported him with an offer of his salary; but Brochero would not disobey orders—publicly at any rate. In private he said in Oviedo's hearing that he wished that Águila would force him to stay. The archbishop during the voyage sought the captains' opinion on the question. Some of them suggested that Águila could easily prevent Brochero from returning so soon by not disembarking the men and munitions.[1]

The belief is persistent that Brochero's real intention was to land at Limerick or Galway. But this belief rests merely on reports received by Sir Geoffrey Fenton and corroborated by one Andrew Lynch, a Galway merchant, that such was the intention of the armada. Lynch had had his information, he said, from one of Brochero's pilots. Very likely the Spanish command allowed this story to circulate among the fleet in order to throw possible spies off the scent. This counter-intelligence device, reminiscent of Operation Overlord of 1944, was a common ruse then as now.[2]

Still Águila would not accept defeat. He talked to Brochero and got him to accompany him to Oviedo's sick-bed to try to persuade the archbishop to go to the north. In spite of his sickness the archbishop would not give way, and his only answer was that he had nothing to add to what he had said in Belém. Much nettled, Don Juan rose to his feet and, saying that that would be the last dispute, left him alone.[3]

1. AGS, Guerra Antigua 3144: Oviedo's answers to D. de Ibarra, 6 Aug. 1602.
2. Oviedo's answers, cit.; AGS, Guerra Antigua 590: Brochero to E. de Ibarra, Lisbon, 14 Apr. 1602; *Cal. S.P. Ire.*, *1601–3*, p. 122: Fenton to Cecil, Dublin, 12 Oct. 1601, old style, and p. 129: testimony of Lynch. Cf. Dulles, *Craft of intelligence*, p. 146.
3. Oviedo's answers, cit.

The fleet sailed on until on the evening of 27 September it reached the Irish coast. Between the Blaskets and Dursey Island it took on pilots preparatory to landing in the morning. That night, however, a storm struck, driving away two galleons and six accompanying craft from the main fleet and upsetting Águila's plans. The mistake of sending great galleons, especially without Irish pilots, on such an expedition, rather than small vessels, was now all too apparent. Brochero asked Águila what was to be done. Don Juan replied that if they could make one of the ports they had determined on with even one ship, he would disembark. Brochero then managed to make Kinsale, where Águila disembarked on 2 October. With his much-diminished force of 1,700 men in twenty-five companies he took possession of the town, allowing the garrison to depart to Cork. Don Juan, still against Oviedo's judgement, had deliberately avoided Cork.

Of the ships driven away by the storm Zubiaur's galleon *San Felipe* with three hookers spent the next five days in a vain attempt to renew contact with the other ships or alternatively to make Kinsale or Castlehaven. A south wind was now blowing, and Zubiaur resolved to make for Teelin. On his first attempt he reached lat. 53°N. before the wind turned him back. When the wind shifted to the south again he tried a second time for Teelin, only eventually to be driven far to the south. He therefore sailed for home and came in to El Ferrol. With Zubiaur were López de Soto, Centeno, and Oleaga, as well as the infantry captains Castellanos, Arbe, and Barragán. The four ships carried between them eight infantry companies, 674 men in all. To add to the misfortune they carried most of the munitions and match for the arquebuses, which left Águila very short.

With the men from the galleon *San Pedro* and the hooker *León Dorado*, both of which also had been separated from the main fleet by the storm but managed eventually to make Kinsale, Águila had by 9 October a force of 3,300 or 3,400 men at his command.[1]

Little as it was, here was a Spanish army in Ireland. Would Munster rise? Surprisingly it was Águila himself whose action prevented this from happening, when he rejected an offer made on behalf of his

1. AGS, Guerra Antigua 3145: Brochero to Philip, Cascaes, 6 Nov.; Guerra Antigua 3144: Águila to Philip, Kinsale, 8 Oct.; López to same, from *San Felipe*, Ferrol, 22 Oct.; and to Caracena, 22 Oct.; account (by López) of adventures of *San Felipe* (22 Oct.); Guerra Antigua 3143 and 3145 (*Epistolario de Zubiaur*, pp. 70–2): Zubiaur to Caracena, three letters, from *San Felipe*, 22 and 23 Oct.; Guerra Antigua 3145 (*Rep. Nov.*, i. 362–3): Oviedo to Philip, Kinsale, 6 Oct.; Guerra Antigua 589: Oviedo to Philip, 1 Aug.; Guerra Antigua 3144: report by Albornoz. Cf. *Pac. Hib.*, i. 274–85; O'Sullivan, *Kinsale*, pp. 193–6.

fellow chiefs and himself by Daniel O'Sullivan Beare, who ruled the peninsula between the Kenmare river and Bantry Bay. O'Sullivan offered to provide two thousand men, a thousand armed and another thousand to be armed by Águila, in order to block Mountjoy's road and prevent a siege until the arrival of the northern armies. In excuse for Águila it can be said that he was extremely disappointed to learn[1] that Florence MacCarthy and James Fitzthomas had been committed to the Tower. One of the chief reasons for landing in Munster had been the expectation that these two would second the Spaniards. Once Águila had secured his base, he would, reinforced by the troops of Florence and Desmond, have taken the field with both infantry and cavalry, the latter on mounts supplied by his Irish allies. His hopes were shattered; these allies and any others who were well-affected to Spain had been taken prisoner, and he had excuse for suspecting of proven loyalty to the government those who now came to offer service. He would wait until he had assurance from O'Neill and O'Donnell before trusting them. It was a fateful decision, for as later events were to show there were still, in spite of O'Sullivan's record of loyalty hitherto and in spite of Carew's precautionary ruthlessness, the embers of revolt left in Munster.[2]

Out of the province then 'nobody worth a garron'[3] but only a few followers of Florence MacCarthy came in to Águila. Ruling the local Irish out of his reckoning and commanding such a small, poorly armed, and poorly provisioned force, without *maestres de campo*, Don Juan dismissed the notion of taking the field and decided to fortify himself as best he could until he was reinforced by the armies of Ulster and by Spain.

The harbour of Kinsale runs straight from the entrance in a northerly direction for about a mile and a half before turning sharply westwards to where the river Bandon meets the sea. The town, built on the northern side of this bend, lay almost on an island, as its whole eastern side was bounded by the sea, which was almost connected with Ballinacurra Creek; this creek in turn ran from the Bandon along the town's west and north sides.

Parallel to Kinsale harbour on the east, separated from it by a

---

1. *Cal. S.P. Ire.*, 1601-3, p. 84.
2. AGS, Guerra Antigua 3144: memorial by López de Soto, 22 Dec.; O'Sullivan Beare, *Hist. Cath. Ibern. comp.*, p. 224; Butler, *Gleanings from Irish history*, pp. 31-8.
3. *Cal. S.P. Ire.*, 1601-3, p. 119.

promontory a mile or more wide, and extending to cut off the approach further to the north runs Oyster Haven. North again from Oyster Haven but less than a mile from the town is Knockrobin Hill (268 ft.); south-west of Knockrobin and due north of the town is Camphill or Spital Hill (also 268 ft.). West again of these are two other hills, Ballinacubby and Kippagh. The terrain to the eyes of the Spaniards was very rough, uninhabited land, with great marches and rivers, most of them without bridges, so that (they saw) to besiege any place ordnance must be brought by sea.[1]

Rincorran Castle stood on the east bank of the harbour, about a mile from the entrance. It commanded the harbour in two directions, both southwards towards the entrance and westwards towards the town. This castle Águila garrisoned. On a little promontory half a mile across the bay from the town and just where the harbour turned from northward to westward stood another castle, Castle-ny-Parke or Castle Park, which commanded the town and its anchorage. Águila put another garrison here.

Don Juan lost no time in advising O'Neill and O'Donnell of his arrival, but by 10 October he had had as yet no answer to several appeals sent to them to come and join him. He already feared that they would not get through the barrier of fortresses erected to the south of their mountain fastnesses. The news of the Spaniard's coming spread quickly, and Hugh O'Neill soon knew of it, but he shared Águila's fear. He could not understand why Águila, seeing he had not sufficient forces to take the field, would not remove to Killybegs, Sligo, or even Galway, where he himself might join him.[2]

But as Águila looked northwards to the four hills that dominated the town, he felt himself trapped in a pit, *un hoyo*. Mountjoy told the council that Kinsale had 'a good wall, and many strong castles in it', but to Don Juan it was merely a slate wall, a bare two and a half feet wide, without moat or traverse, and he felt his situation to be more vulnerable than in the open field. Mountjoy later conceded that the town was weak against cannon, but maintained that it was impossible to place artillery anywhere but that the Spaniards commanded it. This invites the comment that if they did, it was with shot from the

1. AGS, Guerra Antigua 3144: report by Sandoval, Mar. 1602.
2. AGS, Estado 620: news from London, 20 Dec. 1601, old style; Guerra Antigua 3143: O'Neill to Águila, 12 Oct.: copy sent by Águila to Philip, with letter of 31 Oct.

castles more than with guns; Águila made good use of what artillery he had retained, but it was light.[1]

Don Juan rejected the notion of removing to a better port. Cork he had ruled out, and he feared that if he set about removing, the enemy would have time to prepare for his disembarking elsewhere, for example, at Castlehaven. He was afraid too to take the risk of having the ships scattered once more by putting to sea along this gale-tossed coast. He had had to send pilots to Baltimore to bring to Kinsale the *León Dorado*, which carried the companies of Captains Pedro Henríquez de Tejada and Francisco de Piños.[2]

On 9 October Brochero, accompanied apparently by Captain Albornoz, who was sent by Águila to report to Philip, left Kinsale with the royal ships. The admiral left behind 5,000 quintals of biscuit, still being unloaded from the hookers, while the *León Dorado* had brought another 600. This was deficient provisioning in Águila's reckoning. Brochero's withdrawal, as Águila complained, exposed the disembarkation to fire from the enemy, who were able to come into the mouth of the harbour and gain control there. The Spaniards had lost access to Kinsale by sea, and would therefore find the defence of the town so much more difficult.

But in view of the antipathy between them, Águila refused to take the responsibility of countermanding Don Diego's orders to sail, and the latter was adamant that he must go. He had now food aboard for his sailors for only twenty-one days, which would certainly not see him through winter and was dangerously little for the return voyage in the weather at this time of year. He mistrusted his foreign sailors pressed for service from ships in Lisbon. Don Juan charged that Brochero had thrown the food so carelessly on the shore that most of it was broken in pieces and was damp. The munitions too disembarked by Brochero on the shore or even in the sea were not, he complained, nearly enough.

To all this Don Diego retorted that the foreign sailors were fleeing and that he had had to put a Spanish guard over each to stop them. His ships were anchored half a league from the town, but he had taken everything to the town in boats. Águila, he pointed out, was in

1. AGS, Guerra Antigua 3144: Águila's report to Philip, 8 Oct. and (*Pac. Hib.*, i. 280–5) report by Albornoz; Moryson, *Itinerary*, iii. 25, 35: Mountjoy to English Council, 17 Nov. and to Cecil, 23 Nov.

2. AGS, Guerra Antigua 3144: Águila to Philip, Kinsale, 31 Oct.; *consulta*, 12 July 1603; Guerra Antigua 3145: Brochero to Philip, Lisbon, 17 Nov.

Kinsale with all his men, with control over the town and its citizens. Why then did he not take the food from the boats and put it under cover and take the artillery and other stores to their proper place?

As to control of the harbour, Brochero maintained that Don Juan could secure control by taking artillery off the ships to fortify Castle Park. Don Diego offered him as much artillery as he wanted for fortifying it. Águila agreed that by fortifying Castle Park he could keep the entrance open for ships from Spain and make himself secure in the town. He knew that Castle Park was the key to Kinsale. But the castle was too weak as it stood, and he would need to build a proper fort there, enclosed within a strong four-walled stockade, where he could mount artillery. For that he needed lime, and to man the fort he needed more men than he could spare from the defence of Kinsale and of his uncovered munitions. For the want of men and materials too he was unable to throw up fortifications on the landward side of Kinsale. Besides, he had no horse for moving heavy artillery about, and he needed in any case to spare his meagre supply of powder for the muskets and arquebuses. So although Brochero made repeated offers of artillery to him, and was joined in his pleas by Oviedo and the other ecclesiastics, Águila yielded to their importunities sufficiently to disembark only two field-pieces and two demi-cannon; the rest of the artillery he returned with Brochero. The two leaders could not agree on anything and Brochero made all haste to depart. The next day, 10 October, the hookers (all but the *León Dorado*, which left Kinsale on 30 October) sailed too, and Águila was left to cope as best he might with the Irish winter and the English enemy.[1]

He still had hopes of help from Spain and asked for men and materials to fortify Castle Park. He wanted also (he wrote) to build a fort at the entrance to Cork harbour, so as to starve Cork into surrender. Kinsale and Cork, he reckoned, would be bases for an invasion of England when large reinforcements came from Spain.

Cavalry were perhaps Águila's greatest lack. The enemy were collecting all the cattle and corn round about and breaking the mills, and with their cavalry were coming daily up to the walls of Kinsale. Don Juan had his men sally out time and time again against them, but to little effect. He was worried by the fear of cavalry reinforce-

---

1. AGS, Guerra Antigua 590: Brochero to E. de Ibarra, Lisbon, 14 Apr. 1602; Guerra Antigua 3145: Brochero to Philip, Lisbon, 17 Nov. 1601; Guerra Antigua 3144: Águila to Philip, 8 and 31 Oct.

ments coming to the enemy from England. He soon found that Irish cavalry were of poor quality and would be of no use to him. Irish cavalrymen, who rode without stirrups, held their spears by the centre over the shoulder—fought, as Águila said, 'with half-pikes'; their hobbies were very light and they could not meet the English in equal combat. But Don Juan's experienced eye soon saw what in fact O'Neill had already demonstrated in combat, that the native Irish with training would make good infantrymen. Husbanding his treasure rather too well (he was preoccupied with the need to supplement his men's rations of dry tack with meat bought from the Irish), he sought more money from home in order to buy Irish soldiers over from the queen. But he needed reinforcements from Spain too, and they should come, he desired, in ships able to do battle with those that Elizabeth was preparing.[1]

The Spanish force was, in fact, too small unless reinforced and it had come none too early if the rebellion were to be saved from collapse. It had taken Mountjoy and Carew less than two years to break the rebellion in Munster, where Carew's campaign had been especially efficient, and in Leinster. Mountjoy hoped by a third expedition into Ulster before the end of 1601 finally to stamp out the revolt in its last stronghold.

By March 1601 Carew was master of Munster and was able to send troops into Connacht. The 'sugan' earl and Florence MacCarthy were both taken and were sent to England on 24 August 1601 to be committed to the Tower. Just as the lord deputy established garrisons in Leinster to keep the O'Mores, O'Conors, and O'Byrnes subdued, so did Carew maintain his grip on Munster by putting garrisons in a number of castles south of the Shannon. Sir George concentrated his forces at the towns of Cork and Limerick, since he expected the Spaniards to land at one or other of these ports. Here too he gathered in provisions and tools for siege-work. If the Spaniards had landed anywhere else Carew did not know how the English army could have been provided until the following summer 'with victuals and carriage to lodge by them'.[2]

In Ulster the way was prepared for the final onslaught. From Lifford, Niall Garbh, Docwra's ally, had gone to seize Donegal abbey and

1. AGS, Guerra Antigua 3144: Águila to Philip, 8 and 13 Oct.; Guerra Antigua 3145: Brochero to Philip, Cascaes, 6 Nov.; Guerra Antigua 589: Águila to Philip, Avila, 25 July 1602; Guerra Antigua 587: Bertendona to Philip, 6 Nov.
2. Cal. S.P. Ire., 1601–3, pp. 118–19, 120.

maintained it against Red Hugh's siege. South of the Ulster line of
defences, which ran from the river Erne to Loch Neagh, Mountjoy had
a chain of garrisons running all the way from Boyle abbey in north
Connacht, through Brefni and south Monaghan, where he had conquered the barony of Farney, to Lecale. Docwra's total of effectives
was reduced to 1,675, but at Carrickfergus Chichester commanded a
force of 850 foot and 150 horse; while in the garrisons between Dundalk and the Blackwater Mountjoy had 800 foot and 100 horse. In
Lecale he had 150 foot, in the Pale and adjoining parts 3,150 infantry
and 175 horse, and in Connacht 1,150 foot and 62 horse.[1]

With these bases in Connacht, the north midlands, the Pale, and
Ulster ready for concerted action, the lord deputy was now prepared
to launch a final offensive on Ulster. But as rumours of the intended
Spanish invasion gathered force Mountjoy, in September, went south
to Kilkenny, leaving the garrisons behind. He was thus prepared for
the alternatives of combining with Carew against the Spaniards, should
they come, or of fighting another winter campaign against the enemy.[2]

At news of the Spaniards' arrival Mountjoy gave orders for the
bringing of troops from the Pale, the northern garrisons, and Connacht
to Cork and went there himself, arriving on 7 October. Carew could
guarantee him supplies of victuals for two or three months and had
also a good supply of munitions in stock. The lord president had arrested all the lords he mistrusted and taken pledges from the others;
thus the leading men of the province remained loyal from the coming
of Águila until those of the south-west defected with the arrival of
Zubiaur at Castlehaven in December.[3]

Mountjoy sought by burning and proclamation to deprive the
Spaniards of corn and cattle. Lack of ordnance and rainy conditions
delayed his taking the field, but on 10 October he sent out from Cork
a strong force, reckoned by the Spaniards at 1,000 foot and 500 horse,
to test the Spaniards' strength. Águila, with loss to himself of fifteen
or twenty men, beat them off.[4] By 26 October the lord deputy was
able to leave Cork, and that night he encamped at a point five miles
from Kinsale. He now had under his command a force of about 6,800

1. *Cal. S.P. Ire.*, 1601–3, p. 27; *Pac. Hib.*, i. 231–2; Moryson, *Itinerary*, iii. 11–13; Falls,
Mountjoy, pp. 160, 162; E. M. Jones, 'The Spaniards and Kinsale 1601', in *Galway Arch. Soc.
In.*, xxi (1944).

2. Hayes-McCoy, 'Strategy and tactics', in *I.H.S.*, iii. 269; Moryson, *Itinerary*, ii. 445.

3. *Cal. Carew MSS.* 1601–3, p. 179; *Pac. Hib.*, i. 286–9; Moryson, *Itinerary*, ii. 451–3, 464; iii. 13.

4. AGS, Guerra Antigua 3144: Águila to Philip, Kinsale, 31 Oct.; Guerra Antigua 3145:
Brochero to same, Lisbon, 2 Nov. (*recte* Dec.).

foot and 611 horse in list; these included[1] the men he intended for dispatch to the Limerick border in order to hold that country. Of the 4,000 men Cecil had earlier earmarked for Ireland, 2,000 had already arrived there; the other 2,000 would follow, together with ten ships of war. Yet a further 2,000 men would be sent at the end of October.[2]

In Spain meanwhile, the king, on receiving news of Águila's departure, made arrangements to send him 5,000 quintals of biscuit and to raise ten companies of infantry as reinforcements—measures which did not nearly approach in scale those being taken by Cecil.[3]

Before he left Cork the lord deputy issued a proclamation in which he maintained that the Irish had no cause to take up arms against their lawful sovereign and that the war was unjustly maintained by the pope and the king of Spain. This drew a quick response from Águila, a counter-proclamation which bore the stamp of Oviedo's authorship and in which Don Juan justified his invasion altogether on grounds of religion. These grounds were the excommunication of Elizabeth and the appeal by the Catholic Irish to the pope and the king of Spain for help against the English, who were treating them cruelly. Águila then called on the Irish Catholics, telling them that the pope ordered them to take up arms for the defence of the faith: *summusque pontifex . . . vobis imperat ut arma in defensionem fidei vestrae sumatis.*[4]

Águila's claim answered the demands of propaganda rather than of truth. Pope Clement VIII, who had removed the Papacy from dependence on Spanish might, had given Águila no order for the Irish Catholics to rise. The fruit of Clement's diplomacy was the reconciliation with the Church of Henry IV in 1593 (he was solemnly absolved on 17 September 1595), a reconciliation that paved the way towards the effecting of peace between the two Catholic powers in 1598. Relations now between Rome and Madrid might be somewhat strained,[5] but this was an inconvenience that Clement's well-directed policy could afford.

1. Falls, *Elizabeth's Irish wars*, p. 295, appears to be inaccurate here.

2. *Pac. Hib.*, i. 290–1, 293, 294; *Cal. Carew MSS. 1601–3*, pp. 179, 180; Moryson, *Itinerary*, ii. 464–6, 457–8; ii. 1–15, 41; O'Sullivan, *Kinsale*, pp. 42–3; Falls, *Mountjoy*, pp. 166–7.

3. AGS, Guerra Antigua 3144: junta to Águila, to Moura, and to Juan de Pedrosso, Vallid., 3 Oct.; Águila to Philip, 13 Oct. (The answer to this letter, dated 4 Dec., was never received by Águila. Cf. *Pac. Hib.*, ii. 103.)

4. AGS, Estado 1570; VA, Borghese, ser. III, vol. 65C, f. 12 (*Archiv. Hib.*, iii (1914), 244–5). There are other copies in BM Add. MS 5847 (Cole Papers), pp. 316–17, and elsewhere (cf. NLI, *Report of the council of trustees, 1951–2*, pp. 48, 83, 94). The proclamation is dated 31 Oct. (Cole Papers).

5. Cf. Ranke, *History of the popes*, ii. 44, 104–14; Hinojosa, *Los despachos*, pp. 348, 355–6.

The pope therefore appointed Father Mansoni, an Italian Jesuit, as his legate *a latere* to Ireland, instead of the Spanish Franciscan desired by O'Neill. Clement refused to proclaim a religious war in Ireland, to enfeoff Ireland under the Spanish crown, or to excommunicate the Catholics who refused to support Hugh. When Águila sailed Mansoni was not even with him.[1] Small wonder then that the nuncios, Buffalo in Paris and Frangipani (whose distrust of O'Neill's motives has already been noted), were horrified at Águila's indiscretion. Frangipani forecast serious danger to Catholic interests in England and Flanders, while Buffalo recorded the displeasure of the king of France, who was 'grieved that his holiness has placed more confidence in the king of Spain than in him'.[2]

But there is another side to the picture. Although it is true that the pope did not make support for Águila a matter of conscience for Irish Catholics, Clement did not deny all support to O'Neill and to the invasion. He did recognize O'Neill as captain-general of the Catholic army in Ireland and did grant the chief's supporters the crusade indulgence. Clement had gone as far as he could to meet O'Neill's and Philip's wishes in the appointment of a nuncio. The pope could not and would not decide against the loyalist Catholics, but he had appointed a legate to Ireland. The appointments of Oviedo to Dublin and Lombard to Armagh (he was provided on 9 July 1601) must also be considered in the general reckoning. The truth is simply that Clement VIII, in line with his general policy did not wish to pronounce between conflicting Catholic interests; he sought to reconcile them as far as possible and to maintain his influence over both.

Águila's proclamation, the Bulls of indulgence, and even a threat of excommunication against recalcitrants from the bishop of Cork, all broadcast wholesale in Munster, failed to arouse the province.[3] One reason was that the priests of Munster were preaching, as Oviedo found to his distress, that the Irish should take up arms against the Spaniards and their Irish allies. Oviedo had some discussions with these priests on the matter, but they refused to give up their position until

1. F. M. Jones, 'The Spaniards and Kinsale 1601', in *Galway Arch. Soc. Jn.*, xxi (1944), 20; 'Pope Clement VIII (1592–1605) and Hugh O'Neill', in *I.C.H.S. Bull.*, no. 73 (1953); *Mountjoy*, p. 122.

2. VA, Borghese, ser. III, vol. 65C, p. 11 (*Archiv. Hib.*, iii (1914), 246 and xxiv (1961), 63): Buffalo to cardinal secretary of state, 25 Jan. 1602.

3. *Cal. Carew MSS, 1589–1600*, p. 523: Bull of indulgence, 18 Apr. 1600; *Archiv. Hib.*, iii. 244; *Pac. Hib.*, i. 295–8; AGS, Guerra Antigua 3145 (*Epistolario de Zubiaur*, p. 94): Zubiaur to Philip, 29 (? 22) Dec.

the Holy See deprived loyal Catholics of the sacraments and excommunicated them.[1]

Don Juan was therefore left to his own resources, which were poor. Unable to erect proper fortifications to guard sea or land approaches, he garrisoned Rincorran and Castle Park so as to impede as far as possible the approach of English shipping to Kinsale, and entrenched his outposts at Camphill, so as to command to some extent land access to the town. The lord deputy's tactical answer to both measures was swift and effective. Without as yet tools for entrenching, so that his men had to lie in the open, he encamped on 27 October at the foot of Knockrobin Hill, near the present village of Brownsmills and at the head of Oyster Haven. This useful inlet, as well as protecting Mountjoy's left flank and rear, gave him a waterway up which supplies landed by ship could be ferried to the very camp at high tide and thus bypass Kinsale. At the same time he could to some extent prevent the approach by land of victuals to the Spaniards. Don Juan saw the danger, but in ten days' skirmishing failed to drive the English back from Knockrobin.

He saw little to comfort him as at the end of a month in Ireland he took stock of his position. He was badly outnumbered, with only 2,500 effectives now, who were pitifully inexperienced and shivered in their thin clothes in the raw late-autumn Irish weather. Don Juan wished that money and reinforcements would come; if only they did, many of the Irish would join him. Yet knowing this he continued to spare his own money. When he came back to Spain he still had 59,000 ducats with him. His niggardly policy is as hard to justify as it is to explain.

For food Águila's men had only a little rotten biscuit and water. Every day more of the poor wretches were falling ill because of so little to eat and so much to do; the remainder were harried by the enemy's continuous attacks and were called to guard duty so much that the arms never left their hands. No wonder some deserted. Don Juan had another worry, for supplies of fuse for the arquebuses were running critically short.[2]

His main problem however was that he was separated from O'Neill by the length of Ireland. Six or seven weeks previously O'Neill had been warning Ensign Sandoval that on no account must the Spanish army land south of Limerick. With Florence MacCarthy and James

1. AGS, Guerra Antigua 591: memorandum by Oviedo, with letter to Ibarra, 31 Mar.
2. AGS, Guerra Antigua 3144: Águila to Philip, Kinsale, 31 Oct.

Fitzthomas both in the Tower, and with Carew's grip on Munster firm, the invaders would have no support in the south. O'Neill had indirect news of the Spanish landing within a week or so of Águila's coming. By the time, a few days later, that Danvers began to draw off the northern garrisons Hugh was well aware that Águila's army was too small to take the field in Munster. He waited for Don Juan to take to sea again and come north to Sligo or Killybegs. He did not know of Águila's objections to removing from Kinsale. Don Juan at the end of October received Hugh's message asking him to come to the north. This merely confirmed him in his belief that he should have gone to Donegal Bay in the first place. He became even more embittered against Archbishop Oviedo and Cerdá, and took out his spite on them by accusing them of following their own ends in insisting that the armada should go to the south.[1]

The rancour between Oviedo and Águila was unfortunate, as was the lack of confidence between Don Juan and his captains. These officers were aggrieved that Águila did not appoint colonels or majors from among them, or appoint a council of captains to advise him. The archbishop became a centre of disaffection, around whom formed a group of disgruntled captains, who blamed Águila for not fortifying himself properly to landward or seaward, for not purchasing mounts from the Irish, and for not buying the services of the Irish themselves.

Away in the north, with the garrisons from Armagh, Blackwater, and the Newry out of the way, O'Neill was engaged from 10 October in daily incursions into Monaghan, the Fews, Brefni, and the Pale. He had two objects in this: he wanted, firstly, to win back the border lords who had submitted, Ever MacCooley MacMahon of the Farney, Tirlagh MacHenry of the Fews, MacMahon, Maginess, Sir Oghy O'Hanlon, and O'Reilly; and secondly, he wished by devastating Louth to force Mountjoy to draw back to the defence of the Pale.

To O'Neill's consternation, however, it gradually began to appear that Águila was tamely allowing himself to be besieged in Kinsale and that Mountjoy was not going to give up the siege. The privy council in Dublin called in vain upon the lord deputy to come to the aid of the harassed Pale gentry like Sir Edward Moore and the bishop of Meath; the lord deputy was not to be turned aside from the real task of the moment, which was to eject the Spaniards from Ireland.

1. AGS, Guerra Antigua 3144: O'Neill to Águila, 12 Oct.; copy sent with letter, Águila to Philip, 31 Oct.

O'Neill was thus in a dilemma. O'Donnell was summoning his Tyrconnell and Connacht levies to rendezvous at Ballymote. But O'Neill's newly won border allies pointed out with considerable trepidation that their departure would leave their countries open to attack from the garrisons, should they be augmented, or even from an army of Scots if, as the council were suggesting, such an army should descend on Ulster. King James VI, at news of the Spanish landing, had offered Elizabeth aid of troops. That 'wisest fool' in Christendom, as the shrewd Henry IV called him, showed his astuteness in this crisis by allowing Sir Robert Cecil to guide him in taking proper steps to secure the succession.[1]

O'Neill's hesitation at this moment indicated, as Seán O'Faolain's excellent analysis has shown, neither incompetence nor cowardice. The Spaniards, in spite of their pleas for his assistance, could surely stand siege in a walled town indefinitely against much superior numbers. The hardship of winter weather would tell more on besiegers than besieged. The expected reinforcements from Spain, especially if they landed at a better-chosen port, must restore the advantage to the Irish and Spaniards. It was entirely foreign to O'Neill's character and completely out of keeping with the tactics which had brought him such considerable successes to leave the security of his fastnesses and march his main force at this season of the year, lightly equipped as they must be if they were not to be bogged down, through an unfriendly country the long distance to Cork. Both Chichester and Fenton doubted that O'Neill would, as Fenton said, 'go up now when he will have to strive against rivers and waters and will have to meet the extremities of winters'.[2]

And even arrived in the south, what could O'Neill achieve? He must be confronted with Mountjoy's and Carew's armies on open ground where he would no longer have the advantages of cover and mobility. And must his men lie in the open, with only beef to eat after what slender supplies of meal and butter they could carry were exhausted, to engage in the wholly unaccustomed work of besieging an enemy?

Yet within three weeks of his first hearing of the Spaniards' arrival, he had decided to go to Kinsale. Given the weighty considerations urging him to remain at home, the proven ability of the Spaniards to stand siege and his real doubts about the wisdom of his going to the

1. *Cal. S.P. Ire.*, 1601–3, pp. 81–165; *Cal. Carew MSS*, 1601–3, p. 154.
2. Cf. *Cal. S.P. Ire.*, 1601–3, pp.152–3, 163, 187; O'Faolain, *The great O'Neill*, pp. 247–51.

south, it was not such a long delay. But although O'Donnell, who for his matchless speed of movement went first to draw off pursuit, left Ballymote on 2 November and O'Neill followed a week later, it was a fortnight after that again before anyone on the government side realized Hugh's real intention of going to Munster. Though closely watched, still 'closer in his resolutions' was O'Neill.

Red Hugh reached Ikerrin in north-west Tipperary and halted. And O'Neill held off, waiting to see what the besiegers would do in view of O'Donnell's proximity.

IX · SIEGE

Ciúnas, ná cómhnaidhe, tathamh, nó tionnabradh . . .
A.F.M., ad. an. 1601[1]

THE ACCOUNT of the early skirmishes at Kinsale is all from the English side and some of it strains credulity.[2] But of the English gain when on the night of 4 November Sir John Barkley drove the Spaniards out of their trenches, enabling Mountjoy to advance camp there can be no doubt. It was a further victory when Captain Taaffe forced the Spaniards to slaughter some cattle and sheep that Águila had grazing on the Castle Park peninsula. Taaffe's objective had been the capture of the animals, and in this he had failed. But the English could be satisfied: Águila had lost much valuable food. More than that, he had given occasion to the critics in his own camp to declare that he could have killed and salted these animals beforehand.

From his new encampment on Spital Hill Mountjoy began a damaging bombardment, to prevent which Águila had not strong enough forces to mount an effective sortie though time and again he tried. And out of range of Águila's musket-fire Mountjoy's cavalry still ran the country at night, burning the corn.[3]

Ships arrived at Oyster Haven from Dublin, bearing provisions and artillery for Mountjoy. Soon the lord deputy had a battery firing on Rincorran; this battery was aided by fire from the pinnace *Moon* stationed in Kinsale Harbour. The *Moon* also prevented Águila from sending reinforcements to Rincorran. On 11 November Mountjoy forced the surrender of the fort. The garrison yielded on condition that they be allowed back to Spain. The lord deputy agreed to this

1. 'Nor quiet, rest, sleep, nor repose . . .'
2. The journals kept by Stafford (Carew's secretary) and Moryson (Mountjoy's secretary) are evidently the common source for the accounts of the siege in Moryson's *Itinerary*, *Pac. Hib.*, *Cal. Carew MSS.*, and *Cal. S. P. Ire.*
3. AGS, Guerra Antigua 3144; Águila to Philip, 31 Oct.; *Pac. Hib.*, i. 298–302; cf. *Ir. Sword*, ii (1954), 72.

condition because he wished to avoid delay and to impress the
Spaniards with his clemency; he in turn was impressed with the stubborn resistance set up by the commander of the castle, Ensign Paez de
Clavijo. The town, Charles saw, would be stoutly defended, and he
wished for more artillery to bombard it.[1]

But at least there was heartening news of reinforcement of troops
coming: Elizabeth promised him a further 5,000 levies, 4,000 for Kinsale and 1,000 for Loch Foyle. The Spanish council of state were ig-
norant of the scale of the help being prepared in England to help
Mountjoy and were deaf to the appeals of López de Soto to send
strong reinforcements of men and material to Águila and to pile up
supplies at Corunna. Preferring to listen to Castel-Rodrigo when he
said that Águila's fleet had sailed properly supplied, the council were
making wholly inadequate plans for reinforcing Don Juan. These
plans, completed on 25 November, were that nine ships under
Zubiaur's command would sail from Corunna, carrying 900 men and
2,000 quintals of biscuit and flour, wheat, and rye; while Cerdá, now
recovered from his bout of malaria, would sail from Lisbon with four
ships carrying 150 or 250 men, together with 4,500 quintals of biscuit.
These two small squadrons would carry as well powder, fuse, and
lead, with pick-axes, shovels, and other materials and implements
required for fortifications and artillery-trains. Galleons could not go
to Ireland in the wintry weather, and so Águila would not get his
cavalry; but an effort must be made to send a company of lances, or
heavy cavalrymen. Águila was encouraged to try to raise two companies of arquebusiers in Ireland.[2] Ibarra, the secretary of the council
of war, learned on 12 December that England was planning to send
six to seven thousand men, with artillery, aboard thirty ships, to
destroy Águila before Spanish reinforcements arrived, and had sent
four large galleons, well-armed, to patrol the Straits of Dover. This
report contained enough of the truth to show the scale of the English

---

1. *Pac. Hib.*, ii. 1–17; Ó Clérigh, *Beatha Aodha Ruaidh*, i. 312–14.
2. AGS, Guerra Antigua 3144: dispatches from council of war to Castel-Rodrigo and
others, Vallid., 31 Oct. (*Epistolario de Zubiaur*, pp. 73, 74–5), and La Serreta, 16 Nov.; Guerra
Antigua 3144, 3145 (*Epistolario*, cit., pp. 75–6): dispatches to Águila and others. 25 Nov.
(*Rep. Nov.*, i. 363–4), and to Águila and to Zubiaur, Vallid., 27 Nov.; Guerra Antigua 3144;
Castel-Rodrigo to Philip, Lisbon, 6, 7, 8, and 16 Nov., and to Ibarra 5 Nov.; López to Philip,
15 Nov., twice, 21, and 28 Nov.; Brochero to Castel-Rodrigo, Cascaes, 5 Nov.; Zubiaur to
Caracena, 23 and 24 Oct. (*Epistolario*, cit., pp. 71–2); Guerra Antigua 3145: Brochero to
Philip, 6, 7, and 17 Nov., and to junta, 2 Dec.; Guerra Antigua 587: Caracena to Philip, 6, 14
and 22 Nov.; López to Philip, Corunna, 6 Nov.; Moryson, *Itinerary*, iii. 20–3.

counter-attack, but alarming as it was it did not galvanize Spain into action.[1]

The fact that Águila's bases were a thousand miles away in Lisbon and Corunna was now all too apparent, while Mountjoy's were much more convenient in Chester, Bristol, and Barnstaple. How much further away again from Kinsale was Madrid, the capital whose selection by Philip II in preference to Lisbon—or Brussels—has been so justly censured as a grand political and strategic error. And as if Madrid was not remote enough the business of state was now regularly conducted from Philip's hunting-lodges in the mountains around Madrid, Valladolid, or Zamora![2]

When news was brought to the besiegers of Kinsale that O'Donnell was approaching Munster and that O'Neill as it was wrongly thought was but a few days behind, Mountjoy on 16 November fortified his camp on its northern side; and next day Carew led off two regiments on what he suspected would be a vain attempt to intercept the elusive Red Hugh. Sir George marched to the Suir, where he lay on the east side of the river in the vicinity of Golden across the path that he thought O'Donnell must take.[3]

O'Donnell burned his boats by coming south, for his departure meant the fall at last of Ballyshannon (the key to the western passage from Munster to Ulster) to the English. It was a desperate throw, which only victory in the south could justify. The Erne was Red Hugh's Rubicon. He eluded Carew by a famous night march of thirty-two Irish (forty English) miles over an opportunely frozen defile of the Slieve Felim range on 2 December. He then rested for a week in Connelloe in Limerick while he sought to constrain the lords of that part of Munster to his side.

The lord president was back at Kinsale on 6 December. He had been joined on the way by the young Lord Clanricarde, with a regiment of foot, and by Donough O'Brien, the third earl of Thomond, who had brought 1,000 foot and 100 horse from Bristol. All these troops were now quartered in a new camp under Thomond on the slopes of Ballincubby Hill, on the west side of the town. This camp was set up with the double objective of preventing a junction between the Spaniards and O'Donnell and of investing the town more closely.

1. Guerra Antigua 587: F. de la Riva Herrera to Ibarra, 17 Nov.
2. *Cal. S.P. Ire.*, *1601–3*, pp. x–xi; Braudel, *Méditerranée et monde méditerranéen*, pp. 773–4, 883; Gounon-Loubens, *Administration de Castille au xvie siècle*, pp. 43–4.
3. *Pac. Hib.*, ii. 9–10.

Carew and Clanricarde remained with Mountjoy in the great camp on Camphill.[1]

From Connelloe O'Donnell came on to Bandon. He now had the allegiance of Thomas Fitzmaurice, Lord Kerry, of Clanmaurice, who had come with him from the north; John O'Conor Kerry, of Carriga-foyle; and many other leading men of west Munster; but notably not Donal MacCarthy Reagh, who commanded the territory extending from Bantry Bay to the Bandon river, or Cormac MacDermot Mac-Carthy, lord of Muskerry, who ruled over the watershed of the River Lee from Ballincollig westwards. Fear of MacCarthy More domina-tion kept Cormac still loyal, and he came to the aid of Mountjoy during the siege of Kinsale. With Florence now in the Tower, his rival Donal, base son of the dead Clancarty, was again recognized by O'Neill as MacCarthy More. Florence's brother, Dermot Maol, also joined the northern leaders.[2]

O'Donnell arrived at Bandon on or before 12 December, and estab-lished communications with Águila.[3] O'Neill, in turn, leaving his son in charge behind him, left his territory a week after All Saints. He chose the eastern exit, over the northern Blackwater and Boyne. The companies from his own territory of Tyrone attending him were estimated in number at 4,060 horse and foot, while Red Hugh's re-ported muster was 4,000 foot and 3,000 horse. These estimates must be received with a certain reserve. If Sir Geoffrey Fenton may be taken as an authority, the effective rising-out at O'Neill's command, even making allowance for 'cowkeepers and horseboys', would fall far below this estimate. O'Neill was accompanied by many other Ulster lords and their contingents and by John, son of Thomas Roe, earl of Desmond. In Leinster he was joined by Captain Richard Tyrrell, of Brenockton, Co. Westmeath, who had pledged himself to O'Neill in return for a colonelcy, when the Spaniards came, and the lordship of Westmeath. Tyrrell led between four and six hundred men. 'Many other Leinster rebels' also joined Hugh.[4]

1. Ó Clérigh, *Beatha Aodha Ruaidh*, i. 298–310, 318–20; *Cal. Carew MSS., 1601–3*, p. 187; Docwra, 'Narration', in *Celtic Soc. Misc.* (Dublin, 1849), pp. 255, 257, 258–9; *Pac. Hib.*, ii. 10–17; O'Sullivan Beare, *Hist. cath. Ibern. comp.*, pp. 226–7.

2. *Epistolario de Zubiaur*, p. 80; Ó Clérigh, *Beatha Aodha Ruaidh*, i. 332–3; Butler, *Gleanings from Irish history*, pp. 13, 106–37; S. T. MacCarthy, *The MacCarthys of Munster*, pp. 64–85; *D.N.B.*, entry Florence MacCarthy.

3. AGS, Guerra Antigua 3144: Águila to O'Donnell, Kinsale, 14 Dec. 1601.

4. *Cal. S.P. Ire., 1601–3*, pp. 187, 141; AGS, Guerra Antigua 592: agreement between O'Neill and Tyrrell, Dungannon, 2 Jan. 1598; *A.F.M., ad. an.* 1601; *I.H.S.*, ii. 264–5.

Hugh, purposely going slowly, spent some time pillaging and burning in the Pale and came on by way of west Meath and east Munster to join his ally at Bandon River. The traditional site of O'Donnell's encampment is somewhere to the west of Inishannon, along the north bank of the river in the barony of Kinalmeaky. O'Neill had joined O'Donnell here it seems by the evening of 15 December. The two chiefs had done well in transporting their armies three hundred miles in the depth of winter. They had crossed fifty swollen rivers by flinging wooden bridges across them, as well as many others that took them up to the belt or breast. The gamble taken, it seemed, had been worthwhile. Not only had O'Neill and O'Donnell overcome all obstacles on their march southwards but, they were reassured, a relieving force of 3,000 Spaniards had landed at Castlehaven and would provide all the stiffening that O'Neill could demand for his unproven levies. Their delight was to be short-lived.[1]

Now began a war of nerves, but it was not Mountjoy's which broke. Forced by the grim opposition of the Spaniards and the news of the arrival of the Irish to change tactics, the lord deputy gave up his present attempt to carry Kinsale by assault following an intensive bombardment, and instead set about drawing his investment of the town tighter.

With Rincorran taken, Mountjoy had next sought possession of Castle Park in preparation for the assault on Kinsale. Águila, learning of Carew's departure, had sent out a sortie, but the Spaniards met with such hot resistance that they retreated and remained unaware of the reduced state of Mountjoy's numbers. With only 2,500 effectives, many raw men among them, to command, Don Juan was afraid to leave the town defenceless and risk a general engagement.

At this critical point large reinforcements came to the English. Thomond's men had to be sent to Cork to rest, but an equal number of men came into Waterford and a day later (24 November) Sir Richard Levison, admiral of the queen's Irish fleet, came into Kinsale with the warships and the remaining 2,000 reinforcements.

Subjected to gunfire from the camp and from the warships now in control of the harbour, Castle Park capitulated after four days.[2]

Archbishop Oviedo was furious, and blamed Aguila for the loss of

---

1. Moryson, *Itinerary*, iii. 27–8; *Epistolario de Zubiaur*, p. 126: report of Zubiaur's adventures, Luarca, 14 Jan. 1602.
2. Moryson, *Itinerary*, iii. 38–44.

Rincorran and Castle Park. He dwelt bitterly on the fact that Águila had rejected the advice proffered by Brochero and himself to fortify Castle Park. Oviedo believed that Águila had shown great irresolution. He had not only not fortified the castles but he had thrown up no other defences and had shamefully let the forts be taken. Womanlike he had let himself be invested by land and sea and had repelled the Irish who wished to come in, so that not only did they not come in but some of his own soldiers deserted.[1] A story was later carried back to Spain by Deacon Pedro de Colmenares (no friend of the archbishop's, it is true), to the effect that Oviedo had had certain of the captains to visit him in his house. Colmenares could name most of these officers: Muñeza, Cuellar, Cardenosa, Jaén, Navarra, Jara Millo, Don Pedro Morejón, Henríquez de Tejada, and perhaps one or two others. At their secret meetings Colmenares alleged that criticisms of Águila's courage were freely exchanged, Oviedo going so far as to say that Águila wished to hand them over to the enemy and enter the service of the queen.[2] Whatever the truth of this tale, it is certain that relations between the archbishop and Águila were marked by mutual distrust.

Mountjoy now had men, artillery, and victuals in plenty. With the reinforcements he had under him a list total of 11,500 foot and 857 horse. This included Carew's detachment of 2,100 foot and 320 horse, which had not yet returned. A flying squadron of 1,050 infantry relieved of watch duty was detached from the total to answer alarms.[3]

Strangely enough Mountjoy and his council chose not now to attempt to breach the town but to continue the siege, bombarding at the same time the Spaniards' houses. Thus, they thought, hunger and exposure would decimate the Spaniards. Exposure was killing Mountjoy's own men at the rate of forty a day (6,000 of the besiegers— Stafford, López, and Oviedo all agree—were actually to be lost during the siege), but remembering how desperately men of Águila's command had fought in a similar situation in Brittany, when three hundred of them under siege at the Pointe Espagnole had sold their lives

1. AGS, Guerra Antigua 3145: memorandum by Oviedo, 27 Jan. 1602.
2. AGS, Guerra Antigua 3144: declaration by Colmenares.
3. Moryson, *Itinerary*, iii. 40–3: *Cal. S.P. Ire.,1601–3*, p. 200, errs by defect in stating that the list in Munster stood on 4 December at 9,650 foot and 675 horse. Reinforcements had landed at Loch Foyle on 24 November, bringing the number of effectives there and in Donegal up to 1,685 men (in list 3,000), apart from officers; a force of 295 foot and 13 horse landed at Carrickfergus on 25 Nov. (*Cal.*, cit., pp. 174, 176, 178–80 189).

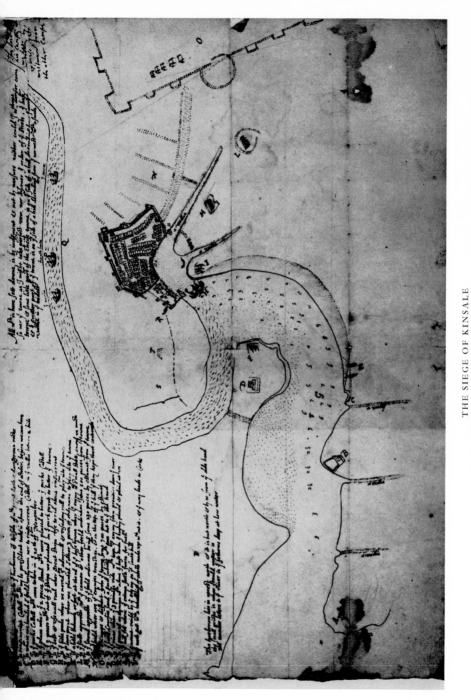

THE SIEGE OF KINSALE

A contemporary copy of a map made probably by Paul Ivye, at the end of November 1601

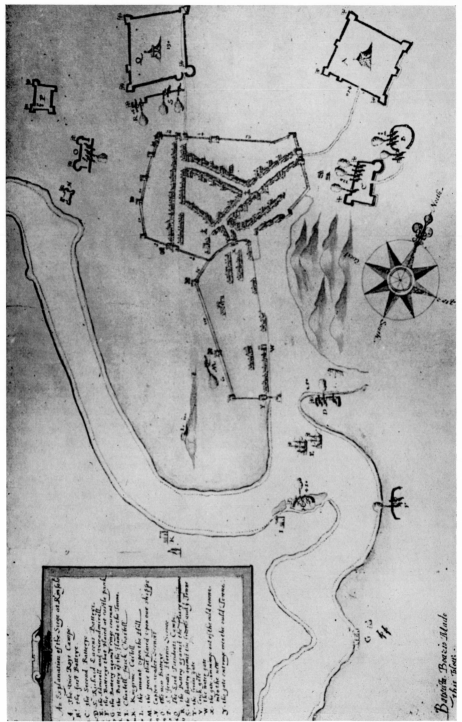

THE SIEGE OF KINSALE

A contemporary plan by Baptista Boazio

dearly, Mountjoy did not relish a hand-to-hand encounter at a breach with the Spaniards.[1]

The lord deputy now set up two batteries, one near the camp on the north-east side and the other on the Castle Park peninsula. The former had a cannon, demi-cannon, and four other pieces; three culverins from the latter played on the old town on the north-east side. On the night of 3 December the English in the face of frost, enemy fire, and Spanish sortie worked furiously to dig parallels nearer the town on the north-east side on commanding ground and two nights later raised another battery at this point. Levison also bombarded the old town from the admiral and vice-admiral, which were now moored in a little pool between Castle Park and the town and near the blockhouse or fort defending the old or 'base' town.

The combined effect of Carew's return with Thomond and Clanricarde and of the news that O'Donnell maintained his advance made Mountjoy change his plans and try what a breach might do. The three culverins for their precision firing were removed to the east battery, and the bombardment was continued until 8 December, when Águila contemptuously rejected a call to surrender. But two days later the east gate and a great part of the wall next to it were broken down.

Mountjoy, still cautious, launched a 'bravado' by 2,000 infantrymen led by Sir John Barkley on this breach, not as an actual assault but rather to discover whether an assault were possible. At least, so said the English, in spite of their numbers. After an hour's sharp fighting, with the Spaniards lodged in a trench outside the breach, the English found their answer and withdrew. The Spanish troops, inspired by the careless contempt for the English displayed by one of their captains, Morejón, the similarity of whose name to his own intrigued Fynes Moryson, had again proved themselves stout defenders.[2]

That night and the next day, 12 December, the English established a fort closer to the town than Thomond's camp, on the west side. When night had fallen on 12 December the lord deputy manned this fort with seven companies, leaving some divisions of Thomond's men on guard without. Mountjoy designed these troops to second the artillery that was to be planted nearby; the trenches besides the gun-emplacements on the east side he also manned with seven companies. Águila's outposts on Compass Hill south of the town noted all this;

1. Cf. Falls, *Mountjoy*, pp. 33–4.
2. Moryson, *Itinerary*, iii. 38–40, 44–50.

the Spaniard saw the lines of investment being drawn tighter around him both to west and east, cutting off the entry of even the limited supplies he was getting and eliminating any hope of communication with the approaching Irish; he foresaw that his men and defences were to be subjected to an even heavier bombardment and that the general assault must now be imminent. He determined to do what he could to remove or at least lessen the danger.

The day was very wet and the rain increased as darkness fell. An hour after dark, at eight o'clock, Águila's men, in number about 1,500, made their sortie. They attacked the trenches on the east and spiked two guns before they were made to give ground, then fell on the new fort on the west side and took it, broke down the platform prepared for the ordnance that was to be placed there on the next day, and filled the trenches before they were made to retire by Clanricarde. The captains leading the sortie insisted that they would not have retired but for Águila's repeated orders to them to do so.[1] Accounts of the sally are conflicting, the English claiming that they had killed two hundred Spaniards with little loss and that only one cannon was spiked and that but temporarily, while Zubiaur heard that the Spaniards had slaughtered 1,500 English. Águila made a more conservative claim, four hundred enemy dead for the loss of only a few Spaniards, among whom were Captains Bernardino de Soto, son of Pedro López, and Charles MacCarthy ('Zarate'). But Mountjoy, who admitted that it was a 'strong salley', now gave up the idea of an assault, towards the preparation of which he had been working and fighting night and day for over a week, and more particularly for the last two days. The approach of the northern Irish and the arrival of the Spaniards at Castlehaven with, it was said at first, 3,000 men, increased, whatever he might say, Charles's anxiety to take the town. But Águila's demonstration of mettle under attack and the strength of his counter-attack deterred him. Equally they impressed the hitherto cautious lords of the south-west, who now flocked to Castelhaven in numbers.[2]

The folly of sending out expeditions that were so small that they resulted, as Don Martín de Padilla, Adelantado of Castile, complained, 'more in annoying than in punishing the enemy', was now being

1. AGS, Guerra Antigua 3145: paper from Philip for the information of the council, 1 Apr. 1603.
2. Pac. Hib., ii, 32–42; Epistolario de Zubiaur, pp. 80, 127; A.F.M., ad. an. 1601.

borne in upon the Spanish administration. In December Spain decided to reinforce Águila with three cavalry companies, to be sent before the end of the month, and with a Portuguese *tercio* of 2,000 infantry, to be sent later. These orders increased the viceroy of Portugal's testiness. In view of the levy in Portugal of a regiment already ordered for the Indies, where, he asked, could the men be found? And where in Portugal was there suitable embarkation for cavalry?[1]

Given this situation, it was some sort of achievement when Spain was able to send General Pedro de Zubiaur back to Ireland. Zubiaur, it is true, suffered ill-luck on this voyage too; setting out from Corunna on 6 December with ten ships, he landed at Castlehaven five days afterwards with only six, the others being driven back to Spain. Kinsale had been Zubiaur's goal, as he was bringing supplies to Águila, but luckily for him a contrary wind had kept him out of it, so that he escaped destruction or capture by the English warships there.

Zubiaur had with him food, arms, and artillery for Águila's use and a total of 621 infantry under the command of the veteran Captain Alonso de Ocampo. López de Soto described the men as being of very poor quality, even the Gallegos who had served two years in the Azores; some of them, he said, were jail-birds, including one whole company of Portuguese, and they were naked as well. That they could also fight and die like true Spanish infantry these men so unflatteringly described would soon show.[2]

Don Pedro, who would have earned marks from Machiavelli for *virtù*, displayed an intrepidity and a gift for improvisation which belied his sixty years. He set about making the best of his misfortune in not gaining Kinsale, if misfortune it was. Ocampo wanted to go home again, but López sided with Zubiaur. The latter gave out an exaggerated account of his numbers, a stratagem which boomeranged when O'Neill refused to believe that the Spanish reinforcements were less than 3,000 men. But for the moment the stratagem achieved its purpose in inducing the lords of Castlehaven, Baltimore, and Bantry to put him in possession of their harbours. Sir Finnin O'Driscoll More

1. AGS, Estado 840, f. 166 (*Cal. S.P. Spain, 1587–1603*, pp. 690–1; cf. pp. 688–9): Padilla to Philip, Pto. de S. María, 10 Dec.; Estado 840, ff. 273–4 (*Cal.*, cit. pp. 681–2): council of state to Philip, 11 Dec.; Guerra Antigua 3144: Castel-Rodrigo to Philip, twice, 11 Dec.

2. AGS, Guerra Antigua 3144: Ocampo to Philip, Castlehaven, 21 Dec.; López to Philip, Baltimore, 6 Mar. 1602; Moryson, *Itinerary*, iii. 60. Cf. Guerra Antigua 3143 (*Epistolario de Zubiaur*, p. 122), and summary in Estado 840, f. 157 (*Cal. S.P. Spain, 1587–1603*, pp. 683–4): inventory by Juan de la Concha, Corunna, 7 Dec.; *Cal. S.P. Venice, 1592–1603*, p. 492: Cavalli to doge and senate, Paris, 5 Feb. 1602.

held Baltimore, with its castles of Donnelong on Inisherkin island and Donneshed on the mainland. Sir Finnin, as Carew's secretary said, 'never in the course of his whole life had been tainted with the least spot of disloyalty', but Zubiaur was able to take advantage of discord between him and his eldest son Cornelius to secure control of the castles. Sir Finnin's cousins of Glen Barrahane Castle on Castlehaven Bay gave it over to the Spaniards, who also received Daniel O'Sullivan's castle of Dunboy or Berehaven on Bantry Bay. In each case Zubiaur made a formal treaty with the Irish lords, taking the strongholds in the name of the king of Spain.

Don Pedro decided to hold Baltimore harbour as a place for future Spanish landings. Glen Barrahane was only a tower with a little ravelin before it and was indefensible landwards, but Zubiaur, who did not need Águila's warning that Admiral Levison would come to attack him, placed six artillery-pieces on the barbican at the foot of the tower, to cover the entrance to the harbour. He strengthened the tower, repaired the ravelin, and made an esplanade, setting up the six pieces. In Donnelong he placed Captain Andrés de Arbe with eighty soldiers and nine guns.

Dermot O'Sullivan, Daniel's brother, brought young Captain Saavedra to Dunboy on 20 December and there Saavedra installed himself with sixty soldiers and eight pieces. Zubiaur's coming brought a general rally of the lords of south-west Munster to Castlehaven, where they took oaths of homage to Philip before López de Soto. Zubiaur armed 1,000 men with 350 arquebuses and 650 pikes; the other 2,000 soldiers commanded by these gentlemen must await the arrival of further arms from Spain. Daniel O'Sullivan Beare set about assembling his force of a thousand men, while Cornelius O'Driscoll, who claimed that his father now adhered to the Spanish cause, raised a company of horse.[1]

Of the other leaders who now declared for Philip, López was most impressed by the MacCarthys who, he declared, were greater than the Mendozas in Spain.[2] The brothers Donough Moyle and Finnin,

1. AGS, Guerra Antigua 3144: Ocampo to Philip, Castlehaven 21 and 25 Dec.; Guerra Antigua 3145: López to Philip, 20 and 25 Dec.; Estado 188: López to Franqueza, 1 Feb. 1602; to Philip, 12 Feb.; to Zubiaur, 13 Feb.; and to Franqueza and to Caracena, 15 Feb.; Guerra Antigua 3145 (*Epistolario de Zubiaur*, p. 68): Zubiaur to Philip, 19 Dec.; O'Sullivan Beare, *Hist. Cath. Ibern. comp.*, pp. 225, 226; *Pac. Hib.*, ii. 41.

2. Nicholas Browne wrote in 1596: 'At this tyme these Irishe septs [i.e. the MacCarthys] are of greater force and strength than they weare these 300 years.' Quoted, Butler, *Gleanings from Irish history*, p. 10 n. 11.

the sons of Sir Owen ('of the parliament') MacCarthy Reagh with almost all the Clan Carty of Carbery swore allegiance to Philip. So did Donal, O'Neill's MacCarthy More, and the imprisoned Florence MacCarthy's brother, Dermot Maol. Among others doing homage were Daniel O'Donovan, Felim MacCormac, and his brother, and among the Geraldines John O'Connor Kerry, the Knight of Kerry, and Thomas Fitzmaurice, the baron of Lixnaw. The captains Richard Tyrrell and his elder brother, Walter, and William Burke came to join Daniel O'Sullivan; between them they commanded 600 men.

By his display of verve Zubiaur had secured the adherence of the gentlemen of west Munster, who had already noted Águila's success in defending Kinsale and spoke very enthusiastically of his repulse of the English assault of 11 December, in which they believed 1,500 English had been killed. As O'Neill approached their borders they realized too from past experience the wisdom of joining him. It was no doubt in order to stiffen their resolution that O'Neill sent the Tyrrells to join them. Yet, as noted by López, not a single hamlet in Cork or elsewhere, apart from this south-western corner, declared for Philip.[1]

Mountjoy in turn now strengthened his defences in preparation for a siege, and at the same time set about investing the town completely so as to starve it out. All the horse were drawn into the lord deputy's camp, and Thomond's camp, strengthened by the posting to it of Wilmot's regiment, was moved nearer Kinsale, towards the south gate. The ordnance from both eastern and western platforms was hauled into Mountjoy's camp. Two small forts were erected between Thomond's camp and the water to the south so as completely to debar access to the town. Parallels linked up these forts with Thomond's camp, and then with Mountjoy's. The town was now completely surrounded. The English fleet held the harbour, and the investment was continuous from Scilly Point north-eastward to Camphill and thence westward to the Bandon river.[2]

It took Mountjoy a fortnight of very stormy weather thus to prepare, but now he was invested in turn. O'Neill had a total force of

1. AGS, Guerra Antigua 3145 (*Epistolario de Zubiaur*, p. 85): Zubiaur to Philip, 20 Dec.; Guerra Antigua 587 (*Pac. Hib.*, ii. 47–9): Daniel O'Sullivan to Philip, Camp near Kinsale, 29 Dec. (original Irish, with Spanish trans.); Guerra Antigua 3144: López to Philip, Corunna, 20 Mar. 1602; *Relación*, in *Epistolario de Zubiaur*, p. 124.
2. Cf. O'Sullivan, *Kinsale*, pp. 60–1.

perhaps 6,000 infantry and 800 horse under his command.[1] This was besides the Munster Irish who now came in. The Irish besiegers prevented supplies of grass and water, corn and grain, straw and fuel from entering the English camps. Many men and horses began to die of hunger and cold within the camps and the English did not even dare emerge to bury their dead. O'Neill and O'Donnell hoped that plague and illness would soon do their work for them by destroying the enemy army.

Sickness and desertion played havoc with the English; the severe winter weather was causing sentinels to drop dead at their posts, killing men in dozens each night and causing hundreds to run off. Deprived of forage the horses were starving. On the other hand, Águila's position had materially improved. O'Neill was able to send him in cows and other supplies between the two camps, as the English knew, and, unknown to the English, by way of the Castle Park peninsula in spite of the battery there. The meat came as a welcome addition to the hard tack which had been the sole food of the Spaniards up to this. The spirit shown by Águila kept Mountjoy, as he himself admitted, 'at bay'. He could not carry his approaches any nearer or put his battery into effect. Levison's fleet also now had to perform the double duty of guarding the entrance to Kinsale and the storeships there (for the English had no magazines ashore) and of patrolling the coast so as to prevent another Spanish landing at Baltimore or Bantry. Mountjoy urged London to send him reinforcements of four thousand men as well as reinforcements for Levison.[2]

In spite of his threatening situation, however, Mountjoy continued the work of extending his approaches and erected new platforms from which to bombard the west wall, where he now hoped to make a new breach. Águila opposed these preparations with shot from the castles in the walls and with sallies; in a sortie on 27 December the Spaniards broke down one of the platforms.[3]

Both Águila and the Irish leaders urged Zubiaur to send men to join O'Neill. But Don Pedro himself was attacked by Levison, on

1. There are discrepancies in the accounts, but cf. AGS, Guerra Antigua 3144: dispatch by Cerdá with letter, Castel-Rodrigo to Philip, 24 Jan. 1602, and Estado 620: news from London, 26 Dec. 1601, old style. Estado 620: another estimate from England, of 5,000 men altogether, 5 Jan. 1601, old style, is too low.

2. AGS, Estado 620: news from London, 5 Jan. 1601, old style; Guerra Antigua 3145: Philip to council, 1 Apr. 1603; Ó Clérigh, *Beatha Aodh Ruaidh*, i. 326; Moryson, *Itinerary*, iii. 62–80.

3. *Pac. Hib.*, ii. 44–5.

Sunday, 16 December, when the admiral with four galleons and three lesser craft sailed into Castlehaven harbour. The arrival of Daniel O'Sullivan with five hundred foot and some horse prevented Levison from landing his men, and Zubiaur because of contrary winds could not come to close quarters; so the battle was fought with artillery, Zubiaur replying from the land to Levison's fire.

The English squadron anchored closer than Zubiaur, had he had better soldiers, would have allowed, and on the Sunday the English fire drove one Spanish ship, the *María Francesa*, aground. But that night Zubiaur landed more artillery from the grounded ship. He personally directed the fire on Monday and Tuesday, and Levison felt it so hotly that he would gladly have retired but that the wind was against him. At last on Wednesday he managed to have himself towed or warped out but had to leave behind his mooring anchors and cables. The honours lay about even; one Spanish ship had been sunk and seemingly two of the English squadron never made it back to Kinsale. But Levison had failed to dislodge the doughty Zubiaur.[1]

That general in his enthusiasm for his schemes to conquer Ireland, Scotland, and England sent urgent pleas home for the necessary aid in men, ships, equipment, and food; but these appeals could not shake the lethargic administration. O'Neill's intention was, once Don Pedro's contingent of Spaniards had joined him, to force a break-through to Águila. But Zubiaur and López, heartened by beating off Levison's attack, meant to hold the three ports for Spain and dismayed O'Neill and disgusted Águila by retaining the bulk of their Spaniards in the castles that they had received. Zubiaur sent to join the Irish in the week before Christmas only two hundred Spaniards under four captains and Daniel O'Sullivan Beare with 700 Irish, followed by O'Sullivan's brother with 500 more Irish. In Donneshed Zubiaur placed nine cannon and planned to install himself there; Christmas over, he loaded boats with ten pieces and sent them off to Dunboy. He kept six pieces, which he meant for Águila, on two ships at Castel-haven.[2]

1. AGS, Guerra Antigua 3145: López to Águila, Castlehaven, 15 (?) Dec. 1601; Guerra Antigua 3144: Sandoval's account; Ocampo to Philip, 25 Dec.; Águila to Philip, Cork, 19 Jan. 1602; Guerra Antigua 3145: Zubiaur to Philip, 19 Dec.; López to Philip, 26 Dec. Cf. *Epistolario de Zubiaur*, pp. 87, 125-7, 136-7; *Pac. Hib.*, ii. 43-4; O'Sullivan Beare, *Hist. cath. Ibern. comp.*, pp. 225-6.

2. *Epistolario de Zubiaur*, pp. 68-70, 84-91: Zubiaur to Philip, 19, 20, 22, 24, 25, 27, and 30 Dec.; AGS, Guerra Antigua 3145 (*Epistolario de Zubiaur*, p. 127): Zubiaur to Caracena, 22 Dec., and summary of adventures; Guerra Antigua 3144: memoranda of 22 Dec.; Tyrell to

The two hundred Spaniards, even if they carried six standards and eight drums, were hardly enough to transform the Irish army from an amateur into a professional force which could be relied on to stand the test of battle. O'Neill was bitterly disappointed. His men, good guerrillas although they were, were wanting in experience of pitched encounters where troops needed discipline to press home a charge against an unyielding foe or to receive in turn a charge and not panic. Even Hugh's greatest victory at the Yellow Ford was won against an army on the move and with its divisions strung out too much.

The Irish had even less experience of fighting against an entrenched enemy. It would be difficult for O'Neill, as Carew said, 'to force trenches or fight upon hard ground'.[1] Águila wanted the Irish to come up and occupy some point to which he would sally out to join them. The two Hughs accompanied by one of the Spanish captains, Francisco Ruiz de Velasco, went on Sunday 23 December to within a musket shot of Kinsale to make reconnaissance. They had a plain view of the enemy's position, with Kinsale at his back, the sea with his warships on his left flank, and on his right the Bandon, on which Thomond's right wing rested.

The Irishmen pointed out to Ruiz that Mountjoy's men were lodged in trenches a lance-length in height, and emphasized that they were better armed and had artillery. This Ruiz saw; the trenches in fact were so high that they could only be climbed with ladders. Moreover, O'Neill's army numbered only 6,000 infantry and 800 horse effectives, in opposition to Mountjoy's 10,000 foot and 1,000 horse. Ruiz, however, urged him to go up; the Spaniards, he maintained, cared nothing for trenches and would open a way through for the Irish. O'Neill therefore agreed to stake all on an attempt to break through to Águila, but he delayed fulfilling his promise. For another ten days he remained where he was, some five miles from Kinsale, and did not move camp.

There was reason in this; the winds continued westerly and no help therefore could be expected to reach Mountjoy, whose food supplies were failing. In the continued stormy weather the English army, in

1. *Cal. S.P. Ire.*, 1601–3, p. 241: Carew to Cecil, 26 Dec., old style.

López, Berehaven, 3 Mar. 1602; Águila's answers to Diego de Ibarra, 29 Mar. 1602; Águila to O'Neill and O'Donnell, 28 Dec. (Moryson, *Itinerary*, iii. 23), and to López; Guerra Antigua 591: López to Philip, 27 Mar 1602; Guerra Antigua 3145: López to Philip, 20 and 25 Dec. 1601.

mud to its knees, was losing great numbers through exposure: on
Carew's testimony the 6,000 English levies were practically all con-
sumed by death, sickness, and desertion.[1] O'Neill's own men were
dying of hunger; he was without biscuit and had only meat to offer
them. But he could endure that, as the sufferings of the enemy were
greater. Unfortunately Águila's troops too were in great extremities,
and Don Juan kept urging the Irish to move up to the attack. He sent
Ensign Bustamante with guides to conduct O'Neill to a rendezvous,
promising that he himself would sally out there as soon as he heard
the Irish giving battle.[2] Prompted by this encouragement, the Irish
leader decided to accede to Águila's pleas and on Friday, 28 December,
gave orders to move up.[3]

The consequences of the delay in communication between Águila
and his government now became apparent. At the time when O'Neill
was deciding in response to Don Juan's pleas to move up to Kinsale
the council of state were considering the Irish situation on the basis of
reports that were a month or in some cases two months old. The
council then had to rely on information from Águila that was no more
recent than the end of October, on news of Zubiaur's return to Corunna,
and on rather more recent news, which was quite correct, that Elizabeth had dispatched thirteen warships with 4,000 men to Ireland.
Águila's situation as it had been at the end of October, besieged by
Mountjoy, short of provisions, and in particular need of cavalry, was
known to the council; but of Zubiaur's return to Ireland and of the
arrival in Munster of the northern Irish they did not know.

Unaware of the speed with which Águila was urging matters to a
decision in Ireland, the council believed that the war there would be
prolonged until the summer. Then, they agreed with the Adelantado
of Castile, Elizabeth would be in a position to assemble a force in
Ireland large enough to gain the country.

To counter that threat Spain must take effective measures in the
spring. This was all the more necessary as there was reason to suspect
that Elizabeth would persuade France to break off relations with

1. *Cal. S.P. Ire.*, 1601–3, pp. 216, 234.
2. AGS, Guerra Antigua 3144: Ruiz de Velasco to López, 22 Dec.; O'Neill and O'Donnell
to López, Irish camp, 22 Dec.; Ruiz to same, 23 (? 24) Dec.; account by Sandoval; Guerra
Antigua 3145: López to Philip, 25 Dec.; (*Rep. Nov.*, i (1955), 115–6): memorandum by Oviedo,
27 Jan. 1602.
3. AGS, Guerra Antigua 3145 (*Epistolario de Zubiaur*, p. 94): Zubiaur to Philip, Castlehaven, 29 Dec. 1601; *Pac. Hib.*, ii. 49.

Spain and unite with England in expelling the Spaniards from Ireland
and in raising the siege of Ostend. Victory in Ireland for Spain would
impress France and Scotland and put a curb on English support of the
Dutch. Thus Philip II's Atlantic ambitions were revived by his son.

The council therefore approved once more its decision of a fortnight
or so earlier to dispatch three companies of light cavalry as soon as
might be and to levy and send off as quickly as possible afterwards a
Portuguese *tercio* of two thousand men. The cavalry, under the command of Captain Duarte Núñez, would comprise two hundred and
twenty effective lances, made up of the companies of the count of
Puñoenrostro, Don Pedro Pacheco, and Don Sancho Bravo, and would
embark at Lisbon. The council added to these earlier orders a fresh
measure authorizing the raising of regiments of Walloons and Germans in Flanders, under the direction of the archduke. These troops
should land at Kinsale or at whatever port in Catholic hands O'Neill
and O'Donnell might designate.

Meanwhile Águila would be supplied with meat, wine, and vege-
tables. Orders were sent to him and the northern Irish to join forces,
but not to risk battle if the enemy were too great.

Juan de Contreras Gamarra, late commissary-general of light
cavalry in Flanders, wanted an army of 14,000 infantry and 1,200
horse sent from Dunkirk to Ireland. This was to forestall any move by
France; but the idea was rejected by the council because of lack of
money and because such an army, to be raised in Flanders, Italy, and
Spain, would not be ready by the spring.

The council in fact were apprehensive of more immediate threats
to Spanish safety from both France and England than from Ireland,
however events might develop there. Elizabeth was preparing, so
intelligence reported, a fleet of twenty armed galleons to attack Ceuta
and Tangier, in retaliation for the Spanish invasion of Ireland. Thoroughly alarmed by this report, the council as well anticipated attacks
on the Indies by English warships and on the Spanish kingdoms by
France. A series of orders reflecting the gravity of the concern felt by
the administration was issued at the beginning of January to put
Ceuta, Tangier, and the Caribbean ports on the alert and the militia
and cavalry of the Spanish kingdoms at the ready to meet attack.
Greatest emphasis was placed on the preparation of the galleys of
Spain and Italy. New galleys were ordered, and all were to be armed
and manned with the Spanish infantry in Italy. These manned war-

ships were to be used not, as the Adelantado wanted, to reinforce
Águila, but to deal with any possible attack from France. In effect, the
larger considerations of Spanish policy meant the denial to Águila of
vital support.[1]

1. AGS, Estado 840, ff. 158, 160-7 (*Cal. S.P. Spain, 1587-1603*, pp. 695-9): reports, letters,
and *consulta* of 22 Dec.; Estado 840, f. 157 (*Cal.*, cit., pp. 692-5): Castel-Rodrigo to Philip,
11 Dec. (not Sept.); Guerra Antigua 3144: Philip to Castel-Rodrigo, Vallid., 20 Dec.; council
of war to F. de la Riva Herrera, 20 Dec. and to Castel-Rodrigo, Vallid., 31 Dec.; Guerra
Antigua 591: council of war to Águila, Castel-Rodrigo, Caracena, Duarte Núñez, etc.,
Vallid., 4 Jan. 1602.

X · ROUT

When, without stratagem,
But in plain shock, and even play of battle,
Was ever known so great and little loss,
On one part, and on the other?
Shakespeare, *Henry V*, Act iv, Sc. viii

THE STORM CLEARED on Sunday, 30 December, and Mountjoy renewed his bombardment of Kinsale, breaking down 'a good part' of
the wall of the town. He made another trench beneath the remaining
platform and completed it that night in spite of thunder and light-
ning.[1]

Reports now began to come in from his scouts of the approach of
the Irish army. Eventually, towards the night of Monday 31 December, the Irish appeared in view on a hill, Coolcarron, between the
English and Cork, and bivouacked that night on the other side, at
Belgooly.

O'Neill had brought up his whole army; O'Donnell, Tyrrell, and
the Munstermen who had come in were there, while Ocampo had
joined them,[2] leaving Captain Barragán behind in Castelhaven as his
deputy, and had taken over command of the two hundred Spanish
infantry. Mountjoy was reduced to 7,000 men and was planning to
send his horses, which lacked fodder, to Cork. When he saw the Irish
force come into view the lord deputy exclaimed, report goes, 'This
kingdom is lost to-day.'[3] Although the English were not deceived by
the show of Spanish standards, O'Neill had now cut Mountjoy's land
supply-line from Cork, though the sea-route remained open; and to
the west, over the Carrigaline river, the whole country was declared
for O'Neill and Spain.

1. *Pac. Hib.*, ii. 45–7, 49; AGS, Guerra Antigua 3145 (*Epistolario de Zubiaur*, pp. 94–6):
Zubiaur to Philip, 29 and 30 Dec.
2. AGS, Estado 188: Águila to López, Kinsale, 17 Jan.
3. AGS, Guerra Antigua 3144: report by Cerdá, with letter, Castel-Rodrigo to Philip,
Lisbon, 24 Jan.

That night and the following night the Spaniards launched strong attacks on the new English trenches beneath the platform on the west, while during the intervening day they harassed the English with shot from the walls and turrets. O'Neill's horse and foot too kept appearing that same day on the crest of Coolcarron. Thus Spaniards and Irish sought to keep Mountjoy's army always at the ready and so expose it to fatigue and the rigours of the cold, stormy weather. The English artillery returned the Spanish fire, but now with no intention of making a breach. O'Neill was too close at their backs, and Mountjoy, put on his guard by intercepted letters from Águila to O'Neill, awaited the Irish attack.[1]

A line of hills runs from Coolcarron on the north-east to Horsehill on the south-west. A rather wide valley lies between this line and the other line of ridges on which the English emplacements were situated, the ground sloping upwards from the valley in gentle, undulating fashion towards the English position. At the south-western end of the valley, near where White Castle creek flows towards the Bandon river, was fought the battle, of inglorious memory for Irish arms, of Kinsale.[2]

Early in the morning of 3 January the Irish moved up 6,000 foot and 800 horse from Belgooly.[3] Tyrrell commanded in the van his men of Meath and Leinster and the Munster Irish, perhaps a thousand men, together with Ocampo's two hundred Spaniards. The main Irish force, the battle, was led by O'Neill himself and was formed mainly of his own Cenél Eoghain levies, while O'Donnell commanded the rear of Tyrconnell and Connacht men.

The Irish planned, as Águila had proposed to them, that at about daybreak Tyrrell's vanguard should have placed itself at an agreed position between Thomond's camp and the west fort. Here, Águila had insisted, they would be quite safe. When Tyrrell had made known his presence there by musket-fire or some other predetermined signal Águila should sally out to join him. Then together they should at once, or perhaps after they had all retired to the town and re-formed, attack Thomond's camp. At the same time the combined Irish battle and rear should fall on Mountjoy's, the main camp.

Such is the substance of what we know from the available evidence.[4]

1. *Cal. S.P. Ire., 1601–3*, p. 239; Moryson, *Itinerary*, iii. 74–5.
2. Cf. O'Sullivan, *Kinsale*, pp. 67–8.
3. AGS, Guerra Antigua 3144: Ruiz de Velasco's estimate of 22 Dec. to López agrees nearly with that of Ocampo. Cf. Moryson, *Itinerary*, iii. 81.
4. Cf. Appendix I.

That the plan was betrayed to Carew for a bottle of whiskey by one of the inner council of Irish lords, Brian MacHugh Oge MacMahon, is a story in which the classical daemons of Irish tragedy, drink and treachery, appear and one, moreover, which receives authority from Carew himself. Nevertheless, the story is a fabrication, composed later with perhaps the intention of damaging MacMahon's name.[1] The letters that he had intercepted and the information brought by his spies were enough to put Mountjoy on his guard. He saw that an attack that night was extremely probable, but its precise design was unknown to him.

An hour before midnight he was warned that the attack would come before dawn. He therefore ordered his troops to be in readiness and positioned Power's squadron volant, with Sir Richard Graeme's scouts in front, beyond the west of the main camp and close to the main guard of cavalry.[2]

An army of the time moving into battle went with the horse in the lead, then the foot in order: van, battle, and rear. But the rivalry between Cenél Eoghain and Cenél Conaill, that was as old as the eighth century and that with the formation of the alliance between the two Hughs seemed to have died, was in fact only dormant and now awoke again. O'Donnell had favoured attack, while the wiser O'Neill had not; the latter's preferred course had been to harry the lord deputy and subject his army to exposure and famine, while avoiding a direct encounter. But O'Donnell's view had prevailed in council, and now out of the argument grew bitter animosity. The younger chief would not yield precedence to the older, and so the divisions marched out shoulder to shoulder instead of in order. 'Their chiefs were at variance,' say the Four Masters, 'each of them contending that he himself should go foremost in the night's attack; so that the manner in which they set out from the borders of their camp was in three strong battalions, three extensive and numerous hosts, shoulder to shoulder, and elbow to elbow.' They soon lost contact with one another and went astray as well. It was close to daybreak when O'Neill came in view of the English scouts. By now Tyrrell should have been in position for Águila to come out of the town, but the plan had misfired. Tyrrell was not in position and Águila stayed in.

1. *Pac. Hib.*, ii. 53–5; AGS, Estado 620: news from London, 17 Jan., old style. Cf. P. Moore, in *Clogher Record*, i (1956), 100–105.

2. *Cal. S.P. Ire.*, 1601–3, pp. 241–2; *Pac. Hib.*, ii. 55–6.

Warning came from Graeme to Mountjoy of the enemy's presence, and the lord deputy ordered a general stand-to. While the men were arming he sent his marshal, Wingfield, ahead. The marshal returned with confirmation of Graeme's report. Mountjoy's immediate concern was to guard against attack from Águila, if the latter should become aware of O'Neill's presence, and he ordered the main part of his army, under Carew, to stay within the encampments, five regiments within his own camp and four within Thomond's, to defend them against possible assault by Don Juan. He sent all the horse with the support of two regiments of foot, those of Sir Henry Ffolliott and Sir Oliver St. John, forward to join Power. These three regiments made a force of some 1,500 to 2,000 men and the horse numbered four or five hundred. Expecting O'Neill to attack in front, Mountjoy chose a battleground before and in front of Thomond's camp and the west fort that was joined by trench to this camp. This ground, which was open, suited the English and besides offered them the advantage of flanking fire from Thomond's camp.[1]

O'Neill, however, did not advance. From the crest of the ridge in front of Millwater Ford, to which after recognizing the English scouts he had gone forward, he saw the three regiments and the cavalry confronting him. The Spaniards had not come out of the town, and with the English prepared for him he would have to fight on ground of their choosing, which he was not willing to do. He therefore went back and ordered his men to withdraw over the ford. The retreat led over boggy ground, and he hoped to prevent the English from crossing or at least to renew contact with his other divisions and face the enemy on firmer ground. The Spanish captains with him at once questioned his orders and he told them that he feared the enemy would sally out and cut off his passage. Ocampo advised him to draw up his men in battle order and cut his way through to Águila. It was impossible, the Spanish captains urged, that the enemy would leave his trenches having Águila in his rear. If indeed he did so, all the better, for Don Juan would at once leave Kinsale to attack him.[2] The Irish leader, however, refused to take the risk, and continued his withdrawal, while the English cavalry under Sir Henry Danvers followed him up to Millwater.

1. *Cal S.P. Ire.*, *1601–3*, p. 240: Carew to Cecil, 26 Dec., old style; AGS, Estado 620: news from London, 10 and 17 Jan., old style (300 horse and 1,600 foot on the queen's forces); *Pac. Hib.*, ii. 57; Hayes-McCoy, 'The tide of victory and defeat', in *Studies*, xxxviii. 314.

2. AGS, Guerra Antigua 3144: report brought by Sandoval on 9 Feb. from Castlehaven; *Pac. Hib.*, ii. 57.

The lord deputy, seeing his opportunity, at once decided to pursue. This, in view of the Irish numerical superiority, was taking a great risk; but the danger was outweighed in Mountjoy's mind by the fact that the further he followed the greater must be the chance that any engagement would take place out of earshot of Kinsale; and in the country beyond the ford, a 'fair champion' as he was told, he could hope to avoid an Irish ambush.

The Irish now, followed by Danvers's cavalry, which were accompanied by Wingfield, had crossed the boggy ground to firm land beyond, near White Castle. About half an hour had gone by since first contact had been made with the enemy and O'Neill's supporting divisions were coming up. He therefore began to embattle his army, with Tyrrell in the centre, his own battle forming the right, and O'Donnell coming up with the rear to form the left wing. Marshal Wingfield saw an opportunity in this confusion, and he and the dashing Clanricarde obtained permission from Mountjoy, who was following up with the regiments of foot, to attempt a charge.

Power's infantry had come up to support the cavalry; from this infantry the eager Wingfield took a hundred shot and sent them in, together with a hundred horse, to drive back the Irish loose shot whom O'Neill had appointed to hold the crossing. A sharp musketry engagement followed, which it seems was heard in Kinsale. Águila, however, suspected that this firing was an English ruse to draw him out and rejected Oviedo's appeal to lead out his men. Repulsed at first, the queen's shot after being reinforced drove back the Irish, and the marshal, Clanricarde, Graeme, and Captains Taaffe and Fleming, all hot for a fight, crossed over with their horse.

These English cavalry contingents, finding themselves confronted by O'Neill's own division, the Irish main battle, immediately charged. Finding the Irish horse stand firm, they did not press home the attack but wheeled off to their flank. The Irish cavalry raised a great shout, but their exultation was short-lived. By now two other cornets of horse, Mountjoy's own and Carew's, had come up, together with the remaining two regiments of infantry. Again the English horse charged and this time the Irish cavalry broke and fell in upon the ranks of their own foot. Wingfield now with his cavalry took the Irish foot in the rear while his infantry attacked them in front. The sharp fighting in 'plain ground' was too much for the Irish, who were further dismayed by the flight of their horse, composed as it was of their leading men,

The Siege of Dunboy, June 1602

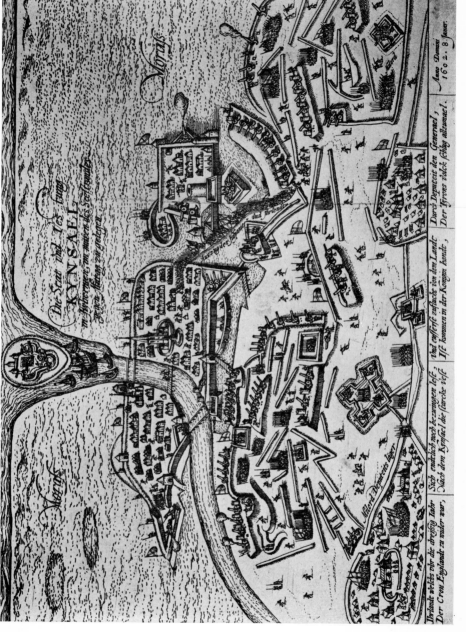

A PUBLISHED GERMAN PLAN OF THE SIEGE OF KINSALE, 1602

and they in turn broke and fled, a disordered mob. They were too demoralized to retreat on their van and rear, which were in any case too far removed from them. The English cavalry pursued them as they ran, butchering them mercilessly.

Only at this late stage did Tyrrell in the centre go to O'Neill's support; with the object of putting himself between the pursuers and the main body of English foot he began a flank movement. But St. John's regiment, sent in by Mountjoy, attacked Tyrrell's men as they were wheeling. Tyrrell's division after a short resistance gave ground and retreated to a hilltop behind. Ocampo's Spaniards, who were with the Irish van, were not so fleet of foot and stood up to the attack of Mountjoy's troop of horse, under Godolphin, until many of them were killed. Ocampo with forty-nine others surrendered, while about sixty escaped to Castlehaven. Tyrrell's foot, although they had removed in good order and although the main English attack was concentrated on the Irish battle, now followed the example of the battle in taking to their heels.

O'Donnell's men had given no support, probably because they were stationed too far off. Now in turn they became demoralized; they were not attacked, but the sight of the two other battalions being routed and the example of the fugitives who ignored Red Hugh's exhortations to turn and fight was too much for them and they too fled.[1]

Such was the rout—*derrota*, as the Spaniards truly called it—of the Irish chiefs at Kinsale. The English cavalry had won the day and the lord deputy in knighting young Clanricarde on the field (his second knighthood) acknowledged that his fiery zeal had played a major if not decisive part in the victory. The Irish horse, on the other hand, had offered only token resistance to the English cavalry and O'Neill had not been seconded by O'Donnell. The English claimed capture of 2,000 arms which O'Neill's men in their precipitate flight threw away, and O'Neill lost all his baggage and cows. The English pursuers, some companies of horse and infantry, followed, doing great execution for about a mile and a half, which was as far as the half-starved horses could go. Estimates of the Irish losses vary, O'Neill admitting to 500 dead, Águila putting the number at 1,000, and the English claiming to have accounted for fourteen captains and up to 1,200 men dead. The most acceptable figure seems to be somewhere between 500 and 1,000 Irish dead, chiefly from the battle; the English horse were too

1. *Pac. Hib.*, ii. 58–61; *Trevelyan Papers*, pt. ii, p. 105; *Cal. S.P. Ire., 1601–3*, p. 242.

exhausted to do more execution. The English losses were few: by their own account, which is probably true, fewer than a dozen men were killed, although many of the horses lay dead or wounded.[1]

Meantime what of Águila? His men were all ready in arms waiting to go out as soon as the Irish gave their signal. When the firing of musketry and arquebuses was heard they displayed, at least Archbishop Oviedo so reports, great eagerness to join the battle. But as they prepared to take the field Águila ordered them back, and when they showed impatience at being restrained he issued an edict declaring that the Irish were not engaging the enemy but that the firing was an English stratagem designed to draw them out. This edict duly quietened them.[2]

Then at the end of the battle the English fired a volley in token of victory. This at last Don Juan decided was the Irish signal to him that they had engaged the enemy, and he sallied out to help. But the real nature of the situation became apparent to him at once when he saw the Spanish colours being carried by the English and he beat a hasty retreat. The English drove some forty or sixty badly wounded soldiers into the town to let Águila know the disaster that had befallen his allies. The relentless Mountjoy spared no Irish prisoners and hanged many, some two or three hundred it was said, within sight of the town.[3]

The brief fight at Kinsale was of disastrous consequence for native Ireland. The Irish armies were now dispersed and their Spanish allies were again encircled in Kinsale, with the enemy in control of all land and sea approaches. While the Spaniards at Castlehaven deplored the opportunity that had been missed they were unaware that the Irish had been faced with a task really beyond their powers. A half-hour's resistance by the chiefs would, as López said, have ensured victory.

1. *Pac. Hib.*, ii. 60–1; AGS, Estado 620: news from London, 17 Jan., old style; Guerra Antigua 3144: Castel-Rodrigo to Philip, 24 Jan., with report by Cerdá (estimate of 300–1,500 dead); account by Sandoval (500 Irish and 90 Spanish casualties, between dead and captured); Guerra Antigua 3145: Águila to Philip, Cork, 26 Feb.
2. AGS, Guerra Antigua 3145 (*Rep. Nov.*, i (1955), 115–116; *Epistolario de Zubiaur*, p. 138): memorandum by Oviedo for king and royal council, 27 Jan.
3. *Pac. Hib.*, ii. 62; Moryson, *Itinerary*, iii. 81–2; AGS, Estado 620: news from London, 10 and 17 Jan., old style. López's story that Don Juan sallied out and killed four hundred of the enemy and gained seven standards and some English pieces receives no other confirmation, and in spite of its circumstantial detail cannot be accepted. Oviedo, if it were true, could hardly accuse Águila of cravenness or worse. Oleaga, who carried this story with him from Castlehaven on 6 January, left before there was time properly to sift the truth of the rumours about what had happened at Kinsale.

For the combined Irish and Spanish forces had had a considerable local superiority in numbers to the enemy and (as Ensign Sandoval pointed out) ought, considering Don Juan's successes in his sallies, to have had easy victory. Yet, López decided, to maintain this was to forget that in the ability to conduct an engagement the Irish were altogether without experience. They were without military discipline and up to the time of the battle of Kinsale they had conducted the war by means of ambuscades in rough country, with each man acting individually. They had no idea of any other method of fighting or of battle-formation. So they had carried on the fight for over eight years, and their success had given such hope of conclusive victory that the relief of Águila was taken for granted when the chiefs arrived. This belief was supported, as Oleaga suggested, by two factors: the fear shown by the lord deputy who began to entrench himself very strongly on all sides, and the declaration of the Munster Irish for Águila. The chiefs came a great distance, overcame a thousand difficulties and upsets, gamely endured hunger and fear, only to fail at the important hurdle.[1]

O'Neill's forces, hotly pursued by St. Laurence, fled in disorder from the battlefield, the infantry throwing away their arms to lighten themselves. About 140 were drowned crossing the Blackwater; others going by way of Connelloe lost 200 of their number in the river Moy and at Owen Abbey; carriages were abandoned; and the wounded were cut down in north-west Munster. It would seem that O'Donnell retired his men, who had been only very lightly engaged, in better order and came to rest on a hill eight miles away. O'Neill, who had lost all but a fraction of his army, was with him. Next day, 4 January, O'Neill wrote to Águila that he could no longer help him since enemy devastation in his own territories called him home. He then set out for the north again. A report said that he led home only 600 troops out of the 6,000 that he had brought to the south. The latter figure was exaggerated by at least one-third, but the former may be near the truth.

Soon Richard Owen was seeking on O'Neill's behalf to negotiate a pardon for the chief. But O'Neill's feelers produced such unacceptable terms from Mountjoy, including agreement to the shiring of his country, that he gave up the negotiations.[2]

1. *Epistolario de Zubiaur*, p. 133.
2. *Pac. Hib.*, ii. 93, 95–100; AGS, Guerra Antigua 3144: Águila to Philip, Cork, 11 Feb.; Guerra Antigua 3145: same to same, 26 Feb.

O'Donnell gave command of the army of Tyrconnell to his brother Rory, who led it home by way of Connacht. Red Hugh himself went to join Zubiaur. O'Neill's intention was that O'Donnell would remain with Zubiaur and his Spaniards until further reinforcements should come from Spain. Only if such help came would the native cause now survive. Captain Richard Tyrrell escaped westwards and eventually installed himself with some of his men in the castle on Cape Clear; the rest of his companies were dispersed in west Cork, Kerry, and Limerick.[1]

On Saturday, 5 January, Hugh O'Donnell arrived at Castlehaven to tell the astonished Spaniards of the rout of the Irish army, seven or eight thousand men in number, by an enemy force of only 500 men. The young chief, as he confessed, was still at a loss to explain the defeat. Next day Zubiaur, accompanied by Sebastián de Oleaga, took ship for Spain. Red Hugh insisted on accompanying them, although Zubiaur and López insisted that King Philip would be displeased at his leaving when his men so badly needed encouragement. O'Donnell felt strongly that only by appealing in person to Philip could he secure the help that Ireland needed. He took with him his confessor, the Franciscan Father Florence Conry, and some captains.[2]

Prospects of adequate help from Spain were now, however, poor in the extreme. The duke of Medina Sidonia, the luckless sea commander of the 'invincible' armada, reported that shipping was in a poorer state in his command of Andalusia than it had been for forty years. The native Spaniards were rapidly giving up seamanship. The duke's well-known pessimistic outlook had not improved with the years, but in fact he could find no-one in Cádiz or San Lucar to take the risk of bringing food or clothes to Ireland.[3]

But from Lisbon the five ships that Moura had been preparing since October sailed out for Ireland on 1 January, with Captain Martín de Ballecilla in command. Ballecilla was captain of the *San Pablo*, flagship of the Atlantic fleet, and had already been in Kinsale with Brochero. They carried two infantry companies, together with a supply of

1. AGS, Guerra Antigua 3144: account by Sandoval; Estado 620: news from London, 10 Jan., old style; *Pac. Hib.*, ii. 69–70, 116; Guerra Antigua 3144: O'Neill to Philip, from his camp, 16 Jan., with covering letter, Zúñiga to Philip, Ostend, 14 May; Águila to Philip, 17 Jan.

2. *Pac. Hib.*, ii. 64; AGS, Guerra Antigua 3145: Zubiaur to Philip, Luarca, 15 Jan.; (*Epistolario de Zubiaur*, p. 99): López to Philip, two letters, Castlehaven, 6 Jan.; Estado 1745: memorandum by 'Mac Dermud', 2 Apr. 1603.

3. AGS, Guerra Antigua 592: Medina Sidonia to Philip, San Lucar, 5 Jan.

biscuit. Three were driven back to Spain by contrary winds and Ballecilla arrived off Kinsale with the other two on 14 January only to
learn that Águila had surrendered; whereupon he returned to Lisbon.[1]

The same day that Ballecilla arrived off Kinsale Zubiaur was making
port at Luarca in Asturias. From Luarca Oleaga brought the news of
the rout at Kinsale to the king on Saturday, 20 January. Zubiaur
repeated Águila's complaint that Don Juan had been placed in an
impossible position in an indefensible hollow in unfriendly country.
Castlehaven, Baltimore, and Berehaven were, Don Pedro maintained,
more easily defensible than Kinsale, and Philip should strengthen
their land and sea defences. Philip ought also, he proposed, send an
armada to Limerick, to take Limerick or Galway and effect a junction
with O'Neill and O'Donnell at Galway.[2]

Águila had already surrendered to Mountjoy on 12 January. His
men were now down to 1,800 effectives, and of the 800 or so others
who were ill some ten to twelve were dying every day. He was without two great advantages which commonly enabled a besieged place
in that age to hold out indefinitely against attack: control of the water
approaches, enabling reinforcements or supplies to land, and strong
fortifications. It was knowledge of these weaknesses, coupled with his
belief that the Irish had failed him, first in refusing to give battle and
then in withdrawing, that prompted him to seek honourable terms
when he was not without certain advantages over Mountjoy. For the
wind still favoured ships from Spain and Águila had six weeks' food—
though only bread and wine—against the lord deputy's six days'
provisions. Mountjoy's fleet was almost without food. In spite of the
three breaches he had made in the walls and in spite of the three forts
at the western side designed to prevent Águila from sallying out, he
had no hope of taking the town by storm, his men were so weakened
and discontented.[3] Águila had made three vigorous sorties from his
western gate since the battle, two on 4 January, which by their own

1. AGS, Guerra Antigua 591: memorandum by Ballecilla, Corunna, 18/20 Jan. 1602;
Guerra Antigua 592: statements by A. Carreno y Baldés, 13 Jan.; Guerra Antigua 3144:
Castel-Rodrigo to Philip 9 Jan. and (with report by Cerdá) 24 Jan.; Águila to Ibarra, Kinsale,
18 Jan.; Guerra Antigua 3145: Riva Herrera to Philip, Santander, 13 Jan.; statement by
Aguilar, 13 Jan.; Iguizcuiza to Caracena, Vivero, 14 Jan.; Mexía to same, Ribadeo, 14 Jan.;
Guerra Antigua 592: Caracena to Philip, 27 Jan.

2. *Epistolario de Zubiaur*, p. 138; AGS, Guerra Antigua 3145: Zubiaur to Philip, Luarca,
15 Jan., and Corunna, 21 Jan.

3. *Pac. Hib.*, ii. 85; AGS, Guerra Antigua 3145: Oviedo to Philip and his royal council,
27 Jan.

admission 'crased' five English pieces, and one the following night, and had been repulsed only after difficult fighting. Mountjoy feared from conversations with his Spanish prisoners that a relieving force must soon come from Spain and overcome his own fleet. His main strength lay in his cavalry, but he had no oats for his horses. He was anxious to strengthen his grip on the country again and acutely aware of the fact that the Spaniards held three other strongholds in Munster. The lord deputy, therefore, was glad to accept Águila's terms.[1]

In the articles of composition signed by the rival commanders on 12 January Don Juan agreed to surrender Kinsale and the forts of Castlehaven, Baltimore, and Berehaven. He undertook that his men would not bear arms against Elizabeth, no matter what reinforcements might come from Spain, before their return home. In guarantee of good faith Águila agreed to remain behind until the second embarkment, should two echelons of shipping be necessary to take his troops back to Spain. Three captains, Pedro Morejón, Pedro Zuazo, and Diego González Sigler, would remain behind as pledges when all the others had gone.

Mountjoy agreed for his part to give Águila enough shipping and victuals (to be paid for by Don Juan) to transport his men, whether Spaniards or others, back to Spain with all he had, his arms, artillery, money, ensigns, and so on. Archbishop Oviedo is alone in saying that the ships were to be provided within a month, for none of the various versions of the articles of capitulation contains such a clause. Finally it was agreed that there would be a cessation of arms and a truce at sea until the Spaniards were shipped home.[2] Fr. Archer, S.J., understanding that Águila during the three days' discussions which it took to conclude the peace was consenting to hand him over to the English, escaped to join the Spaniards at Dunboy. There he found his fellow Jesuit, Brother Dominic Collins.[3]

On 19 January the lord deputy, taking with him Águila and many of his captains, removed to Cork. From there he intended to conduct a campaign to extinguish the revolt in Munster. Águila agreed to hand

1. AGS, Guerra Antigua 3144: report by Sandoval, Mar. 1602; Águila to Philip, Cork, 19 Jan.; Guerra Antigua 591: Águila to Ibarra, Kinsale, 18 Jan.; Estado 620: news from London, 2 Feb., old style; Epistolario de Zubiaur, p. 319: account of Zubiaur's experiences, 25 Jan.; Pac. Hib., ii. 71–7.

2. AGS, Guerra Antigua 3145: Oviedo to Lerma, Kinsale, 26 Jan.; Pac. Hib., ii. 78–81; Cal. S.P. Venice, 1592–1603, p. 496; VA, Borghese III, 65 C, f. 41 (Archiv. Hib., iii (1914), 247–8): articles of capitulation.

3. Archiv. Hib., xvii (1953), 11.

over the castles of Castlehaven, Donneshed (or Baltimore), Donnelong, and Dunboy, and so informed López de Soto.[1] But the return home of the Spaniards from Kinsale and the handing-over of the castles was held up for a month because of bad weather.[2]

In the period of waiting neither Don Juan nor Oviedo, who had remained in Kinsale, was idle. Each set down for Philip's benefit his own opinion of what had been amiss with the handling of affairs and of what was now to be done. Oviedo blamed Don Juan for not keeping open the entrance by sea to Kinsale or a passage for O'Neill and O'Donnell to enter by land. He blamed him also for turning away the Irish who had offered service and for not keeping his word to join O'Neill on the morning of the battle.[3]

While the archbishop wanted Spain to disregard the treaty, Don Juan had given up the fight. He credited Mountjoy with having 10,000 veterans of the wars in 'Flanders, France and Brittany' in Ireland now, with four to five thousand levies to come. In fact Mountjoy had just cashiered 2,000 men in list, and the new English levies existed yet only in intention. The truth was that Don Juan had turned against the Irish and now lent a ready ear to everything the astute lord deputy told him. Águila accused the Munster Irish, some of whom were now eagerly seeking pardon from Mountjoy, of double-dealing, as he did O'Neill for now negotiating through Richard Owen with the queen. Águila had fault to find with Brochero and the ecclesiastics who had supported him for insisting on the landing in the south. He had fault too to find with Pedro López: if López had sent the bulk of his men to O'Neill, said Don Juan, the Irish would not have failed to take the position he himself had assigned them. In regard to the castles, what López and Zubiaur should have done, Don Juan contended (and it is impossible not to agree with him), was make the Irish keep secret their declaration for Philip and let them remain in possession of all the castles but one.

Don Juan found three causes for the Spanish failure in Ireland. In the first place, he said, it was possible to take any port in Ireland; a Spanish expedition might yet take Cork. But to defend a port was the trouble. If Águila had been sent to join the chiefs in the beginning, he

1. *Pac. Hib.*, ii. 85–9, 110; AGS, Guerra Antigua 3144, Estado 188: Águila to López, Kinsale, 17 Jan.
2. AGS, Estado 188: López to Philip, Castlehaven, 22 Feb.
3. AGS, Guerra Antigua 3145 (*Rep. Nov.*, i. 115–16): Oviedo to Lerma, 26 Jan., and to king and council, 27 Jan.

would have had time to fortify some places, to which reinforcements could have been sent. Secondly, Zubiaur had not heeded Águila's order to send his men to join O'Neill. Thirdly, Brochero when he returned from Kinsale should have gone directly to Corunna (for report said he had had time) and come back with reinforcements to Águila.[1] He might have added, but did not, another cause: Spain's failure to heed Zubiaur's advice to keep Brochero's ships at Kinsale throughout the winter.

1. AGS, Guerra Antigua 3144: Águila to López, Kinsale, 17 Jan., with note added by López; Guerra Antigua 3145: Águila to Philip, 11 Feb.; same to same, 26 Feb.

XI · WITHDRAWAL

Thus was Tyrone made the tennis-ball of fortune, and abandoned by Spain's over-prized greatness.

Thomas Gainsford, *The true exemplary and remarkable history of the earl of Tyrone* (1619)

I cannot believe that Your Majesty is planning to send an army to Ireland, for that I hold would be the course of least value and most risk, with failure almost certain.

Don Diego Brochero to Philip, 4 June 1602[1]

THE SURRENDER OF ÁGUILA was cruel luck for the lords of the southwest, whose long record of loyalty prior to the coming of Zubiaur would not now preserve them from the vengeance of the lord deputy. Their decision to throw in their lot with the Spaniards and O'Neill had been a mistake, and now they must pay the penalty. But they could not believe that Spain would abandon them. Daniel O'Sullivan Beare and the O'Driscolls therefore renewed again their oaths of fidelity before López, and vowing to maintain themselves against the English until the end of May, even if they did lose their castles, retreated with two or three thousand men to a mountain pass five leagues from Castlehaven.

López de Soto, although he agreed with these lords that they had been unjustly treated, handed over the castles to the English when they came to take delivery. Captain Harvey took over Castlehaven Castle on 22 February and Donneshed and Donnelong Castles on 7 March. López was interested to see that the English soldiers were even more dispirited and miserable than the poor wretches of Gallegos who had come to Castlehaven; until now he had thought that no soldiers could be inferior in quality to these. On 12 March, Pedro López, Barragán, and the garrisons set sail for Spain, taking with them the seven cannon from Donnelong. On board the three ships were four

---

1. *No me persuado que V. Md. trate de meter gente en Yrlanda, porque lo tengo por cossa de menos substancia, mas arriscada, y casi cierto el ruin subcesso.*

hundred and thirty men from Castlehaven, Donneshed, Donnelong, and Dunboy in eight companies.[1] They were in Corunna by 20 March. Richard Tyrrell vacated the castle at Cape Clear, in which Harvey placed a guard; but Captain George Flower was prevented by the harsh weather from reaching Dunboy from Berehaven.[2]

The news of the defeat at Kinsale caused great alarm in Spain. The government feared that England would now be free to send more troops to Flanders and to dispatch her sea forces to help the Dutch and prey on the Spanish treasure fleets. Ironically, the English also expected a fresh attack by Spain on Ireland, to retrieve the situation there. But Lerma, for want of 'ships, soldiers, sailors, arms and munitions', could not consider strong reinforcements at short notice. With Velada, Idiáquez, and Fray Gaspar he devised a plan to send a small flotilla at once, either to remove Águila to a better position or to retire his army to Spain.[3] The council of war planned to follow up this force with an army of 6,000 men, 3,000 Portuguese and 3,000 levies, to be sent as soon as possible.

But that these plans would ever materialize was doubtful in the extreme. There was a dearth of men in Portugal. Moreover, the men returned from Ireland told such tales of the harsh and poverty-stricken conditions there as to frighten others from going. In any case transports could not be found to take an army to Ireland. Finally, even if such a large army as was planned could be raised, it was very unlikely, as the council well knew, that it could be withdrawn from Spain.[4]

While the council were in fact still debating what ought to be done for Ireland Ensign Retés landed at Corunna on 25 February with news of Águila's surrender. Retés was followed within a fortnight by the

1. *Pac. Hib.*, ii. 115–16; AGS, Guerra Antigua 3144: López to Philip, Baltimore, 3 and 6 Mar., and Corunna, 21 Mar.; memorandum by López 28 Feb.; Guerra Antigua 591: Barragán to (Philip), Vivero, 22 Mar.

2. AGS, Guerra Antigua 3144: López to Philip, Corunna, 20 and 21 Mar. and 2 Apr.; Águila to López, 17 Jan. with note by López; Guerra Antigua 591: López to Philip, 27 Mar.

3. AGS, Estado 840, f. 48 (*Cal. S.P. Spain, 1587–1603*, pp. 699–703): *consulta* by junta of four, Valdavida, 29 Jan.; f. 34 (*Cal.*, cit., p. 703): Philip to Águila, Mansilla, 30 Jan.; f. 35: Philip to López, 31 Jan.; Estado 188: López to Zubiaur, 13 Feb.; Guerra Antigua 591: Philip to Caracena and to Caracena (*recte* Zubiaur), Zamora, 13 Feb.

4. AGS, Guerra Antigua 589: *consultas* by council of war, 25 Jan. and 8 Feb.; Estado 840, f. 47 (*Cal. S.P. Spain, 1587–1603*, pp. 703–4): Franqueza to Lerma, 13 Feb. 1602; Estado 840, f. 159 (*Cal.*, cit., pp. 705–7): *consulta* by council of state, Vallid., 21 Feb.; Guerra Antigua 591: royal schedules to Águila and others, Zamora, 13 Feb.; Guerra Antigua 3144: Castel-Rodrigo to Philip, twice, Lisbon, 11 Dec. 1601; Guerra Antigua 590: memorandum by council of state, Vallid., 13 Feb. (?).

ships carrying Legoretta's *tercio*, 1,374 men in all, led by Ocampo. As a result the Spanish administration called off all preparations and decided merely to send 20,000 ducats to the lords of Berehaven, Castlehaven, and Baltimore.[1]

There in south-west Munster things had taken a dramatic turn. Daniel O'Sullivan, with Tyrrell and Father Archer, had been refused pardon by Mountjoy. When Castlehaven was handed over the news was brought straightaway to O'Sullivan, who was also told that his own castle of Dunboy was next to be delivered up. This was more than the proud chieftain would stand. Stationing a thousand men near Dunboy, he, Father Archer, and another priest sought and gained admission from Saavedra. That night Daniel admitted two hundred of his followers through the cellars, and the next day after a short struggle he wrested possession of Dunboy from Saavedra. This was on Saturday, 23 February.[2]

Associated with O'Sullivan in his coup were many of the lords of the south-west, and others rallied to his side. Supporting him now he had Denis O'Driscoll of Castlehaven, Daniel MacCarthy More, Sir Finnin O'Driscoll's son Cornelius, and O'Sullivan More's son Daniel. Sir Finnin himself had already returned to the queen's allegiance, but all his followers were with Cornelius. With O'Sullivan also were Captain Richard Tyrrell and his brother Walter; Richard came, although he realized full well the futility of O'Sullivan's action.[3] The Tyrrells and William Burke, brother of Redmond the baron of Leitrim, brought between them a thousand men. A number of the principal men of the Desmond connection, among them Thomas Fitzmaurice, baron of Lixnaw, the Knight of the Valley, and the Knight of Kerry, came too. In all these lords commanded 3,000 men, armed according to the Irish fashion, except for the 350 who had received arquebuses from Zubiaur and the 650 who had received pikes. Many others waited to see the outcome of O'Sullivan's stand before declaring themselves.

O'Sullivan made as brave a show as he could. He put 150 men to

1. AGS, Guerra Antigua 591: Caracena to Philip, Corunna 9 Mar. Cf. Estado 188: same to same, 27 May; Guerra Antigua 589: *consulta* by council of war, Vallid., 14 Mar.; Guerra Antigua 591: Philip to Caracena, Vallid., 19 Mar.; Guerra Antigua 3144: Ocampo to Philip, Corunna, 8 Mar.

2. AGS, Guerra Antigua 591: Águila to Philip, Corunna, 2 Apr. 1602; Guerra Antigua 3144: Saavedra to López, 23 Feb.

3. AGS, Guerra Antigua 3144: Tyrrell to López, Berehaven, 3 Mar.

guard Dunboy and stationed 1,200 outside to skirmish. He sent the Spaniards to be embarked with López at Baltimore, but retained their artillery and three of their gunners.[1] He held the castle for the king of Spain, he declared, and would render it up only at Philip's order. López, far from displeased at O'Sullivan's coup, urged the king to send help to Dunboy before April.[2]

Águila, on the other hand, was annoyed at Daniel's impulsiveness. He suspected that Carew and others were urging on Mountjoy that the seizure of Dunboy excused him from being any longer obliged by the treaty. Yet, although it has been alleged that he offered to win back Dunboy for Mountjoy, the fact is that Don Juan stoutly maintained that the treaty was in no way affected by O'Sullivan's action and that the lord deputy was still bound to return to him the artillery in Dunboy. The latter, to his credit, agreed with Don Juan and promised when he had regained the castle to embark the artillery for Spain, provided that O'Sullivan received no voluntary Spanish help to enable him to defend the castle.[3] Mountjoy foresaw little difficulty in taking an Irish castle when the time came.

O'Sullivan too was aware that Dunboy would be difficult to defend against English bombardment. He planned to make a last stand, should it come to that, on Dursey Island and placed Cornelius O'Driscoll with sixty men there. Cornelius with three pieces fortified the island to the best of his ability.[4]

As for Mountjoy, he was more concerned with O'Neill than with O'Sullivan. Taking Carew with him, he set out on 19 March for Dublin; from there the lord deputy planned to attack O'Neill in Ulster. Águila meanwhile, taking advantage of the first fair wind for Spain, set sail and landed at Corunna on the evening of Palm Sunday, 31 March. With him came Archbishop Oviedo. The army was now all returned: some 2,200 men from Kinsale and some 440 from the other ports. Don Juan had brought back besides his munitions a treasure of 59,000 ducats. Before he left he heard that Richard Owen had gone to England to treat of pardon for O'Neill. All in all his experience in

1. AGS, Guerra Antigua 3144: Saavedra to López, Berehaven, 23 Feb.; López to Philip, Baltimore, 6 and 21 Mar.; O'Sullivan to López, Berehaven, 23 Feb.; Guerra Antigua 591: López to Philip, Corunna, 27 Mar.; Guerra Antigua 590: O'Sullivan's replies to López, Ardea, 17 June; Pac. Hib., ii. 118–20; P. O'Sullivan Beare, Hist. cath. Ibern. comp., pp. 234–5.

2. AGS, Estado 188: O'Sullivan to Caracena, 25 Feb.

3. AGS, Guerra Antigua 3144: López to Philip, Baltimore, 6 Mar.; Águila to López, Cork, 28 Feb.; Guerra Antigua 3145: Mountjoy to Águila, Cork, 23 Feb., old style.

4. Pac. Hib., ii. 127–9.

Ireland had left him with a thorough distaste for all things Irish and an equal regard for the English and their greatness.[1]

There in effect the matter rested. López continued to plead for support for O'Sullivan in Dunboy and for a force to re-take Castlehaven and Baltimore.[2] But Spain would do no more, and the troops being levied were already being redirected to the Indies. The efforts still being made by the archduke to raise private Irish soldiers in Flanders to go to O'Neill's aid could then be of little avail.[3] O'Donnell was entertained with fair words by the governor at Corunna and this encouraged him in his pathetic belief that an armada would yet go to Ireland this summer and fortified him against abuse flung at him by the Spaniards returned from Ireland, who maintained that the Irish had betrayed them at Kinsale. Supported by the ever-faithful archbishop of Dublin, he kept up his pleas for an auxiliary force to keep the war going until summer had brought the armada.[4]

In Oviedo's mind there was no question but that Philip would come to Ireland's rescue. His concern was rather with the problem of winning over the loyalist Irish, on whom the queen's strength depended. His association with Ireland went back over a quarter of a century, during which period he had visited the country seven times in all. Heart and soul committed to O'Neill's cause, he was convinced that the great need was to get from Rome a clear order forbidding Catholics to oppose O'Neill and the Spaniards. In Munster he had found the priests urging their flocks to take arms against the Spaniards and their Irish allies; these clergy had thus effectively prejudiced the success of the expedition. Until such a definite order as he wanted came from Rome, Oviedo knew from discussions with these priests, they would continue to preach political obedience to the crown. Philip, he decided, must renew at Rome the attempt, defeated by the Anglo-Irish in the previous year, to secure from the pope a *motu proprio* forbidding

---

1. AGS, Guerra Antigua 591: Águila to Philip, 2 Apr.; López to same, 31 Mar.; Oviedo to Ibarra, 31 Mar. All Corunna; Guerra Antigua 590: attestation by López, 2 Apr.; Guerra Antigua 3144: Caracena to Philip, 23 May, with musters of 14 Apr. and 15 May; *Pac. Hib.*, ii. 136.

2. AGS, Guerra Antigua 3144: López to Philip, Castlehaven, 3 Mar; Guerra Antigua 591: same to same, Corunna, 27 Mar.

3. AGS, Guerra Antigua 592: Philip to Medina Sidonia and to the commissioners going to Lisbon, Vallid., 30 Mar.; Estado 620: Zúñiga to Philip, Nieuport, 23 Apr., and Ostend 14 May.

4. AGS, Estado 188: O'Donnell to Philip, Corunna, 21 and 22 Mar.; Caracena to same, 21 Mar.; *consulta* on these letters; Estado 840, f. 5: Philip to Caracena, 3 Apr.

all the Irish under severe censures to take arms against the Spaniards and O'Neill in their fight for the Catholic faith.

The archbishop, did he but know it, was wasting his breath. Lerma saw himself well out of the Irish war and had no desire to enter that arena again. After all, he had shown England that the queen was not immune from attack in her own sphere of interests, and as the main strength of the expedition had returned home, the demonstration had been worth the cost.

But even the indolent Lerma agreed that the Irish account could not be written off just like that. Charges and counter-charges were being hurled about. Wearisome though they were, some effort must be made to deal with them. While López de Soto refused to agree with Águila that Spain must withdraw from the Irish theatre, Oviedo accused the general of both ineptitude and cowardice. López, who was undoubtedly a meddler, again quarrelled with the archbishop over the conduct of the hospital and complained that Oviedo had been ready on the slightest occasion—*por quítame essa paja*—to impede him at Kinsale.[1] Don Juan, while he agreed with López in accusing Oviedo of interference, charged that López himself had refused to obey his orders. He himself, of course, had done his best at Kinsale. Had not Mountjoy come under censure from his own side for not holding Águila to ransom? The lord deputy, said Águila, would not have made peace had he not mistakenly believed that Águila had had food for three months; and had Don Juan not by continuous sallies deceived him into thinking that the Spaniards were greater in number than was the case? Mountjoy had not realized that so many of the Spaniards were ill.

Lerma, in face of these and other reproaches cast so freely by the leaders of the expedition against one another, had no option but to refer the matter to the council of war, which reported back on 6 April that a full investigation was necessary. Lerma, on the advice of the council, appointed Castel-Rodrigo at Lisbon, Caracena at Corunna, and Diego de Ibarra of the council of war at court to collect evidence.[2]

Philip, also on the council's advice, rejected López's proposal to send a force of 3,000 men before the end of April to Berehaven, but agreed

1. AGS, Guerra Antigua 591: López to Philip, Corunna, 23 Apr.
2. AGS, Guerra Antigua 3144: note on folder enclosing López's papers: Guerra Antigua 589: *consulta* by council of war, Vallid., 6 Apr.

to send a cargo of arms and munitions with money to O'Sullivan, to show that the king was not deserting him.[1]

The commission of inquiry soon had in its hands the testimony of Diego de Brochero. Don Diego gave his account of the disputes over the port of disembarkation and of his quarrel with Águila over the landing of the provisions and munitions at Kinsale and over his departure from Kinsale. With the substance of his account the reader is already familiar.[2] Brochero was now a member of the council of war, and the council on his advice ordered a halt to the levy of infantry in Portugal. Brochero also advised Lerma against sending another expedition to its doom in Ireland. Spain, he suggested, should rather keep the war alive by sending a subsidy of 100,000 ducats to the chiefs.[3]

Knowing that the king was in receipt of such advice, and denied permission to go to court to counter it, Hugh O'Donnell ate out his heart in Corunna. He begged first for a force of 2,000 men and then even a smaller force to take with him to Ireland, and finally at least to be himself allowed to go to fall fighting besides his friends in the north. But his appeals were in vain; Brochero had convinced the council of state, which now endorsed the council of war's decision against sending 3,000 men, as being too small a force, to Berehaven.[4]

The Adelantado stood alone in the council for attack, and strong attack on Elizabeth. He proposed to lead an army of 25,000 men against England, 14,000 of his own and the rest to be raised in Flanders by Fedérico Spínola. The stout-hearted old warrior had in his enthusiasm forgotten what his shrewder brother-councillors saw, that if such a force as Spínola offered to raise materialized in Flanders it would get no further, for the archduke would appropriate it. But not to discourage Don Martín altogether, the council suggested that he might be provided with a sum of 1,000,000 ducats in order to finance an expedition by Fedérico Spínola, not to England now, but to Ireland.[5]

---

1. AGS, Guerra Antigua 3144: dispatches from López, Baltimore, 6 Mar, and Corunna, 21 Mar.; Guerra Antigua 589: *consulta* by council of war, Vallid., 10 Apr.

2. Cf. pp. 109, 113–14, *supra*.

3. AGS, Guerra Antigua 587: *consulta* by council of war, Vallid., 20 Apr.; Estado 188: Brochero to Philip, Lisbon, 4 June.

4. AGS, Estado 840, ff. 76–7, 73 (*Cal. S.P. Spain, 1587–1603*, pp. 709–12): O'Donnell to Philip, Corunna, 15 and 25 Apr.; Estado 840, f. 68: Caracena to Philip, 25 Apr.; Estado 840, ff. 32–3 (*Cal.*, cit., p. 713. Hume's summary is inaccurate): *consulta* by council of state 1 May.

5. AGS, Estado 840, f. 36 (*Cal.*, cit., pp. 713–15): *consulta* by council of state, Aranjuez, 13 May.

For the English invasion Ambrosio, Federíco's brother, had raised 9,000 Italians. With these he left Italy on 2 May 1602 and marched through Burgundy to Luxembourg. At Puerto de Santa María Federíco made ready eight galleys and left on 14 April, but in a sea-fight with Richard Levison and William Monson off the coast of Portugal he lost two and so reached Lisbon with only six.[1]

This was the position when in May the Adelantado put forward his plan. It was, however, now clear, if not to the Irish, that Lerma would send no further aid of any substance to Ireland. Red Hugh O'Donnell throughout April and May continued to cherish hopes of being sent back to his country with a force of 2,000 men, the forerunner of a full-sized army to be sent to Ireland before winter. But his repeated calls for this force went unanswered.

Instead on 24 May Ensign Diego de Cuenca sailed from Corunna in the *Santiaguillo*, carrying 20,000 ducats in money and some supplies for distribution to O'Sullivan, the O'Driscolls and other southern leaders. Governor Caracena advised these lords by letter that they could expect an abundance of similar supplies in the near future.

Pedro López de Soto strongly supported the sending of aid to O'Sullivan, and sought to convince the administration of its obligation, on both spiritual and material grounds, to maintain the Irish Catholics in their struggle. Pedro López appealed to his king in the latter's role of defender of the faith; not only the Irish, he said, but the English Catholics put their trust in the king of Spain. So far, said López, the help sent to Ireland had been too small, and both time and landing-place had been wrong.

Besides supernatural there were human motives which must, López believed, inspire Spain in this matter. Spanish aid to Ireland, he said, would leave England with her hands full in Ireland and prevent her from embarrassing the sea-lanes which the plate fleets took or from aiding the rebels in Flanders. This was shown, Pedro pointed out, when the Spaniards landed at Kinsale, for the queen then withdrew her galleons and men from Ostend. Even were Ostend to capitulate, Maurice would still maintain the struggle in the Low Countries, and a diversion in Ireland would yet be useful for preventing England from giving him anything but weak support.

López went on to suggest that Spain use Ireland as a base for launching an attack, with ten to twelve thousand men, on England,

1. Rodríguez Villa, *Ambrosio Spínola*, pp. 32–5, 51.

as soon as that country divided on the succession question. He made proposals for sending immediate help, perhaps in May, to Ireland, and especially to Daniel O'Sullivan Beare, before Dunboy was forced to surrender.[1]

But although George Kerr, the Scottish exile, who had long been working for a Spanish invasion of Scotland, now put the interests of Ireland first and supported López in his demand for an invasion of Ireland, he did so in vain. Father Florence Conry attended the court at the Escorial from June onwards, trying to get a licence for Red Hugh to come to court; but without result. Meanwhile O'Neill had turned to Archduke Albert for help. But his request for four shiploads of munitions and other war-stores was merely referred by Albert to Philip, who on the advice of the council of state ignored this request too.[2]

Ireland was in fact written off; but in spite of the council of state's lukewarm attitude towards the Adelantado's proposals, Lerma and Philip were still attracted towards the idea of an attack on England. The king consulted Brochero, who advised that an attack by ships of high freeboard on England was bound to fail. With galleys, on the other hand, Don Diego thought it would be very easy to conquer England, but difficult thereafter to hold the country. His own suggestion was to send ten to twelve galleys, which he himself offered to command, well-manned with good, seasoned troops, to burn and pillage around the English coast and make Elizabeth come to terms.

But Philip had another idea. Without taking Albert (or Brochero) into his confidence the king instructed his ambassador Zúñiga that Ambrosio Spínola and his Italians (6,000 thought Philip, going on the Adelantado's figures, but in reality 9,000), with 5,000 Germans and Walloons, must go to Lisbon, there to embark on Fedérico's galleys. Fedérico would be given eight of the galleys of Spain to bring his total up to eighteen. A thousand Spaniards at Lisbon, as Castel-Rodrigo was instructed, would also be embarked. Philip wrote asking Albert not to impede Ambrosio:

. . . I ask you to allow Marquis Spínola . . . to go with his 6,000 Italians where he wishes, and not to detain him a single hour. Where he is going Your

1. RAH, Colección Salazar, L, t. 24, ff. 61–8v: P. López de Soto, 'Causas divinas y humanas, que obligan a amparar a Yrlanda', May 1602 (?).
2. AGS, Estado 840, f. 201 (*Cal. S.P. Spain, 1587–1603*, p. 718): *consulta* by council of state, 13 Feb. 1603; Estado 620: Albert to Philip, Camp at Oster d, 23 May 1602; Estado 2023: *consulta* by council of state, 15 June.

Excellency will still have him very near you, and he will keep the enemy so occupied that it will be as good as if you had them by your side. These men form the basis of his whole design, which you would wreck if you were to detain them.

Fedérico, engaged at Lisbon in repairing and fitting his galleys, was ordered by Lerma to the Escorial for final instructions. The Genoese then embarked a regiment of infantry at Santander, and on 9 September set out on his voyage. On 3 October he reached the English Channel. Here after running the gauntlet of some enemy ships he had his fleet broken up by storm. Two of his ships were lost, two made Nieuport, and he himself with the remaining two limped into Sluys on 16 October.[1]

Meanwhile Albert's siege of Ostend was proving ineffectual and he was being hard pressed by Maurice. Philip was then forced to divert Ambrosio from the proposed English expedition, and to send him in July to assist Don Francisco de Mendoza, the admiral of Aragón, who was besieging Diste. There for the rest of the summer Ambrosio served.[2]

At the same time the inquiry into the conduct of the Irish expedition proceeded. A total of fifty-three men, it was estimated, had deserted the Spanish ranks to join the English side during the siege of Kinsale, between 10 October 1601 and 12 January 1602, and Philip had arrests made among the troops returned to Corunna. Others were arrested because of seventeen barrels of powder not accounted for. Captain Basco de Saavedra was also placed under arrest, but Caracena after investigation satisfied himself that Saavedra was innocent of the charge against him, namely that it was through his negligence that O'Sullivan Beare had recovered his castle. Caracena's heart was not in the inquiry, for the idea of apportioning blame where everyone could be censured appeared to him to be pointless: 'siendo culpas tan generales que por lo menos se escapan muy pocos de cargarlos unos a otros.'[3]

While the inquiry took its snail-like pace, Ireland was left to its fate.

1. AGS, Estado 2224 (Correspondance, eds. Lonchay and Cuvelier, i. 105): Philip to Albert, San Lorenzo, 11 June 1602); Estado 2224: Philip to Zúñiga, 11 June, and to F. Spínola, San Lorenzo, 16 June; Rodríguez Villa, Ambrosio Spínola, pp. 36–7, 51–2.

2. Rodríguez Villa, op. cit., pp. 52–8.

3. AGS, Guerra Antigua, 3144: list sent by Juan Ochoa de Vaztorra, Corunna, 19 May; RAH, Col. Salazar, L, t. 24, f. 73: López to Caracena, 29 May; AGS, Guerra Antigua 591 Philip to Caracena, Aranjuez, 2 May; Guerra Antigua 3144: Caracena to Philip, Corunna, 25 May; Guerra Antigua 592: same to same, 20 May.

Mountjoy and Carew were reducing the country to subjection, Carew with savagery in south-west Munster and Mountjoy, though far from well, with determined ruthlessness in Ulster and the west. The lord deputy was anxious for a quick conclusion of the Irish business. For one reason, the results of his campaign against O'Neill were such as to sicken even an Elizabethan general in Ireland. With sword and famine he attacked O'Neill, and the famine brought cannibalism in its wake.[1] For another reason, Mountjoy could best win the gratitude of his queen by bringing the long costly war to a speedy close.[2] Docwra gained Ballyshannon castle on 4 April, while Mountjoy in June and July laid the foundations of Charlemont Fort on the river Blackwater and of Mountjoy Fort on the shores of Loch Neagh, caused O'Neill to flee from Dungannon to the shelter of Glenconkein Forest, devastated Monaghan, and established Conor Roe, the 'queen's Maguire', in Fermanagh.

Carew had Thomond ravage the country around Bantry Bay, while he himself proceeded westwards by way of Dunnemark to Dunboy. Meanwhile Sir Charles Wilmot had been laying Dingle and Iveragh waste and had driven the Lord of Lixnaw and the Knight of Kerry into Desmond. Carew left Cork on 3 May and arrived at Berehaven on 16 June. O'Sullivan Beare and his confederates were still awaiting with a strong trust the coming of the Spaniards.[3] But Sir George sent a force to take Dursey Island, which fell easily, and he took Dunboy after only one day's siege (27–8 June). After that it was only a matter of stamping out the embers of revolt in south-west Munster; and this was done with grim efficiency. Tyrrell fled to King's County in December and on 13 January O'Sullivan set out on his famous march to Leitrim, which he and the remnant of his following reached after fourteen days.[4]

With grand indifference to the spectacle of Gaelic Ireland writhing in her death-agony, the Spaniards pursued their investigation into the causes of the failure of Águila's expedition. Archbishop Oviedo's evidence to the commission of inquiry covered familiar ground; he had nothing new to add to his earlier strictures on Águila's conduct

1. '... finally [O'Neill and Rory O'Donnell], hoping for help from Spain, never surrendered until innumerable numbers of their people died from pure hunger and until some of them were eating one another ...'; AGS, Estado 840, f. 56: paper presented by O'Neill to Castro, Spanish ambassador at Rome, with *consulta* by council of state, 24 Mar. 1610.
2. Falls, *Mountjoy*, pp. 194–5.
3. AGS, Guerra Antigua 590: dispatches and letters forwarded by Caracena to Philip, Corunna, 28 July.
4. A.F.M.; *Pac. Hib.*, ii. 148–315; O'Sullivan Beare, *Hist. cath. Ibern. comp.*, pp. 234–54.

except on one point. Águila, he said, had entered Kinsale harbour not of his own choice; his ships were there before Don Juan knew where he was. When he discovered his position he was disgusted, but found himself unable to sail to Castlehaven: 'pero que por hallarse ensenados en el Quinzal, antes de acavalle [=acabarle] de reconocer, no pudieron entonces yr a Castelaven.' Afterwards, though, Oviedo maintained, it was quite possible for Águila to go to Castlehaven; why he did not the archbishop could not say.[1]

If Oviedo made charges against Águila, the latter had an advocate who was able to reply to the archbishop in kind. Deacon Pedro de Colmenares had gone to Kinsale with Águila and was there all the time until the treaty. He made allegations about secret meetings between the archbishop and some captains at Oviedo's house, where extraordinary things were said.[2]

The archbishop, said Colmenares, had sent without Águila's order or knowledge certain dispatches to the chiefs. These dispatches were carried by Oviedo's servant, Pedro Ibáñez, who had gone with the consent of Captain Zarate over the wall with them. The day that the chiefs were routed, said the deacon, no fighting was seen, but the musket-fire was heard most plainly. Colmenares spoke of the 'great fear' then displayed by the archbishop and his friends and of their desire to surrender themselves. But his charges of intrigue are vague and were prompted most likely by sheer pique or malice, his own or Águila's.[3] Oviedo's charges had more influence on the minds of the commission, which now in view of the testimony so far collected reduced the matters to be answered by Águila to five heads: 1. The number of men on the expedition being what it was, its destination (as O'Neill and O'Donnell had laid down) should have been Cork or Limerick. But a week out from Lisbon the order was given, in case the fleet should be scattered, to rendezvous at Kinsale or Castlehaven. Where was this change made, why, and on whose advice? 2. Did Águila ask Brochero to stay until another order came from the king? If he did ask, when was it, and where? Were there any witnesses? 3. On realizing the difficulty of defending Kinsale and its harbour, why did not Águila go to Cork? Did he ask Brochero to take the armada to Castlehaven, or elsewhere? If so, when and how? and were there any

1. AGS, Guerra Antigua 3144: Oviedo's answers to D. de Ibarra, 6 Aug. 1602.
2. Cf. p. 120, *supra*.
3. AGS, Guerra Antigua 3144: declaration by Colmenares.

witnesses? 4. On deciding to stay in Kinsale, why did Águila not fortify the place by sea, since reinforcements from Spain would have to land at the port, and by land? Why did he not make use of the houses in Kinsale, erect a fort, and collect all the cattle possible, burning everything else on the enemy? 5. When the chiefs arrived at the place that Águila had, through Bustamante, indicated to them and were, as some said, heard to be fighting, why did not Águila go out, as he had promised, to their aid?[1]

To sift truth from error was not an easy task for the commission in view of the many stories about the expedition that were circulating among the troops at Corunna. For example, it was asserted that the pilot of the *San Pedro* on the voyage to Ireland had bored the galleon, so that it might ship water and be forced to return to Spain. His action, so it was said, had won general approval from the crew, who hated having to go to Ireland. There were suggestions too that Zubiaur could have made Ireland on the first voyage, had he so desired. Such suggestions, reflecting as they did on the redoubtable Zubiaur's bravery and honour, could hardly be taken seriously.

An allegation that was, however, taken seriously by the commission of inquiry was that Don Pedro (or Diego) de Heredia, a sergeant of Captain Zuazo's company, together with twenty or thirty of his men went over to the enemy from Rincorran. Their arrest was ordered.

On the basis of the evidence by now collected the council of war issued some findings. As to why the landing took place at Kinsale the council found that none of the three, Águila, Brochero, or Archbishop Oviedo, was at fault here:

> ... que no hay causa para poner culpa a ninguno de los que llevavan cargo de la armada y de la gente de guerra ny al arçobispo de Dublin, porque no hay cargo que les hazer sobre ello.

In regard to Brochero's returning from Kinsale the council absolved him from blame, since he had borne an order to return with the ships. The manner in which Don Diego had disembarked the victuals and munitions the council did not find worth pursuing. Investigation was to proceed on the other heads of inquiry.[2]

1. AGS, Guerra Antigua 3144: heads of questions to Águila and others (D. de Ibarra's hand).
2. AGS, Guerra Antigua 3143: *consulta* by council of war, Vallid., 21 Oct.; Guerra Antigua 591: Philip to Castel-Rodrigo, Tordesillas, and orders from Philip to Zubiaur and others, Tordesillas, 4 Dec.; Guerra Antigua 3144: D. de Ibarra (?) to Caracena and others, 12 Apr. 1603; resolution by full council, 12 Apr.

Red Hugh O'Donnell wanted not an investigation into the failures of the past but rather action in the present. Still hopeful of Spanish aid, he managed to get a hearing for another proposal. Father Conry suggested it to Fray Gaspar, who put it to the council. The new proposal was that a force of 3,000 men be sent to Ireland; they could easily take Galway, and by keeping 14,000 of Elizabeth's troops busy in Ireland they would relieve the archduke of great pressure. But the marquis of Poza voiced the feelings of the majority in the council when he said that since Flanders made the first call on Spanish resources and since there was not enough aid for both Flanders and Ireland, all the available aid should be sent to the Low Countries, without any diversion allowed.[1] And Philip was forced to agree that this was basic arithmetic.

But at least some money could be found to aid O'Neill and keep the spark of rebellion alive. The premature death of Hugh O'Donnell, on 9 September 1602, further grievous blow as it was to the Irish cause, made Spain hasten the sending of the sum of 50,000 ducats that Philip had decided on in March. It was agreed to send 30,000 ducats immediately to O'Neill, together with a quantity of arms, and the remainder afterwards in two further instalments. Father Conry was indignant at this; it was, he protested, paltry aid. Philip's conscience made him agree sufficiently to decide to send Conry at once with 30,000 ducats to O'Neill, with promise of 10,000 a month to follow, to pay his Irish soldiers and men to be raised in Scotland to carry on the war. Later, it was decided, Cerdá should also go and take the chains and swords previously destined for distribution among the Irish; these were still in Corunna.[2]

But Ireland wanted more substantial help than this. A French ship left Berehaven on 18 July and arrived at a port near Ribadeo, in Asturias, within ten days. On board were the O'Driscolls, Denis, lord of Castlehaven, and Cornelius, son of Sir Finnin. These two came as envoys from the Irish lords, holding out in the south-west still after the fall of Dunboy. With them was Ellen O'Donoghue, widow of Dermot MacCarthy, the brother of Florence. Dermot, after six years' service against the English, had been killed by a musket shot at Dun-

1. AGS, Estado 621: *consulta* by council of state, 22 Oct.

2. AGS, Estado 840, f. 37 (*Cal. S.P. Spain, 1587–1603*, pp. 715–16): Philip's holograph to *consulta* by council of state, 1 Oct. 1602; Estado 840, f. 203: Prada to E. de Ibarra, Vallid., 1 Feb. 1603; Estado 840, f. 202 (*Cal.*, cit., p. 729): *consulta* by council of state, 17 Feb. 1603. Cf. *supra*, p. 69. Oviedo had thought to take these presents with him in 1600.

boy. The Lady Ellen had one daughter with her, her eldest son, a boy of ten years, remaining a prisoner in Cork. Father Archer and Alférez Cornelio Maris, an Irishman who had gone with Zubiaur to Ireland, were also on board to ask for further aid. These together with many other Irish refugees, such as Hugh Mostian, Redmond Burke, baron of Leitrim, and Matthew Tully, O'Donnell's secretary, were given pensions and in many cases places in the Spanish service.[1] But their mission was for all that a failure; the help they asked for Ireland was not given.

By February 1603 no money had been sent to O'Neill, in spite of Philip's decision of the previous October; and Father Conry had given up hope that this decision would ever be honoured. Another palliative measure was now proposed by the council to Philip: Cornelius O'Driscoll, they advised, should be sent to Ireland with a boat-load of provisions for his friends.[2] It was painfully clear that Spain would send no more real help; for her the Irish adventure was over.

The leisurely inquiry was now nearly at an end too. Don Juan del Águila had taken his time to reply to the charges laid against him. Contrary to the common opinion of historians he had not been imprisoned, but had retired to his native Avila. From there he sent his secretary, Gerónimo de la Torre, with a letter to Philip in March. In this letter Águila claimed to have acted throughout the Irish campaign with conspicuous valour. Don Juan forwarded a letter which Pedro López had sent him from Castlehaven, after López's arrival there; in this López had written that he would sent five hundred Spaniards—'one figure five and two zeros more of good soldiers'[3]— to join O'Neill and O'Donnell, together with a thousand Irish. López however, said Águila, had written later to the chiefs to say that he could not send them any men and that they should give battle. Both O'Neill and Don Juan had sought to induce López to send more men to join the Irish, but without effect.[4]

Águila's evidence was considered by the councils of state and war in

1. AGS, Guerra Antigua 591: Caracena to Philip, Corunna, 28 July; schedule for Caracena of list of pensions for Irishmen, 4 Dec., and schedules of various dates for others; Guerra Antigua 589: memorials by Cornelius and Denis O'Driscoll and Ellen O'Donoghue, with covering letter from Caracena, 8 Aug.

2. AGS, Estado 840, ff. 200-1 (*Cal. S.P. Spain, 1587–1603*, pp. 718–19): *consulta* by council of state, 13 Feb. (not Jan.) 1603; Estado 840, f. 206 (*Cal.*, cit., p. 739): *consulta*, 13 Mar. 1603.

3. 'Un cinco de guarismo y dos zeros mas de buenos soldados.' AGS, Guerra Antigua 3145: López to Águila, 15 (?) Dec. 1601.

4. AGS, Guerra Antigua 3145: Águila to Philip, Avila, 29 Mar. 1603. Cf. *supra*, pp. 134–6.

full session on 12 April. The council, of course, were unaware that
O'Neill, 'prostrated grovelling to the earth', as one eye-witness said,
had three days previously submitted to Mountjoy. Esteban de Ibarra
had prepared for the council a list of charges against Don Juan. This
indictment began by reciting that on the day of the battle Águila had
defaulted in his agreement to sally out and meet O'Neill; that instead
of Cork or Limerick he had gone to Kinsale and thereafter had refused
to remove himself from there; and that he had failed to fortify himself properly. He could, the allegation went on, have secured command of the sea approaches and prevented any enemy ship from
entering by making a cavalier on the seaward side and placing there
four pieces. The land at the foot of Rincorran was very suitable for
fortifying in this manner, and there was a wood very near, from which
the enemy had drawn timber to fortify his quarters. There was an
island[1] at the front, on the left, with a very strong tower (the reference
is to Castle Park), which he might suitably have fortified with another
four pieces. It was by way of this island that the Irish Catholics communicated with the Spaniards in Kinsale, sending in news and many
provisions, and that O'Neill and O'Donnell sent in help. As soon as
peace was made the enemy made a fort at the foot of the tower with
four cavaliers and placed at the sea-side four pieces, with which he now
guarded the whole port.[2]

Águila, the charge continued, had a month during which no enemy
appeared. He could have availed of this opportunity to fortify himself,
using the services of five or six hundred of the poor people as pioneers
at very little cost, but he refused. He could have victualled himself
with many cattle, young and mature, and could have used two storehouses of salt belonging to the queen to cook all the meat he wanted;
and he could have baked flour from wheat and barley available within
sight of the walls to provide rations for many days. If he did not want
to barter, he could have bought the flesh very cheaply at four *mara-
vedís* a pound. Thus there was no cause for over nine hundred persons to die of hunger and for the others to live miserably on a ration
of twelve ounces of biscuit and water.

Águila, the recitation continued, could have mounted two hundred
men, for he had saddles and bridles, and there were many horses to be

1. *Pac. Hib.* also describes the promontory on which Castle Park stood as an 'island'.
2. The English on 25 January 1602 began the erection of the great fort at Castle Park.
O'Sullivan, *Kinsale*, p. 99.

bought at from fifty to eighty *reals*. This would have prevented the enemy from taking away the cattle before the eyes of the garrison and coming up to the walls of the castle and town.

Águila was guilty of negligence, ran the next charge, for he had no *maestres de campo*, did not make sergeants major of experienced veterans, did not set up an advisory council of his captains, and treated those who offered advice as ruffians. He allowed the enemy to level the town without placing artillery there to reply, something he could have done in four hours. There was a trench on the landward side which he had occupied from the beginning with one company by day and another by night. Many captains had wanted him to erect a fort there to shelter the town, but Águila would not. The enemy had come and taken it, and had built a fort in which they placed 2,000 men. They had done much damage to the walls, so that if a man halted in the town even his feet were visible to them. A sally had been made on the vespers of St. Lucy,[1] in which the Spaniards had taken the fort and killed many of the men there, making the others flee. Águila had sent three times to make the captains retire and they finally had done so, allowing the enemy to return. This had been the reason why the chiefs had been unable to make the junction, because that was the route they must have followed when coming.

When, in fact, the indictment went on, the northern chiefs came to encamp four leagues away, the captain-general had not resolved on a junction, but had kept them waiting a fortnight, dispiriting them and strengthening the enemy.[2] One day, the final charge read, he had told the chiefs to attack from their last (transit) camp, a league from Kinsale, saying that as soon as the attack had begun he would sally out. He had not done so, and they and the Spanish companies had been lost as a result.[3]

The plenary session of 12 April heard the evidence presented to date, and ordered fuller inquiry on various points. The session advised that Captains Saavedra, Díaz de Navarra, Caja de Cuellar, Jara Millo, and Don Gómez de Vargas should be absolutely discharged and that Captains Cardenosa and Jaén should be acquitted on the charges

1. Cf. pp. 129–30, for an account of this sortie.
2. But as has been seen it was the effort to get López to send his Spaniards to join the chiefs that caused the delay here. Águila was very eager that the Irish should hasten to the attack; of that there can be no doubt.
3. AGS, Guerra Antigua 3145: paper from Philip for the information of the council, 1 Apr. 1603.

against them; if further charges were laid, the door would thus be left open for their punishment.[1] Lerma, it now came to light, had given orders that Brochero, since he had followed his orders very well, was not to be discussed in the inquiry. No doubt his fellow councillors were relieved to be rid of the embarrassment of subjecting Don Diego's record to critical scrutiny. To be in favour is, it must be admitted, often a convenience. Those who are not especially favoured can always, as Águila did (at least, so we are told), console themselves with the thought that in justice they have merited favours.[2]

Águila was diverted from the contemplation of his unrewarded meritoriousness by the need to give some further testimony, this time on the behaviour of two of his officers. Don Juan laid charges of indiscipline against Captain Francisco de Muñeza. In regard to Paez de Clavijo it was true, Don Juan agreed, that Rincorran was weak, but Paez could have held out longer. Águila could not corroborate Paez's excuse that his soldiers left him since Mountjoy had given them passage before the treaty, but he would accept the excuse.[3]

Another plenary session of the council was held exactly three months after the previous one. O'Neill had meantime gone to England, to make his submission to King James. And already Philip had on James's accession sent Juan de Tassis Peralba, now created conde de Villamediana, to congratulate him. Villamediana had left Valladolid in May for the English court. Such a diplomatic gesture meant that peace was in the air. In only three months' time, in fact, on 31 October 1603, Philip's peace commissioners would be leaving Valladolid on a journey that would take them by way of Paris and Brussels eventually to London. Archduke Albert had at the end of 1602 yielded, though with very bad grace, to Philip's insistence that the Spínolas attack England. But when Fedérico was killed off Sluys on 25 May 1603 the final obstacle to peace was overcome. Ambrosio, who had been raising men in Germany and Italy, was in September put in charge of the siege of Ostend. He won great fame in taking that city, but there was to be no Spínola invasion of England.

Lerma's intent was as pacific as James's, and the Irish diversion would not be without its uses to Spain in the peace negotiations.

1. AGS, Guerra Antigua 3144: resolutions by council of state and war, 12 Apr. 1603.
2. González Dávila, *Felipe tercero*, p. 247.
3. AGS, Guerra Antigua 3144: Águila to Philip's secretary (Bartolomé de Aguilar y Añaya), Avila, 16 Apr. 1603.

Besides, the succession (which the attack on Ireland had unfortunately not decided) was now settled. Stern judgements, therefore, were not in order and the councillors found for Águila (and incidentally Brochero, who, while escaping the peril of censure, did not have to forgo praise) on each of the five charges against him. The findings may be summarized as follows:

Firstly, on the matter of the port of disembarkation the finding was that Águila before leaving Lisbon used all proper diligence to select the place most suitable for quick junction with O'Neill and O'Donnell and least open to the English fleets, but he was deprived of choice in everything.

Secondly, in regard to Brochero's return the council found that Brochero did try to stay, but could not because of his order to return as soon as the men were disembarked. Besides, he had left Lisbon with food for but seventy days, and when setting out to return from Kinsale he had food for only twenty.

In the third place, the council inquired why did not Brochero take the army from Kinsale to a better port? He did not do so, it was found, because of lack of food, the fatigue felt by his men, and the possibility that he might have been driven back to Spain by adverse weather. Moreover, Águila did not propose such a removal to him. If they had set about it the enemy would have had time to prepare for their disembarkation elsewhere. The effect of cross-winds on that coast was proved by the fact that the ship carrying Captains Pedro Henríquez de Tejada and Don Francisco de Piños was driven eight or ten leagues from Kinsale and arrived there more than twenty days late, after Águila had sent pilots.

The fourth question to be decided was did Águila fortify himself? Here the council vindicated Águila completely. He fortified Kinsale, the council concluded, within and without as much as was possible. He had to cover up the food from weather and waves, and had not the time, men, or materials to make a real fort. As soon as Brochero was gone he had to spend some days in gathering the victuals, partly from the hulks in which they remained and partly from the sand. The enemy were molesting him before he had the food covered. He did occupy a little castle with a tower in front of it, which in a manner guarded the port, to occupy the enemy until the help of which he was certain came. These places (the council are evidently not very clear on the distinction between Rincorran and Castle Park) were defended, but not as well as they might have been, for from one of them some of the men went over to the enemy. In a place defenceless against attack from above, and with very little food, he had made a heroic stand for three months. Though there was no hope of help from Spain after the rout of the Irish Águila gained very favourable conditions in the treaty.

Finally, as to the battle, the council decided that the chiefs did not arrive at the place appointed them by Bustamante. Thinking that they would, Águila had given orders to go out to help them, although this would have endangered the safety of Kinsale. The men were ready, sentinels were posted, and Águila himself was at the gate, but no-one heard or saw the chiefs fighting. O'Neill and O'Donnell were beaten by a few of the enemy because of their bad order of fighting and their poor resolution. This lack of resolution was shown by their having sent baggage back three leagues that morning, an indication that they did not mean to advance. When a large part of the day had gone by without anything having been heard Águila, leading about a hundred men, sallied out. So many English came to their posts that none seemed to be missing. This proved that they had not been heavily engaged with the Irish.

The council, finding thus for Águila on all points, expressed their opinion that he had done his duty very well, prudently, and bravely, and deserved no blame but rather equal or greater commands. Don Juan, however, did not survive the verdict long, dying as González Dávila complains before he had received any return for his services. He was interred in Barraco, a town which, his pious biographer remarks, thus earned fame for its association with Águila's ashes and his triumphs.

The verdict of the council, though it left certain questions unanswered, was all things considered just. The count of Puñoenrostro, however, gave a dissenting opinion in which he held Águila to blame for not securing the port at the beginning and for not effecting a junction with the Irish. Águila, Puñoenrostro held, failed in his first duty when he entered Kinsale, which was to see if the port could be held and, if it could, to fortify it without an hour's delay, to dig a trench for defence, and then and only then to disembark the artillery and munitions. What he did, however, was to disembark these first and, without fortifying the port, place himself in a pit surrounded by heights. He did not occupy these or any place that would protect his position. If, as Águila and others said, Kinsale was impossible to fortify in this manner, the first day would have made that clear. Brochero remained nine days there, but Águila (who had too few men to be master in a campaign) failed in his first duty, that of reconnoitring. He would have done better, said Puñoenrostro flatly, to return to Spain.

The count's criticism is well made; yet it ignores the fact that Águila did not allow Kinsale to be carried by storm but capitulated only when he saw no hope of further aid from Spain in time and could at the same time negotiate from strength. Most of the criticism that can be made against his conduct of the campaign loses in weight if it is remembered how badly provisioned and equipped the expedition was; how few men he commanded (and that lack of men was certainly the greatest single factor in limiting the operation's success); how he was prevented from sailing to the north as he wished to do and should have done; and how he was left without ships. On the one outstanding point where there was flat contradiction between Águila and his most severe critic, Archbishop Oviedo, namely whether Don Juan knew that the Irish were engaged with the enemy, the council found that he did not know. That this was a reasonable decision cannot be gainsaid; the Irish unfortunately had been unable to make the appointed rendezvous and, whatever appearances might suggest, Águila had to be wary of a stratagem. He is perhaps to blame for urging against O'Neill's better judgement a premature engagement, as O'Donnell is to blame for supporting him in this.

But so could Zubiaur be blamed for not sending all his force to strengthen the unseasoned Irish armies. All in turn could be excused, however: Águila, because the Irish failed to keep the rendezvous; O'Donnell, because (as indeed the Four Masters suggest) he was weary of half a year's sieges, at Derry, Lifford, Donegal, and now against the English besiegers at Kinsale, and all to no effect; and Zubiaur, because the alternative he decided on offered an excellent selection of harbours for the hoped-for reinforcements to choose between. If Archduke Albert and Aragón had been able to conduct a more successful campaign against the Dutch rebels, Spínola might have been freed to create a diversion in England or reinforcements might have been released for Ireland that would have made all the difference to the outcome of Águila's invasion. Águila might, finally, have done better, but he had created a diversion at England's back door, many hundred miles away from Spain, and had brought the bulk of his army home intact. Worse results there might have been.

The council gave Brochero full acquittal; they found that there had been neither lack of care nor fault in his handling of the navigation to Ireland, disembarkation, or return to Spain. King Philip accepted these findings in full and ordered further investigation in the case of others who did appear guilty.[1]

But with Águila and Brochero cleared of all charges, it was not to be expected that very stern action would be taken against the men of lesser rank. Indeed, Spanish interest in Ireland had now diminished, and it was almost two years before judgement was given in the cases of López de Soto and Zubiaur. The former was then deprived of his office of *veedor* for four years and was forbidden to appear within five leagues distance of the court for two years. The council found for Zubiaur on three counts and against him on one unstated in the minute, but presumably the matter of not sending all his men to join the Irish. For punishment, especially in view of the fact that he had been for a long time imprisoned at court, a reprimand was deemed sufficient. So under something of a cloud a notable career closed, for Don Pedro died a few months later.[2]

The archbishop of Dublin lived on for five years, dying on 10 January 1610 in his order's convent of Valladolid, to which he had retired.[3] Strange in his final years must have seemed to him the designs of providence as he worried about his beloved Ireland, now given over to the heretics, or knelt to pray and mourn at the grave of the prince, Red Hugh, whom he had known in all his vigour, or listened to the news about Ireland brought to him by the many Irish refugees who thronged the court:[4] Hugh Mostian, Redmond Burke, Edmund Eustace of Baltinglass, or Alexander Walshe,[5] who would remind him of that voyage that they two and Cerdá had made to far away Donegal. To these and most of all perhaps to Father Florence Conry he would speak of his hopes that Ireland must yet be freed. These hopes he must have thought, when in 1607 the startling news of O'Neill's coming to

---

1. AGS, Guerra Antigua 3144: *consulta* of 12 July, with Philip's holograph thereon.
2. AGS, Guerra Antigua 640 (*Epistolario de Zubiaur*, pp. 109–10, cf. p. 23): *consulta* by full council on cases of López and Zubiaur, Vallid., 12 May 1605.
3. Colmenares, *Historia de Segovia*, iv. 182.
4. Captain Eduardo Geraldino, in an undated memorial (? 1603), said that there were more than 600 Irish and Scots at the court and in other parts of the Spanish kingdoms.
5. The names of these and others at court in 1603 will be found in AGS, Estado 1745.

Europe to raise another expedition was brought to him, would now surely be realized. Were his illusions finally shattered when O'Neill, at English insistence, was refused entry to Spain; or did he cherish until his death the belief that Hugh would prevail on the pope to arouse on behalf of Ireland the conscience of Catholic Europe? One can but conjecture.

France and Spain, under English pressure, both refused to assist O'Neill's plans to return to Ireland with an army, and he was driven to accept asylum in Rome. With the passing of O'Neill, Oviedo, and Águila from the scene there faded the hope of Irish independence won by Spanish aid. A new era was beginning for Europe and for Ireland, and from his vantage-point in Rome (where O'Neill was hospitably treated but not encouraged to hope for papal backing for his restoration) Archbishop Lombard read the signs. The appeal to arms had failed and wisdom for Ireland, Lombard felt, now lay in accepting the bitter fact of her political conquest and concentrating on the preservation of her religious liberty. It was time to explore the possibilities of the text, 'Render unto Caesar', to which de la Field had already appealed. And so as primate of Ireland Lombard set out to promote Catholic acceptance of Caesar, James I, as lawful sovereign of Ireland and to convince the king of the reality of Catholic loyalty. In the new international climate, with religion 'beginning to lose its position as the keystone'[1] of politics, Henry IV was willing to make compromises in France, as was Philip III on both the Atlantic and Mediterranean seaboards. James too, besides accommodation with Spain, was ready to seek compromise with the pope on the religious question. Lombard felt this was a situation to be exploited.[2]

Before the council's findings of 12 July 1603, Cerdá, sent off at last with the money together with munitions for O'Neill, had learned of the latter's submission to Mountjoy, and was already back in Spain accompanied by MacWilliam Burke. A final voyage was made by Denis O'Driscoll on a Spanish ship to take away O'Sullivan Beare and O'Rourke, and the Irish adventure was over.[3]

1. Edwards, in *Measgra Mhichíl Uí Chléirigh*, p. 2.
2. Silke, in *Ir. Theol. Quart.*, xxii (1955), 15–30, 124–50.
3. AGS, Estado 840, ff. 219, 232: *consultas* by council of state, 22 July and 23 Aug.; Cabrera, *Relaciones*, p. 184. On the later history of the O'Sullivans in Spain cf. Hume, *Españoles e ingleses*, p. 268.

APPENDIX I

A NOTE ON THE BATTLE

CHAPTER ELEVEN gives what from the available evidence seems to be the best reconstruction of the intentions of the Irish and their ally Águila on the morning of the battle. Certain evidence from Spanish sources has mistakenly been taken as suggesting that not only would Tyrrell place his force within the town that morning but that the attack on the English, by Águila and Tyrrell against Thomond, and by O'Neill and O'Donnell against Mountjoy, would take place only on the following night.[1] Whether or not Tyrrell's force was to enter the town, the attack was to take place that morning.

The two Spanish authorities in question here are Alonso de Ocampo, who was taken prisoner by the English during the engagement, and Zubiaur. Ocampo's evidence, as given to his captors, does not indicate that the attack was to be delayed until the night of 3 January.[2] What Zubiaur, or rather López for him, quite clearly states is that O'Neill on that morning would occupy a position assigned to him by Águila, whereupon the latter would there and then sally out and join him in a combined attack on the enemy:

Que quedaron de acuerdo con . . . Águila que aquel día [3 January] se pondría con toda su gente en un recuesto donde . . . don Juan le señaló que haziendo cierta señal *que* pudiese salir y dar por su parte en los enemigos.[3]

Zubiaur's account is, of course, at second-hand. On 25 January 1602 Sebastián de Oleaga presented to the council of war a report of events in Ireland from the coming of Zubiaur until the time that he (Oleaga) had left on 6 January. This memorial, made from López's dispatches, is in the hand of Secretary Ibarra, and is printed *Epistolario de Zubiaur*, pp. 134–9.

Whether even the intention was to throw Tyrrell's van into the

---

1. Cf. Hayes-McCoy, in *Studies*, xxxviii (1949), 312–13, and evidence there quoted.
2. Cf. *Cal. S.P. Ire., 1601–3*, p. 240: Carew to Cecil, 26 Dec., old style; p. 241: Power to Cecil, 27 Dec., old style (*Cal.*, cit., p. 241). But cf. *Cal. Carew MSS, 1601–3*, p. 192.
3. *Epistolario de Zubiaur*, p. 128; this statement is repeated almost word for word on p. 137.

town is a moot point. Reports that Tyrrell did design so to place his force, made up of the Irish, estimated at 1,000, and Ocampo's Spaniards, have no confirmation from Spanish or Irish sources. Cavalli, the Venetian ambassador at Paris, who confirms Power's report,[1] learned that Mountjoy intercepted some letters written by O'Neill to Águila, in which Hugh said that on Christmas eve (old style) he would attack with his army the English from one side, and that Águila ought to sortie out with 1,500 of his men from the other, so as to allow the placing in Kinsale of 1,000 Irish and 500 Spanish.[2] This is clearly derived from the English sources. Mountjoy's later dispatches say nothing about an intention to throw Tyrrell's men into the town or to attack the English the following night, but say rather that when Tyrrell had occupied his position Águila would sally out and the attack on the two camps would immediately take place.[3] Later argument among the Spaniards was concerned with whether Águila should have gone out to join the Irish; nothing was said about Tyrrell's going into Kinsale.

1. *Cal. S.P. Ire.*, 1601–3, p. 241.
2. *Relazioni degli stati Europei*, ser. II: *Francia*, i. 41 n. 1: Cavalli to doge and senate, 22 Jan. 1602.
3. *Studies*, xxxviii. 313 n. 1; *Cal. S.P. Ire.*, 1601–3, p. 261.

APPENDIX II

A. MUSTER TAKEN AT BELÉM
30 August 1601[1]

THE MUSTER, taken by Juan de la Peña Zorilla, states that there are forty-three companies of Spanish and Italian infantry under the command of the *maestre de campo* Don Juan de el Águila at Belém.

Tercio *of the* maestre de campo *Don Francisco de Padilla*
(*not counting companies of recruits*)

	By Poll
Padilla's own company	155
Company of Don Christóbal de Ayala	146
„ „ Diego de Vega	149
„ „ Juan Bautista Castellanos	135
„ „ Jusepe de Escobar	149
„ „ Hernando Barragán	92
Companies which came from Andalusia (the others which came were re-formed, as containing few men)	
Company of Gaspar de Molina	129
„ „ Pedro Enríquez de Tejada	55
Companies which came from Galicia	
Company of Pedro Muñiz de Jaén	106
„ „ Juan de Albornoz	102
„ „ Don Francisco de Piños	102
Italian company of Orlando Tesauro	130
Total in *tercio*	1,450

Tercio *of the* maestre de campo *Antonio Centeno*

Centeno's own company	73
Company of Andrés Leal	54
„ „ Francisco Vanegas	54
„ „ Gerónimo de Guevara	64
„ „ Don Bartolomé de Biamonte	44
„ „ Alonso de Ocampo	60
„ „ Francisco Maldonado	66
„ „ Don Sancho de Biedma	61

1. AGS, Guerra Antigua 3144.

	By Poll
Company of Diego de Salaçar	65
„ „ Diego de San Briente	61
„ „ Don Gaspar de Castel Blanco[1]	62
„ „ Don Pedro Xarava del Castillo	66
Italian company of Antonio del Tuffo	132
Total in *tercio*	862

Companies of recruits, to be distributed among both tercios

Company of Francisco Ruiz de Velasco		116
„ „ Francisco Muñeza		110
„ „ Diego González Sigler		113
„ „ Luis Díaz de Navarra		119
„ „ Pedro de Çuaço		107
„ „ Juan Yñíguez de Çarate		107
„ „ Marcos de Porres		113
„ „ Francisco de Heredia		112
„ „ Bernardino de Soto		116
„ „ Christóbal de Cardenosa		113
„ „ Andrés de Arbe		114
„ „ Pedro de Pereda		112
„ „ Miguel Caja de Cuellar		114
„ „ Diego Cascarro		111
„ „ Alonso Xara Millo		113
„ „ Sebastián Graneros		109
	Total of recruits	1,799

Men taken from the castles of Lisbon and San Gián

174 men formed into a company under Don Luis Vela Núñez, and not yet added to a *tercio*	174
Portuguese: 147 soldiers, including certain persons sentenced to serve in Portuguese India, whose banishment was commuted to service with the armada to Ireland. Formed into a company under Roque Pereyra	147

Summary

Tercio of the *maestre de campo* Padilla	1,450
„ „ „ „ „ „ Centeno	862
Companies of recruits	1,799
Men taken from the castles of San Gián and Lisbon	174
Portuguese	147
Total, in 43 companies	4,432

1. Águila allowed him to go home with Brochero, and gave his company to Don Pedro Morejón. AGS, Guerra Antigua 3144: Águila to Philip, 13 Oct. 1601.

B. MUSTER OF ARMY OF IRELAND
1602[1]

This account, by Pedro López de Soto, accompanied a letter from Caracena, 2 April 1602, to the court.

Companies of tercio of Esteban de Legorreta, which came under command of Ocampo

	By Poll
Company of the *maestre de campo* himself	55
„ „ Captain Andrés Leal	34
„ „ „ Juan de Albornoz	64
„ „ „ Pedro López de Jaén	74
„ „ „ Gaspar de Molina	72
„ „ „ Francisco de Eredia	55
„ „ „ Luis Díaz de Navarra	32
„ „ „ Juan Iñíguez de Çarate	67
„ „ „ Francisco Maldonado	42
„ „ „ Diego de San Vicente	42
„ „ „ Don Pedro Morejón	71
„ „ „ Miguel Caxa de Cuellar	61
„ „ „ Don Pedro Jarava del Castillo	52
„ „ „ Pedro de Echaves	45
„ „ „ Don Diego de Biedma	42
Italian company of Captain Orlando Thesauro	110

Companies of tercio of Don Pedro Sarmiento, which came with Águila

Company of the *maestre de campo*	114
„ „ Captain Pedro de Suazo	64
„ „ „ Marcos de Porral	64
„ „ „ Christóbal de Cardenosa	42
„ „ „ Diego de Vega	116
„ „ „ Don Luis Núñez Vela	84
„ „ „ Don Christoval de Ayala	92
„ „ „ Alonso de Xara Millo	49
„ „ „ Diego Cascarro	64
„ „ „ Diego Palomeque	70
„ „ „ Diego González Sigler	53
„ „ „ Jusepe Descovar	105
Italian company of Captain Antonio del Tuffo	108

1. AGS Guerra Antigua 590.

Three companies from Kinsale, which landed at Bayonne

	By Poll
Company of Don Felipe de Beautmonte	129
„ „ Don Gómez de Bargas	51
„ „ Pedro Enríquez	66

Company which landed at Asturias, and is now here

Company of Don Francisco de Piños, with added men	140

The eight companies of Castlehaven, Baltimore, and Berehaven

Company of Captain Hernando Cabeza de Vaca Barragán	65
„ „ „ Francisco Ruiz de Velasco	48
„ „ „ Sebastián Granero	37
„ „ „ Roque Pereyra	41
„ „ „ Alonso de Ocampo	37
„ „ „ Vasco de Saavedra	93
„ „ „ Andrés de Arbe	61
„ „ „ Juan Bautista Castellanos	50

Portuguese companies which came from Lisbon in the hookers and with Ballecilla

Company of Captain Martín Alonso Valiente	95
„ „ „ Chirinos	70
„ „ „ Diego de Aguilar y Castro	62

New companies now come from Castile

Company of Captain Diego de Medina	101
„ „ „ Bernabé de Buitrán	74
„ „ „ Gerónimo de Herradas	77
Total in 47 companies	3,250

Summary

41 companies come from Ireland	2,771
3 „ „ „ Portugal	227
3 new companies	252
Total	3,250

A note by Pedro López says that this muster includes officials and sick, and that between the muster and 2 April over 130 men died. The sick, he adds, are now getting better, and there ought to be over 2,000 effectives.

BIBLIOGRAPHY

I. SPANISH SOURCES

A. *Guides to sources*

The most complete and useful bibliography of Spanish studies is R. Foulché-Delbosc and L. Barrau-Dihigo, *Manuel de l'hispanisant* (Hispanic Soc. of America, 2 vols., N.Y., 1920, 1925), which contains catalogues and inventories of and detailed guides to archival and other sources. The most important bibliography of Spanish history is Benito Sánchez Alonso, *Fuentes de la historia española e hispano-americana: ensayo de bibliografía sistemática de impresos y manuscritos que ilustran la historia política de España y sus antiguas provincias de ultramar* (3rd ed., CSIC, 3 vols., Madrid, 1952). Guillermo Bauer, *Introducción al estudio de la historia*, ed. Luis G. de Valdeavellano (2nd ed., Barcelona, 1952), embodies useful bibliographies. Guides to sources of more particular interest will be found in Pedro Aguado Bleye, *Manual de historia de España*, vol. II: *Reyes católicos—casa de Austria* (8th ed., Madrid, 1959), chap. XIII: 'Casa de Austria 1517–1700: las fuentes', and in Huguette et Pierre Chaunu, *Séville et l'Atlantique 1504–1650* (8 vols., Paris, 1955–9), viii. I, pp. xxi–cxxv. A guide to modern publications during the years indicated is D. Gómez Molleda, *Bibliografía histórica española 1950–4* (CSIC, Madrid, 1955); while the *Índice histórico español: bibliografía histórica de España e Hispanoamerica . . ., 1953–4*, etc. (Centro de Ests. Hists. Internacs., Barcelona, 1955–   ) is a critical index, listing current works, Spanish and foreign. A. Ballesteros y Beretta, *Historia de España y su influencia en la historia universal*, vol. IV, pt. i (2nd ed., Barcelona, 1950), covers the period from Philip II to Charles II and has extensive bibliographies.

A comprehensive guide to Spanish archives is F. Rodríguez Marín (ed.), *Guía histórica y descripción de los archivos, bibliotecas y museos arqueológicos de España que están a cargo del Cuerpo Facultativo del Ramo* (Secc. de Archivos, Madrid, 1921). The Archivo General de Simancas is treated, pp. 129–371. Francisco Sintes y Obrador is author of *Guía de los archivos de Madrid* (Dir. Gen. de Archs. y Bibls., Madrid, 1952). Finally, there is the *Inventario general de manuscritos de la Biblioteca Nacional* (Min. de Educ. Nac., Madrid, 1953–   ).

B. *Archival*

I. ARCHIVO GENERAL DE SIMANCAS

This is the chief source of documentation for the Spanish landings in Munster. *The letters and state papers relating to English affairs, preserved principally in the archives of Simancas*, ed. M. A. S. Hume, vol. IV: *Elizabeth I, 1587–1603* (1889) (*Cal. S.P. Spain, 1587–1603*), must be used with care, and checked at all stages against the originals. There are transcripts of documents in *Epistolario del General Zubiaur, 1568–1605*, ed. Conde de Polentinos (CSIC, Madrid, 1946), and 'Some unpublished letters of Mateo de Oviedo', ed. P. MacBride, in *Reportorium Novum*, i (1955–6), and (faithfully enough translated) in *Pacata Hibernia*.

a. Guides

Guia del archivo de Simancas (Dir. Gen. de Archivos y Bibliotecas, Madrid, 1958) refers to the different printed catalogues that had appeared by 1958. The work of cataloguing is continuing and the most complete list of catalogues will be found in the current hand-list, 'Catálogos del Archivo General de Simancas', available at the archives. As yet cataloguing is far from being completed; besides, the printed 'catalogues' are really only inventories and give for the most part but a very brief indication of the contents of each *legajo* (or bundle of documents).

Of much assistance to the Irish investigator in locating documents are the 'Reports on documents of Irish interest in the Spanish archives', by Fr. Canice Mooney, O.F.M. (1945), in NLI, and by J. G. Healy (1939), in the files of IMC.

These 'Reports' cover the microfilms of Simancas material made for the National Library of Ireland. The 1950–1 *Report of the Council of Trustees* lists these microfilms on pp. 119–21. Fr. Mooney has also reported on the Simancas Archives to the Irish Catholic Historical Committee (*Proc.*, 1955, pp. 18–21).

b. Citation

The two groups (*fondos*) embodying the deliberations of the councils of state and war, respectively Estado (section *Secretaría de Estado*) and Guerra y Marina (section *Guerra Antigua*), were found to be of most value for a study of the invasion. Reference in the present work is given to the section, the number of the *legajo*, and, where, exceptionally, it is indicated, the number of the folio or page. Thus 'AGS, Estado 840, f. 80' refers to Archivo General de Simancas, *fondo* Estado, *sección* Secretaría de Estado, *serie* Negociaciones de Nápoles, *legajo* 840, folio 80. Similarly, 'AGS, Guerra Antigua 3145' refers to the group Guerra y Marina, section Guerra Antigua, series [III], Parte de Mar [=Marina], file 3145. (The group Guerra y Marina is divided into the sections Guerra Antigua, Guerra Moderna and Marina. Guerra Antigua is subdivided into the series Tierra y Mar, Tierra and Parte de Mar.)

2. OTHER ARCHIVES

a. Collections

Real Academia de Historia, Madrid
    MS. Colección Salazar, L, tomo xxiv (Papeles Varios, t. i), ff. 61–76, contains memorials by Pedro López de Soto, written after the defeat at Kinsale and urging further Spanish help.

Museo Naval, Madrid
    Colección Sans (or Sanz) de Barutell, in two series, of 27 and 23 vols. respectively, contains information collected by Barutell in Simancas on shipping used in the expedition. Barutell, who died 1819, has left two inventories in the museum to his collection.

British Museum
    Bergenroth's and Froude's transcripts from Simancas (Add. MSS., vols. 28595–7, 26056 A–C) were already on microfilm in NLI. They have now been largely superseded, as far as the Irish student is concerned, by the microfilms from Simancas in NLI treated above. A number of extracts that are relevant, from the Sloane MSS.,

collections of Cole, Fane, etc., have been microfilmed for NLI. References to them will be found in the 1950–1 *Report of the Council of Trustees*, pp. 35, 43, 44, 48, 50, 51, 71, and 1951–2 *Report*, pp. 51, 83, 94.

b. Printed and calendared material

Relations des Pays-Bas et de l'Angleterre sous le règne de Philippe II, ed. Kervyn de Lettenhove (10 vols., Brussels, 1882–91), has material of Irish interest. Concerning the war in Flanders, *Correspondance de la cour d'Espagne sur les affaires des Pays-Bas au xviie siècle*, eds. H. Lonchay and J. Cuvelier, vol. I: *Précis de la correspondance de Philippe III 1598–1621* (Brussels, 1923), embodies research done chiefly in Simancas and in the Archives Générales du Royaume in Brussels. Correspondence between Archduke Albert and Lerma and others has been edited in the series *Colección de documentos inéditos para la historia de España*, vols. XLII–III. The index vols., CI and CII, of this great series of 112 vols. (Madrid, 1842–95. Cf. *Manuel de l'hispanisant*, ii. 113–79, for contents) should be consulted. A. Rodríguez Villa is editor of *Correspondencia de la infanta Archiduquesa Isabel Clara Eugenia con el duque de Lerma y otras personalidades* (Madrid, 1916).

AGS, Estado 2511, has much documentation on the Boulogne peace conference; transactions and correspondence in Ralph Winwood, *Memorials 1597–1603*, ed. E. Sawyer (3 vols., 1725), i. bk. III.

Two works which illustrate Spanish relations with the Papacy are Ricardo de Hinojosa, *Los despatchos de la diplomacia pontificia en España: memoria de una misión oficial en el archivo secreto de la santa sede*, vol. I (Madrid, 1896), a report on twenty months' research in the Vatican and other Roman and Italian archives; and *Archivo de la embajada de España cerca de la santa sede*, vol. I, ed. Luciano Serrano, *Índice analítico de los documentos del siglo xvi;* vol. II, ed. José M. Pou y Martí, *Siglo xvii* (Rome, 1917). *Archivium Hibernicum* gives transcripts of documents bearing on relations between Spain, Ireland, and Rome during the period from the Vatican Archives, especially vols. II (1913), III (1914), XXIII (1960), and XXIV (1961), for documents from the Borghese collection, and XVII (1953), containing the correspondence of Father Mansoni, S.J. (ed. Rev. F. M. Jones, C.SS.R.). R. A. Breathnach has edited a letter from Donal O'Sullivan Beare to Philip III, in *Éigse*, vi (1952), 314–25, while vol. I of *Spanish knights of Irish origin*, ed. Micheline Walsh (IMC, Dublin, 1960), is relevant.

c. Secondary works

I. GENERAL

Altamira y Crevea, Rafael, *Historia de España y de la civilización española* (3rd ed., 5 vols. in 6, 1913–30; vol. 5 by Don Pío Zabala y Lera).

2. THE ADMINISTRATION

C. Pérez Bustamante, *Felipe III: semblanza de un monarca y perfiles de un privanza* (Madrid, 1950), provides an introduction to the person and court of Philip III. In this connection, F. Tommy Perrens, 'Le duc de Lerme et la cour d'Espagne sous la règne de Philippe III', *Compte-rendu de l'Acad. des Scs. Mors. et Pols.*, xxi–xxii (Paris, 1870); Edouard Rott, 'Philippe III et le duc de Lerme', in *Rév. d'Hist. Diplomatique*, i (1887), 201–16, 363–84; and A. Ferrer del Río, 'El duque de Lerma', in *R.E.*, xviii (1871), 161–87; may also be consulted with profit. Detailed studies on the administration of the reign are lacking. Among works found useful were J. M. Cordero Torres, *El consejo de estado: su trayectoria y perspectivas en España* (Inst. de Ests. Pols., Madrid, 1944); M. J. Gounon-Loubens, *Essais sur l'administration de la Castille au xvie siècle* (Paris, 1860); A. Ballesteros y Beretta, *Historia de España*, cit., vol. IV, pt. ii, chap. I; F. X. Garma y Durán, *Theatro universal de España: descripción ecclesiastica y secular de todos sus reynos y provincias* (Barcelona, 1751), and the court chronicle by Luis Cabrera de Córdoba, *Relaciones de las cosas sucedidas en la corte de España desde 1599 hasta 1614* (Madrid, 1857). Cf. also Ignacio Olagüe, *La decadencia española* (4 vols., Madrid, 1950-1), and Ramón Carande, *Carlos V y sus banqueros*, vol. I: *La vida económica de España en un fase de su hegemonía 1516-56* (Madrid, 1943); vol. II: *La hacienda real de Castilla* (Madrid, 1949). The author has not been able to consult Francisco Tomás Valiente, *Los validos en la monarquía española del siglo xvii: estudo institucional* (Inst. de Ests. Políticos: Coll. Historia Politica, Madrid, 1963).

3. BIOGRAPHY

A particular difficulty that confronts the student of Spanish history is that Spain has no equivalent of the *D.N.B.* The *Diccionario de historia de España* (2 vols., Madrid, 1952) to some extent supplies this lack, as also do *Enciclopedia universal ilustrada europeoamericana*, in course of publication by Espasa-Calpe (Barcelona, 1907–   ), and Louis G. Michaud, *Nouvelle biographie universelle ancienne et moderne* (2nd ed., 65 vols., 1843-65). An incomplete Spanish edition of this work by J. de Burgos, *Biografía universal antigua y moderna* (3 vols., Madrid, 1822) gives additions and corrections for Spain. The *Diccionario biográfico español e hispanoamericana*, ed. Gaspar Sabater (Instituto Español de Estudios Biográficos: vol. I, Palma de Mallorca, 1950), is also useful.

Works which give biographical data on military and naval officers and are besides useful for giving an appreciation of military and naval affairs are José Almirante, *Bosquejo de historia militar de España hasta fin del siglo xviii* (3 vols., Madrid, 1923); Conde de Clonard, *Historia orgánica de las armas de infantería y caballería españolas* (16 vols., Madrid, 1851-9); Cesareo Fernández Duro, *Armada española desde la unión de los reinos de Castilla y León* (9 vols., Madrid, 1895-1903); C. Ibáñez de Ibero, *Historia de la marina de guerra española desde el siglo xiii hasta nuestros días* (Madrid, 2nd ed., 1943); Manuel Juan Diana, *Capitanes ilustres y revista de libros militares* (Madrid, 1851); and Abbot Payson Usher, 'Spanish ships and shipping in the sixteenth and seventeenth centuries', in *Facts and factors in economic history: articles by former students of Edwin Francis Gay* (Harvard, 1932), pp. 189-213.

Other useful works in this connection are Gil González Dávila, *Monarquía de España: historia de la vida y hechos del ínclito monarca, amado y santo D. Felipe tercero...* (Madrid, 1771); Garma y Durán, *Theatro universal*, cit.; *Relazioni degli stati Europei lette al Senato degli ambasciatori Veneti nel secolo decimosettimo*, ed. N. Barozzi and G. Berchet. Ser. I: *Spagna* (this work gives the opinions of Soranzo, Venetian ambassador, 1597-1602, on various counsellors); Mariano Alcocer y Martínez, *Archivo histórico español: colección de documentos...* (Valladolid, 1930), vol. III, *passim*; R. Hinojosa, *Los despachos de la diplomacia pontificia en España: memoria de una misión oficial en el archivo secreto de la santa sede*, vol. I (Madrid, 1896). There are biographies by J. Juderías y Loyot, *Don Pedro Franqueza, conde de Villalonga* (Madrid, 1909); A. Dávila y Burguero, *Don Christóbal de Moura* (Madrid, 1900); Fidel Pérez-Mínguez, *Don Juan de Idiáquez* (San Sebastian, 1935); and Atanasio López, O.F.M., 'Fr. Mateo de Oviedo', in *El Eco Franciscano*, xxvi (1919).

4. FOREIGN RELATIONS

Fernand Braudel, *La méditerranée et le monde méditerranéen à l'époque de Philippe II* (Paris, 1949) (*El Mediterraneo y el mundo mediterraneo en la época de Felippe II*, trans. M. Monteforte Toledo and W. Roces (2 vols., Mexico, 1953)), is a basic work, which does not neglect Philip's interest and involvement in the Atlantic. A. Rodríguez Villa, *Ambrosio Spínola, primer marqués de los Balbases: ensayo biográfico* (Madrid, 1904), includes a number of documents from Simancas relative to the proposed expedition of the Spínolas. Other useful works are Antonio Cerrolaza, *Spínola: un genovés en Flandes* (Madrid, 1946), and J. M. García Rodríguez, *Ambrosio Spínola y su tiempo* (Barcelona, 1942).

Relations with England form the subject-matter of M. A. S. Hume, *Españoles e ingleses en el siglo xvi: estudios históricos* (Madrid, Biblioteca de Derechos y de Ciencias Sociales, 1903); cf. Cyril Falls, 'España e irlanda durante el reinado de Isabel de Inglaterra (1558 a 1603)', in *Segundo curso de metodología y crítica históries* (Estado Mayor Central del Ejercito: Servicio Histórico Militar, Madrid, 1950), pp. 325–54.

The question of a successor to Elizabeth, as it presented itself to Philip III, has been considered by L. Hicks, S.J., 'Sir Robert Cecil, Father Persons and the succession, 1600–1', in *Archiv. Hist. Soc. Iesu*, xxiv (1955). On the Boulogne peace conference of 1600 cf. *Cal. S.P. Venice, 1592–1603*, pp. xxv–vii; cf. also L. Hamy, 'Conférence pour la paix entre l'Angleterre et l' Espagne tenue a Boulogne en 1600: étude historique', in *Soc. Acad. de Boulogne-sur-Mer Bull.*, vii (1906), 434–60.

II. OTHER SOURCES

A. *Guides to sources*

The indispensable guide is *Bibliography of British History: Tudor period 1485–1603*, ed. Conyers Read (Amer. Hist. Assn. and RHS, 2nd ed., New York; 1st ed., Oxford, 1959); this comprehensive work contains a chapter on sources and secondary works relating to Ireland, classified according to subject. R. D. Edwards, *Church and state in Tudor Ireland* (Dublin, 1935), pp. 313–32, provides an exhaustive guide to sources, archival as well as printed and calendared, chronicle material, and modern works. Current writings on Irish history are listed in *Irish historical studies* (Dublin, 1938–).

B. *Archival*

1. MANUSCRIPT

PROL. State papers, Ireland, Elizabeth I–George III.

2. PRINTED

Annála Ríoghachta Éireann: Annals of the kingdom of Ireland by the Four Masters, ed. J. O'Donovan (7 vols., Dublin, 1848–51).
BREATHNACH, R. A. (ed.), 'Elegy on Donal O'Sullivan Beare (†1618)', in *Éigse*, vii (1954), 168–21.
Calendar of Carew papers in the Lambeth library (6 vols., 1867–73).
Calendar of state papers relating to Ireland, Henry VIII–Elizabeth I (11 vols., 1860–1912).
Calendar of state papers and manuscripts relating to English affairs . . . in . . . Venice . . ., *1202–1674* (38 vols., 1864–1947).
Cox, Sir Richard, *Hibernia Anglicana* (2 vols., 1689).

Docwra, Sir Henry, 'A narration of the services done by the army employed to Lough Foyle . . .', in *Celtic Soc. Misc.*, ed. J. O'Donovan (Dublin, 1849), pp. 247–61.

Gilbert, J. T., *Account of facsimiles of national manuscripts of Ireland.* iv. I (HMSO, 1882).

[Haynes, S. ?] *Description of Ireland . . . in anno 1598*, ed. Rev. Edmund Hogan, S.J. (Dublin, 1878).

Historical Manuscripts Commission:
Hatfield MSS, pt. x (1904).
Ninth report, appendix, pt. i (1883).
Tenth report, appendix, pt. v (1885).

Hogan, Edmund, S.J., *Ibernia Ignatiana* (1880).

Irish historical documents 1172–1922, eds. E. Curtis and R. B. MacDowell (1943).

Lombard, Rev. Peter, *De regno Hiberniae sanctorum insula commentarius*, ed. Cardl. P. F. Moran (Dublin, 1868).

MacCarthy, D., *Life and letters of the MacCarthy Mor* (1867).

Mooney, Rev. Donagh, 'De provincia Hiberniae S. Francisci', ed. Rev. B. Jennings, O.F.M., in *Anal. Hib.*, vi (1934), 15–131.

Maps of the escheated counties of Ireland: Ulster 1609 (facsimile, Ordnance Survey Office, Southampton, 1860).

Maxwell, Constantia, *Irish history from contemporary sources 1509–1610* (1923).

Moryson, Fynes, *An itinerary: containing his ten yeeres travell through the twelve dominions of Germany, . . . Scotland and Ireland* (4 vols., Glasgow, 1907–8).

Ó Clérigh, Lughaidh, *Beatha Aodha Ruaidh Uí Dhomhnaill*, ed. Rev. P. Walsh (Ir. Texts Soc., 2 vols., Dublin, 1948 and 1957). Another ed., with English trans.: O'Clery, L., *The life of Hugh Roe O'Donnell, prince of Tirconnell 1586–1602*, ed. Rev. D. Murphy, S.J. (Dublin, 1893).

Ó Huiginn, *The bardic poems*, ed. E. Knott (Ir. Texts Soc., 2 vols., Dublin, 1922–3).

O Lochlainn, C., *Tobar fíorghlan Gaedhilge: deismireacht na teangadh 1450–1835* (Dublin, 1939).

O'Sullivan Beare, Philip, *Historiae catholicae Iberniae compendium*, ed. Rev. M. Kelly (Dublin, 1850).

—— *Selections from the Zoilomastix*, ed. Rev. T. J. O'Donnell, S.J. (IMC, Dublin, 1960).

Persons, Rev. Robert, S.J., *Letters and Memorials*, ed. Rev. Leo Hicks, S.J. (CRS, XXXIX 1942).

Reusens, Chanoine, *Éléments de paléographie* (Louvain, 1899).

[Stafford, Thomas], *Pacata Hibernia*, ed. Standish [J.] O'Grady (2 vols., 1896).

Trevelyan papers, pt. ii: *1446–1643*, ed. J. Payne Collier (Camden Soc., 1893).

Verstegan, Richard, *Letters and dispatches*, ed. A. G. Petti (CRS, LII, 1959).

Wadding papers 1614–38, ed. Rev. B. Jennings, O.F.M. (IMC, Dublin, 1953).

c. *Secondary works*

I. GENERAL HISTORIES

Bagwell, Richard, *Ireland under the Tudors* (3 vols., 1885–90).

Blok, P. J., *History of the people of the Netherlands*, pt. iii: *The war with Spain* (N.Y., 1900).

Cambridge modern history, iii: *The wars of religion* (Cambridge, 1904); *New Cambridge modern history*, i: *The renaissance* (1957), ii: *The reformation* (1958), and iii: *The counter-reformation and price revolution 1559–1610* (1968).

Davies, R. Trevor, *The golden century of Spain 1501–1621* (1937; repr. 1958).

Elizabethan government and society: essays presented to Sir John Neale, eds. S. T. Bindoff, J. Hurstfield and C. H. Williams (1961).

ELLIOTT, J. H., *Imperial Spain 1469–1716* (1963).

ELTON, G. R., *England under the Tudors* (1955).

—— *Reformation Europe 1517–59* (Fontana Hist. of Europe, 1963).

FROUDE, J. A., *History of England from the fall of Wolsey to the defeat of the Spanish Armada* (12 vols., 1856–70; rev. ed., 1862–70).

GARDINER, S. R., *History of England 1603–42* (10 vols., 1883–4).

GEYL, P., *The revolt of the Netherlands 1559–1609* (2nd ed., 1958).

HAUSER, Henri, *La prépondérance espagnole 1559–1660* (Collection Halphen-Sagnac, 2nd ed., Paris, 1940).

HOGAN, James, *Ireland in the European system: 1500–57* (1920).

HUME, M. A. S., *Spain: its greatness and decay* (Cambridge, 1898).

HURSTFIELD, Joel, *Elizabeth I and the unity of England* (Teach Yourself History, 1960).

—— *The Elizabethan nation* (BBC, 1964).

LAVISSE, E., *Histoire de France*, vol. vi (Paris, 1904).

LYNCH, John, *Spain under the Habsburgs*, vol. I: *Empire and absolutism* (O.U.P., 1964).

MATHEW, Abp Davis, *The celtic peoples and renaissance Europe: a study of the Celtic and Spanish influences on European history* (1933).

MacNEILL, Eoin, *Phases of Irish history* (Dublin, 1937).

MERRIMAN, Roger, B., *The rise of the Spanish empire in the old world and in the new* (4 vols., N.Y., 1918–39).

PETRIE, Sir Charles, *Earlier diplomatic history 1492–1713* (1949).

POLLARD, A. F., *History of England 1547–1603* (1910).

PASTOR, Ludwig Freiherr von, *History of the popes from the close of the middle ages*, eds. F. I. Antrobus and others (40 vols., 1891–1935).

RANKE, Leopold von, *History of the popes during the last four centuries*, trans. Mrs. Foster and G. R. Dennis (3 vols., 1913).

TENISON, E. M., (ed.), *Elizabethan England: being the history of this country 'in relation to all foreign princes'* (12 vols., Royal Leamington Spa, 1932–58).

WERNHAM, R. B., *Before the armada: the growth of English foreign policy 1485–1588* (1966).

WILLIAMSON, J. A., *The Tudor age* (1953).

2. SPECIAL STUDIES

a. Unprinted

Ó DOMHNAILL, Séan, 'History of Tír Conaill in the sixteenth century'. NUI Thesis, 1946.

b. Printed

BINCHY, D., 'An Irish Ambassador at the Spanish court 1569–74', in *Studies*, x–xiv (1921–5).

BRADY, Rev. J., 'Father Christopher Cusack and the Irish college at Douay 1594–1624', in *Measgra i gcuimhne Mhichíl Uí Chléirigh*, ed. S. O'Brien, pp. 98–107.

Britain and the Netherlands: papers delivered to the Oxford-Netherlands Conference, 1959, eds. J. S. Bromley and E. H. Kossmann, introd. P. Geyl (1960).

BUTLER, W. F. T., *Gleanings from Irish history* (1925).

DODD, Charles (Hugh Tootel), *The church history of England from 1500 to the year 1688, chiefly with regard to Catholics* (3 vols., Brussels (prob. London), 1737–42; new rev. ed. M. A. Tierney, 5 vols., 1839–43).

DULLES, Allen, *The craft of intelligence* (1963).

EDWARDS, R. D., *Church and state in Tudor Ireland* (Dublin, [1935]).

—— 'Church and state in the Ireland of Michel O'Cleirigh 1626–41', in *Measgra gcuimhne Mhichíl Uí Chléirigh*, ed. S. O'Brien, pp. 1–20.

FALLS, Cyril, *Elizabeth's Irish wars* (1950).

—— 'Mountjoy as a soldier', in *Ir. Sword*, ii (1954), 1–5.

—— 'The growth of Irish military strength in the second half of the sixteenth century', ibid., ii (1955), 103–8.

—— 'Hugh O'Neill the great', ibid., vi (1963), 94–102.

GWYNN, Rev. Aubrey, S.J., *The medieval province of Armagh 1470–1555* (Dundalk, 1946).

HAMILTON, E. J., *American trade and the price revolution in Spain 1501–1650* (Harvard, 1934).

—— *Monetary inflation in Castile 1598–1600* (1931).

HAYES-MCCOY, G. A., 'Ballyshannon: its strategic importance in the wars in Connacht 1530–1602', in *Galway Arch. Soc. Jn.* xv (1931–3), 141–59.

—— ed., *The Irish at war* (Cork, 1964).

—— 'Strategy and tactics in Irish warfare 1593–1601', in *I.H.S.*, ii (1941), 255–79.

—— 'The tide of victory and defeat', in *Studies*, xxxviii (1949), 158–68, 307–17.

—— 'The army of Ulster 1593–1601', in *Ir. Sword*, i (1951), 105–17.

—— 'Irish cavalry, i: the sixteenth century', ibid., i (1953), 316–17.

HENRY, L. W., 'Contemporary sources for Essex's lieutenancy in Ireland', in *I.H.S.*, xi (1958), 8–17.

—— 'The earl of Essex and Ireland 1599' in *Inst. Hist. Res. Bull.*, xxxii (1959), 1–23.

—— 'Essex as a strategist and military organiser, 1596–7', in *E.H.R.*, lxviii (1953), 363–93.

HOGAN, James, 'Shane O'Neill comes to the court of Elizabeth', in *Féilscríbhinn Torna: essays and studies presented to Professor Tadhg Ua Donnchadha (Torna)*, ed. S. Pender (Cork U.P., 1947).

HUME, M. A. S., *Treason and plot: struggles for Catholic supremacy in the last years of Queen Elizabeth* (1901).

JENNINGS, Rev. Brendan, O.F.M., 'Irish swordsmen in Flanders 1586–1610, i: Stanley's regiment', in *Studies*, xxxvi (1947), 402–10.

JONES, Rev. F. M., C.SS.R., 'The Spaniards and Kinsale 1601' in *Galway Arch. Soc. Jn.*, xxi (1944), 1–43.

—— 'Pope Clement VIII (1592–1603) and Hugh O'Neill', in *ICHS Bull.*, new series, ii. no. 73 (1953), 5–6.

—— 'The destination of Don Juan del Águila in 1601', in *Ir. Sword*, ii (1954), 29–32.

—— 'An indictment of Don Juan del Águila, ibid., ii (1955), 218–20.

—— 'The counter-reformation'. Vol. iii. III of *A History of Irish Catholicism*, ed. P. J. Corish (Dublin, 1967).

KEARNEY, H. F., 'The Irish wine-trade 1614–15', in *I.H.S.*, ix (1955).

KELSO, J. B., *Die Spanier in Irland 1588–1603* (Leipzig, 1902).

LONGFIELD, A. K., *Anglo-Irish trade in the sixteenth century* (1929).

LOOMIE, Rev. Albert J., S.J., *The Spanish Elizabethans: the English exiles at the court of Philip II* (Fordham U.P., N.Y., 1963).

LYNCH, J., 'Philip II and the papacy', in *Trans. RHS*, 5 ser., ii (1961), 23–42.

MANGAN, Henry, 'Del Águila's defence of Kinsale 1601–2', in *Ir. Sword*, i (1952), 218–24.

—— 'Comments on "An indictment of . . . Águila"', ibid., ii (1955), 220–3.

—— 'A vindication of Don Juan del Águila', ibid., ii (1956), 343–51.

MEYER, A. O., *England and the Catholic church under Queen Elizabeth* (1916).

MOONEY, Rev. Canice, O.F.M., 'The Irish sword and the Franciscan cowl', in *Ir. Sword*, i (1951), 80–7.

NEALE, J. E., *Essays in Elizabethan history* (1958).

O'BRIEN, Rev. Sylvester, O.F.M., *Measgra i gcuimhne Mhichíl Uí Chléirigh* (Dublin, 1944).

Ó CEALLAIGH, Séamus, *Gleanings from Ulster history; punann ó Chois Bhanna* (Cork U.P., 1951).

Ó DOMHNAILL, Séan, 'Warfare in sixteenth-century Ireland', in *I.H.S.*, v (1946), 48–53.

O'RAHILLY, Alfred, *The massacre at Smerwick 1580* (Hist. and Arch. Papers, ed. S. P. O'Riordain, i. Cork, 1938).

O'SULLIVAN, Florence, *The history of Kinsale* (Dublin, 1916).

POLLEN, J. H., *The English Catholics in the reign of Elizabeth: a study of their politics, civil life and government* (1920).

—— 'The politics of English Catholics during the reign of Queen Elizabeth', in *Month*, c (1902).

—— 'The question of Queen Elizabeth's successor', ibid., ci (1903), 511–32.

—— 'The accession of James I', ibid., ci (1903), 572–85.

PORTER, Whitworth, *A history of the knights of Malta or the order of St. John of Jerusalem* (1883).

QUINN, D. B., 'Ireland and sixteenth-century European expansion', in *Historical studies* (i): *papers read before the second conference of Irish historians*, ed. T. D. Williams (1958).

—— 'Henry VIII and Ireland 1509–34', in *I.H.S.*, xii (1961), 318–44.

READ, Conyers, *Mr. Secretary Walsingham and the policy of Queen Elizabeth* (3 vols., Oxford, 1925).

—— *Mr. Secretary Cecil and Queen Elizabeth* (1955).

—— *Lord Burghley and Queen Elizabeth* (1960).

RONAN, Rev. Myles V., *The reformation in Ireland under Elizabeth 1558–80* (1930).

SILKE, Rev. J. J., 'The Irish appeal of 1593 to Spain: some light on the genesis of the nine years' war', in *I.E.R.*, ser. 5, xcii (1959), 279–90, 362–71.

—— 'Later relations between Primate Peter Lombard and Hugh O'Neill', in *Ir. Theol. Quart.* xxii (1955), 15–30.

—— 'Primate Lombard and James I', ibid., xxii (1955), 124–50.

—— 'Why Águila landed at Kinsale', in *I.H.S.*, xiii (1963), 236–45.

—— 'Spain and the invasion of Ireland 1601–2', ibid., xiv (1965), 295–312.

—— 'Where was "Obemdub"?', in *Ir. Sword*, vi (1964), 276–82.

—— 'Hugh O'Neill, the Catholic question and the papacy', in *I.E.R.*, ser. 5, civ (1965).

WALSH, Rev. Paul, *Irish chiefs and leaders*, ed. Colm O'Lochlainn (Dublin, 1960).

3. BIOGRAPHIES AND BIOGRAPHICAL AIDS

ASTRAIN, A., S.J., *Historia de la Compañía de Jesús en la asistencia de España*, iii: *Mercurian-Aquaviva*, i: *1515–73* (Madrid, 1909).

CLEARY, Rev. G., O.F.M., *Father Luke Wadding and St. Isidore's college, Rome* (Rome 1925).

C[OKAYNE], G. E., *Complete peerage of England, Scotland, Ireland, Great Britain and the United Kingdom . . .*, eds. Vicary Gibbs and others (13 vols., 1910–59).

CORBOY, Rev. James, S.J., 'Father James Archer 1550–1625 (?)', in *Studies*, xxxiii (1944), 99–107.

Dictionary of national biography, eds. Sir Leslie Stephen and Sir Sidney Lee (22 vols., London, 1908–9). First published in 66 vols., 1885–1901.

ESSEN, Leon van der, *Alexandre Farnese, prince de Parme, gouverneur général des Pays-Bas 1545–92*, préface de Henri Pirenne (5 vols., Brussels, 1933–9).

EUBEL, C., O.F.M. Conv. (ed.), *Hierarchia catholica medii aevi, 1198–1503* (2 vols., Munich-Ratisbon, 2nd ed., 1913–14; vol., iii: 1503–92, eds. C. Eubel, G. van Gulik, L. Schmitz-Kallenberg, Munster, 2nd ed., 1923; vol. iv: 1592–1667, ed. P. Gauchat, Munster, 1935).

FALLS, Cyril, *Mountjoy: Elizabethan general* (1955).

FITZGERALD, Brian, *The Geraldines: an experiment in Irish government 1169–1601* (1961).

FOLEY, Rev. Henry, *Records of the English province, S.J.* (7 vols., 1877–84).

GILLOW, Joseph, *Biographical dictionary of the English Catholics* (5 vols., 1885–1903).

HANDOVER, P. M., *The second Cecil: the rise to power 1563–1604 of Sir Robert Cecil, later first earl of Salisbury* (1959).

HAWKES, Rev. William, 'Matthew de Oviedo: birthplace, parentage, place of burial', in *Rep. Nov.*, i (1955), 236–7.

HOGAN, Rev. Edmund, S.J., *Distinguished Irishmen of the sixteenth century: first series* (1894).

JENNINGS, Rev. B., O.F.M., 'Florence Conry, archbishop of Tuam', in *Galway Arch. Soc. Jn.*, xxiii (1948–9), 83–93.

JONES, Rev. F. M., C.SS.R., *Mountjoy 1563–1603: the last Elizabethan deputy* (Dublin, 1958).

Leabhar Chlainne Suibhne, ed. Rev. Paul Walsh (Dublin, 1920).

LODGE, J., *The peerage of Ireland* (7 vols., Dublin, 1789).

LOOMIE, Albert J., S.J., 'Richard Stanyhurst in Spain: two unknown letters of August 1593', in *Huntingdon Library Quarterly*, xxviii (1965), 145–55.

MACCARTHY, S. Trant, *The MacCarthys of Munster: the story of a great Irish sept* (Dundalk, 1922).

MOORE, Philip, 'The MacMahons of Monaghan 1593–1603', in *Clogher Record*, i (1956), 85–107.

NEALE, J. E., *Queen Elizabeth I* (1934; Pelican Books, 1960).

O'FAOLAIN, Sean, *The great O'Neill: a biography of Hugh O'Neill, earl of Tyrone 1550–1616* (1942; repr. 1947).

O'GRADY, S. H., *The flight of the eagle* (Dublin, n.d.).

RENEHAN, Rev. L. F., *Collections on Irish church history*, ed. D. MacCarthy, i: *archbishops* (Dublin, 1861).

SCHENK, W., *Reginald Pole: cardinal of England* (1950).

WALSH, Micheline, *The O'Neills in Spain* (O'Donnell Lecture, Dublin, 1960).

WALSH, Rev. Paul, 'Scots Clann Domhnaill in Ireland', in *I.E.R.*, ser. 5, lxviii (1936), 23–42.

—— *The will and family of Hugh O'Neill* (Dublin, 1930).

—— 'James Blake of Galway', in *I.E.R.*, ser. 5, I (1937), 382–97.

INDEX